Popular Science

WOODWORKING PROJECTS

1985 Yearbook

Popular Science Books

New York

Published by

Popular Science Books
Times Mirror Magazines, Inc.
380 Madison Avenue
New York, NY 10017

ISBN: 0-943822-28-9

Manufactured in the United States of America

Introduction

When I was serving time as the editor of *HANDS ON!* magazine, readers used to call me up daily to talk about woodworking. I made it a point to ask each and every one of them, "What would you like to see in the next issue?" Invariably, the answer came back: "More projects!"

But what sorts of projects? What kinds of woodworking did our readers like to do? More to the point, what kinds of woodworkers were they? To find out, our parent company conducted several surveys. The results were a real eye-opener for me: There aren't just a few general categories of woodworkers and woodworking projects, as I once thought. There are dozens upon dozens! We found a whole spectrum, from the experienced craftsman who builds fine furniture, right down to the "Be Prepared" handymen who keep a few tools and some woodworking plans on hand 'just in case'.

I kept that lesson in mind when I help put together this first *Popular Science Woodworking Projects Yearbook*. We wanted to slake your thirst for projects, but we didn't simply collect a grab-bag of plans. There's something worthwhile in here for every woodworker, no matter what type of woodworking you like to do.

For the fine craftsman who enjoys a real challenge, there's fine furniture of every description from many classical periods — a Queen Anne 'highboy', a Shaker bench, a country interpretation of a Windsor rocker, and a set of ultra-modern occasional tables, just to name a few. We've even put together a project plan so that you can duplicate the famous Chippendale "Gibbs Dresser", the most valuable piece of furniture in America.

Want something easy to brighten up your home or make your life a little more comfortable? This yearbook includes a rolling cart that can be used as a microwave stand, tea cart, or taboret. You've seen cabinets similar to our 'message center' at phone stores for a hundred dollars or more, but you can build one in an afternoon for a fraction of the cost. There's also a fully adjustable shelving unit, wall cabinet, bookcase headboard, kitchen utensil rack, and an ingenious "multi-table" that converts to dozens of different uses.

Are you looking for gift ideas? We offer many quick-and-easy projects that make wonderful presents for friends and relatives of all ages. You'll find reindeer figurines that look as if they're hand-carved, a hanging planter, an inlaid clock, a rattle, and a personalized puzzle/push-toy we've dubbed the "Your-Name-Here Mobile". Want something more elegant, off-beat, very special? There's a wooden briefcase, a tabletop loom, and a rocking cradle.

And we haven't forgotten your workshop or your need for tips and time-saving techniques. There's a chapter to help you design the workbench that's right for you, and a plan for a handsome wooden tool chest like you've seen in some of the better tool catalogues. And we've included an entire *Techniques* section in this book to help you polish your woodworking skills.

As you can see, it took some time putting all this together. Whatever your woodworking interests, I know you'll enjoy it. But to help you enjoy it more, I suggest you take a little time before you dive into any one of these projects. Let me tell you a quick story:

One day I sat down to lunch with our illustrator, Betty Buchelt, and asked her to estimate how many *individual* numbers there are in this book. After a few moment's thought, she gave me an estimate: "Oh, 50,000. Maybe a few more." A few more is right! Later on I made some informal calculations and found she had underestimated by half.

What I'm getting at here is that we had heaven's own supply of numbers to deal with when we put this yearbook together. And all of them have been copied and recopied three or four times — first by the author, then the editor, illustrator, and typesetter. We've checked and double-checked every one of them, but there may be a few wrong dimensions that slipped through the cracks.

Sit down with a calculator and check our numbers *before* you cut good lumber. You know the old proverb: "Measure twice, cut once — and don't trust a woodworking editor any further than you can throw him."

So much for introductions. Enjoy the rest of this book during the months to come. And get in touch with us next year for your copy of the *Woodworking Projects 1986 Yearbook!*

With all good wishes,

Nick Engler
Senior Editor
Popular Science Books

Contributors

Monte Burch ◆ Monte Burch started writing about woodworking as an Associate Editor at *Workbench* magazine. Fifteen years ago, he resigned to become a full-time writer. As a freelancer, he's published over 1,000 how-to articles on home workshop subjects, home repair and maintenance, alternate living, gardening, and outdoor recreation in many major publications. He also has 40 books to his credit, including *Basic House Wiring, The Home Cabinetmaker,* and (just released) *The Complete Guide to Building Log Homes.*

Monte lives in the scenic Ozarks, near Humansville, Missouri, along with his wife Joan and three children. Joan is Monte's better half, even in his freelance business — she takes care of all their correspondence, edits the final manuscripts, and helps with the research. They're planning to start their own publishing business, *Outdoor World Press, Inc.*

Nick Engler ◆ Nick Engler founded the how-to magazine, *HANDS ON!* and managed Shopsmith's publishing department for over three years. During that time, he helped produce not only the magazine, but over 100 project plans, books, manuals, and a syndicated newspaper column for woodworkers.

Today, he writes freelance for many different publications on the subjects of how-to, science, and technology. Nick also serves as Senior Editor for Popular Science Books, and he edited this first *Woodworking Projects Yearbook.*

Nick describes himself as a 'needy' woodworker: "When I need a piece of furniture, I build it. It's a joy to use things day in and day out that you've made with your own hands." Nick lives in a home full of hand-built furniture in West Milton, Ohio.

Bob Gould ◆ Bob Gould has been the Associate Editor of *Workbench* magazine for five years, and he's an avid do-it-yourselfer. Before that he spent 20 years with the United States Air Force, jumping around from base to base — and home to home.

"The first thing I do when I move into a new house," says Bob, "is remodel it to suit my family's lifestyle." He gained a lot of experience as a remodeler during his time with the Air Force. At the moment, he's planning to add two rooms to his present house near Kansas City, Missouri.

Bob also likes to build furniture, particularly reproductions of antiques. (He contributed the "Colonial Cradle" chapter, among others.) When he's not remodeling or building furniture, Bob relaxes by restoring old Porsche automobiles.

Jackson Hand ◆ The late Jackson Hand began his career as the editor of a furniture trade magazine, and became a specialist in wood finishing and antique restoration. Later on, he served as the Editor of several major publications, and contributed articles to *Popular Science, McCall's, House Beautiful, Mechanix Illustrated,* and *Family Handyman.*

Jackson also has several books to his credit, including *How to Do Your Own Wood Finishing, How to Do Your Own Painting and Wallpapering,* and *The Complete Book of Home Repair and Maintenance.* During most of his long writing career, he worked out of his home in Westport, Connecticut.

Jay Hedden ◆ Jay Hedden has been the Editor of *Workbench* magazine for over 25 years, and before that he was the Assistant Editor of *Popular Mechanics.* He's authored several books, including *Best Baths, Successful Living Rooms, Successful Cabinets and Built-ins,* and he's co-authored many other books, such as *Heating, Cooling, and Ventilation, Building Mediterranean Furniture,* and *Solarizing Your Home.*

A woodworker all his life, Jay has designed and built many pieces of furniture. But he recalls his most challenging project was a scaled-down concert harp which his wife now plays. He has also remodeled several of his own homes, and hopes to retire soon in his present home in Leawood, Kansas. He wants to enjoy his woodworking shop, and an extensive collection of hand and power tools that he has accumulated over a lifetime of how-to writing and editing.

Jim McCann ◆ Jim McCann began nailing boards together at his father's knee. Later he got formal training at Eastern Kentucky University, not only in woodworking, but metalworking, electronics, power mechanics, and industrial design.

He joined Shopsmith, Inc. — a manufacturer of power tools near Dayton, Ohio — in 1979 as a Project Plans Specialist, where he helped to design and build over 100 projects for Shopsmith's publishing department, and spent several years as 'Smitty', giving advice to woodworkers in the "Ask Smitty" column in *HANDS ON!* magazine. "That column was just the tip of the iceberg," Jim remembers. "I used to spend 2-4 hours on the phone each day, answering questions from woodworkers all over the country. It took a lot of time — but it was satisfying."

Today Jim is helping woodworkers in another way. He works in Shopsmith's engineering laboratory, helping to design power tools for home shops. He's also inherited his father's tools and has set up shop in Trotwood, Ohio. In his spare time he remains a prolific woodworker.

Burt Murphy ◆ After 25 years in publishing, Burt Murphy has retired to the Hudson Highlands of New York to pursue his special interests in woodworking and antiques.

As Home and Shop Editor of *Mechanix Illustrated* for over ten years, he produced more than 1,000 articles on woodworking and other how-to subjects. There are many other scalps under his publishing belt, including a 22-volume encyclopedia of how-to and nine books on photography. Burt remains a regular contributor to *MI,* and he still writes freelance articles, chapters, and books at every opportunity.

Burt has also restored a landmark building in Cold Spring on the Hudson, New York, where he and his wife, Charlie, collect and trade Victoriana and Sherlock Holmes memorabilia. And if his retirement weren't busy enough, he plans to open a woodworking showroom for gifted craftspersons in the near future.

Bob Pinter ◆ Since he began woodworking ten years ago, Bob has won dozens of ribbons with his projects. (The Shaker Settee, featured in this book, won a blue ribbon at the annual "Artistry in Wood" show, in Dayton, Ohio.) Time and time again, his work has been judged better than that of many professional craftsmen whom he competes against. But even though his work is top notch, he does not count himself as a pro.

"I won't do woodworking for a living," Bob explains. "I do woodworking to *live.*" For Bob, working with wood is unhurried, unpressured, something where he takes time to do it right. "If someone came to me and asked me to build them a Shaker bench in eight weeks, I just wouldn't do it. Putting a deadline on my woodworking removes any reason for doing it. I stop thinking about the bench and just worry about getting it done."

Bob started woodworking in an apartment, building large furniture projects with hand tools. A few years later, he moved to a house and bought some used power tools from a high school. But he still likes to do a lot of his work by hand. "Why should I let the machines have all the fun?" he asks.

And Others ... ◆ It takes more than a few woodworkers to put together a book of woodworking projects. We'd also like to recognize **Linda Watts,** who designed and organized this yearbook, **Betty Buchelt,** who rendered the illustrations, and **Dan Gabriel,** who contributed much of the photography.

And special thanks to Shopsmith, Inc., Sotheby Parke Bernet, and the Metropolitan Museum of Art for allowing us to publish some of their materials.

Contents

Projects

Techniques

PROJECTS

Highboy/Lowboy

Anyway you go, boy, this is one classy addition to your home furnishings.

The pinnacle of classic cabinetry — one of the finest creations in all of furnituremaking — is the Queen Anne 'highboy'. The massive chest of drawers perched atop delicate legs, the sweeping bonnet that reaches to an imposing height give you the impression of strength wedded to beauty, power wielded with grace. A highboy, well designed and well executed, shows what is best about wood and woodworking.

The design is nearly three centuries old, but the term

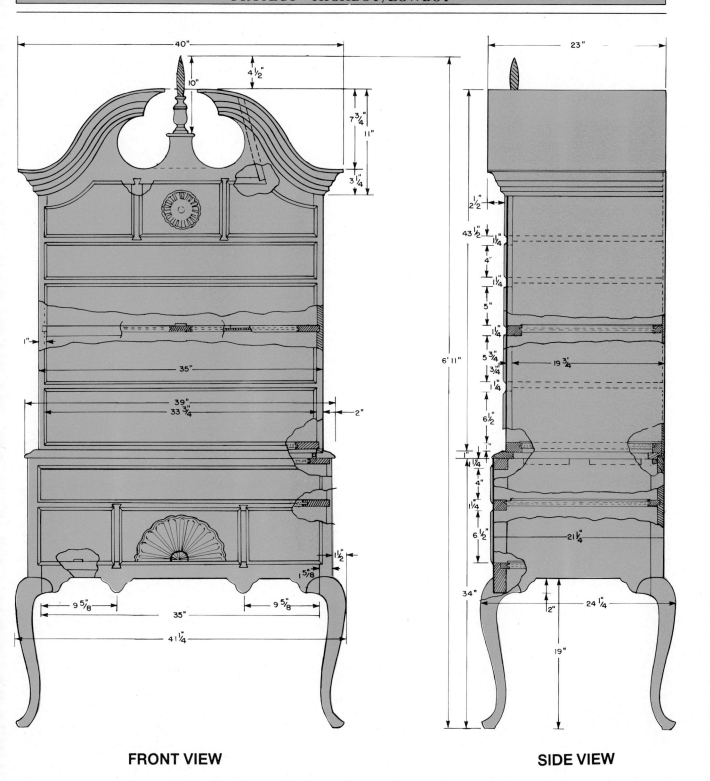

FRONT VIEW

SIDE VIEW

'highboy' is modern. Some eighteenth century inventories mention 'tallboys', but the proper name for this particular piece is a *high chest*. The distinctive design — a chest on a frame — was patterned after furniture imported from the Orient. Early high chests sat on turned legs, but during the Queen Anne period (1725-1750), European and American cabinetmakers borrowed another design element from the East: the cabriole (or 'Queen Anne') leg. The combination of these two design elements turned a somewhat awkward-

looking chest of drawers into a true classic.

A Little Encouragement

As you leaf through this chapter, you'll begin to see why the highboy is one of the high points in woodworking. This is an ambitious undertaking, even for an experienced woodworker.

But don't get discouraged and sigh, "Well, maybe next year . . ." Yes, the joinery is involved — but it's *not* compli-

3

cated. Take a closer look: Almost all the joints are just dadoes and rabbets combined in different ways. The most complex joint is a single dovetail!

Any woodworking project, no matter how complex it seems to be, can be broken down to a series of simple steps. That's the case here. Building a highboy will take a lot of time — there are a lot of steps — but if you can cut dadoes and rabbets, you can do it. All you need is a lot of patience and a positive outlook.

To help you out, I've divided this plan of procedure into simple steps, then grouped those steps into *two* consecutive projects. The first project is a 'lowboy' or low chest. A lowboy is the foundation for the highboy, but it's also an attractive piece of furniture by itself. (See Figure 1.) If you want, you can build just the lowboy portion and stop there. Or you can take a breather after you finish the lowboy, then go on for the highboy when you're ready.

So much for the pep talk. Let's get down to brass tacks.

Building the Lowboy

Choosing Stock — Mahogany was the preferred wood of the Queen Anne period, but many American cabinetmakers worked in native woods. Walnut, cherry, and maple were all common.

> **Tip ◆** Stay away from woods with bold grains such as oak and butternut, or excessively burled woods. Don't let the grain pattern overpower the design.

When you purchase the lumber, remember that you need not build the *entire* project from expensive hardwood. Most professional woodworkers use cheaper 'utility' woods for the parts that don't show. To help you figure how much of each type of wood to buy for this project, I've put together the Bill of Materials as a chart, with the type of wood listed under the "Materials" column. Where I indicate 'hardwood', get a good looking cabinet-grade lumber. 'Hw. Ply.' stands for hardwood plywood — a veneered plywood that matches your hardwood. Where it says 'utility', you can use spruce, poplar, or scraps you have around your

shop. 'Plywood' means just that — I prefer plywood for large, thin panels because it's easy to cut and it doesn't change shape with the weather. Finally, where it says 'maple', use rock maple. These parts rub against other parts, and it's important to use a *very* hard wood so that they don't wear down as time passes.

Legs — Cut the ear and leg stock to size, but leave the stock square until *after* you cut the joinery. If you shape the legs first, it will be next to impossible to line up the mortises and grooves.

Lay out the joints on each leg post. Remember that you're making *three* different legs. The back legs are exactly the same; the front two are mirror images of each other. (See the Leg Joinery Layout illustration). Using a router or a dado accessory, cut the grooves and mortises in the legs. Square off the stopped ends of the grooves with a chisel.

Cut the dovetail slot in the top of the legs by first boring a hole with a 1/2″ or 5/8″ drill bit. Then clean out the sides and bottom with a hand chisel. (See Figure 2.) Don't worry about making this slot absolutely perfect right now; wait till it's time to fit the mating dovetail. Finally, drill holes in the side of the legs to attach the ears and front rails.

Now it's time to shape the legs. For detailed instructions of how to do this, see the chapter on "Cabriole Legs" in the **Techniques** section of this book. Just remember that when you're cutting on your bandsaw, cut with the joinery (holes, grooves, mortises) face down, against the table. And cut the shape of the legs 1/16″-1/8″ oversize to make room for sanding and hand shaping.

Trace the ear pattern on the ear stock, cut the ears, and assemble them with glue and dowels to the legs. Sculpt the legs with rasps, following the sectional views shown with the Leg Pattern illustration. Sand with a medium grit sandpaper — leave the finish sanding until later on.

Sides, Back and Apron — Cut the sides and back, then make the joinery in these pieces according to the Side Layout and the Lowboy Front Corner Joinery Detail illustrations. Remember that the apron gets a 3/4″ x 3/4″ rabbet in the top back corner, to support the bottom dust shield. (See the Side View.) Once again, you can use either a router or a dado accessory to make the necessary grooves, rabbets,

Figure 1. You don't have to build the entire highboy all at once. This project also looks good as a lowboy.

Figure 2. To make a stopped dovetail notch, first drill out the notch with a 1/2″ or 5/8″ bit. Then clean up the sides and bottom with a chisel.

and dadoes. Use a 3/8″ dado or straight router bit to cut the rabbets, and a 3/4″ dado or straight router bit to make the dadoes and grooves.

Tip ◆ If you have trouble with splintering or chipping when you use your dado, check the alignment. The blades and chippers are probably not square to the fence. If that's not the problem, the dado is probably dull.

Cut the stock for the front apron, then make the tenons with a table saw or router. Saw the contours in the bottom of the apron and the sides on a bandsaw, according to the Apron Pattern. Drum sand the edges to remove the millmarks. If you're using hardwood plywood, tape the edges with veneer.

Cut the dovetail in the ends of the front stiles, according to the Front Stile Layout. Then make matching dovetail notches in the top edge of the front apron. Also cut the

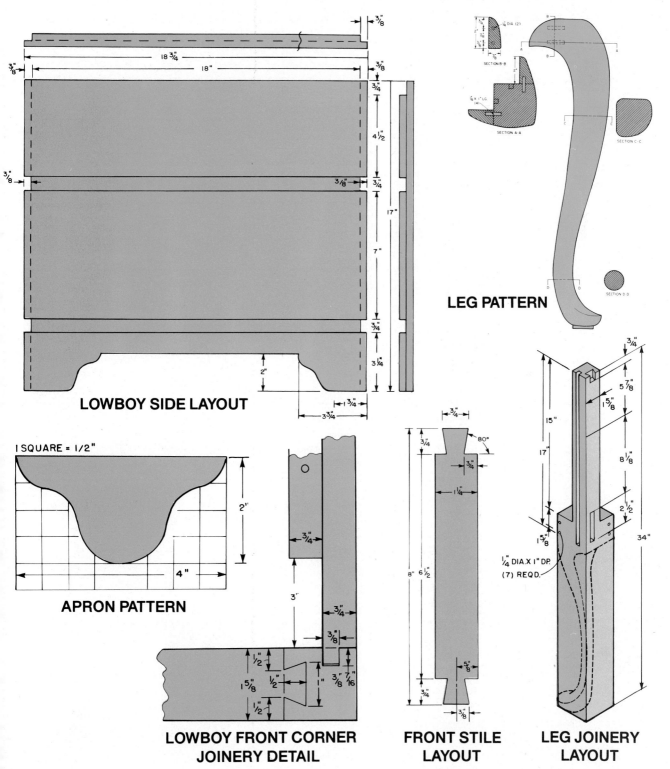

LEG PATTERN

LOWBOY SIDE LAYOUT

I SQUARE = 1/2″

APRON PATTERN

**LOWBOY FRONT CORNER
JOINERY DETAIL**

**FRONT STILE
LAYOUT**

**LEG JOINERY
LAYOUT**

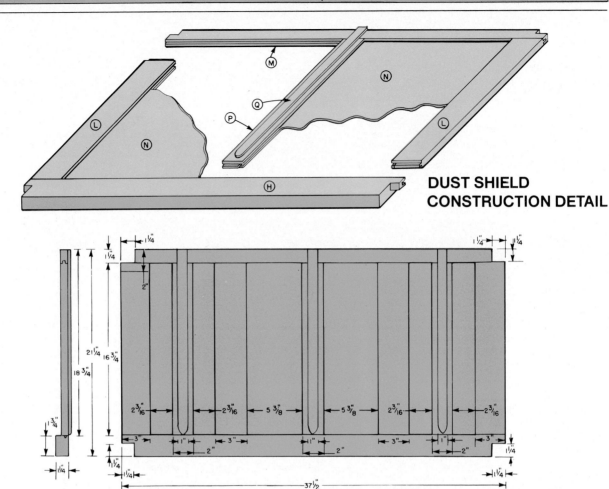

DUST SHIELD CONSTRUCTION DETAIL

LOWBOY LOWER DUST SHIELD LAYOUT

dovetail in the top front rail, following the Lowboy Front Corner Joinery Detail.

Dust Shields — Cut stock for the lowboy dust shields — rails, panels, drawer guides and supports. Saw grooves on the inside edge of the front and back, and on both edges of the middle rails and drawer guide supports. Then cut the tongues on both ends of the middle rails and supports. (See Figure 3 and 4.) Notice the upper lowboy dust shield has only two middle rails and one drawer guide support, as shown in the Dust Shield Construction Detail. The bottom dust shield has four middle rails and two guide supports. For the positions of these rails, refer to the Lowboy Lower Dust Shield Layout.

Before you assemble the dust shields, notch the front and back rails, and drill these rails where they are joined to the legs. Also, make two dovetail notches in the front rail of the upper dust shield, in the same way you made the dovetail notches in the legs.

Remember, the front rails for each shield are different thicknesses, as shown in the Side View and Dust Shield

Figure 3. A router attached to a table is very handy for making the joints in this project, especially on the small pieces.

Figure 4. You'll also find that a dado accessory mounted on your table saw is useful. Shown here is how to make the tenons on the ends of the dust shield rails.

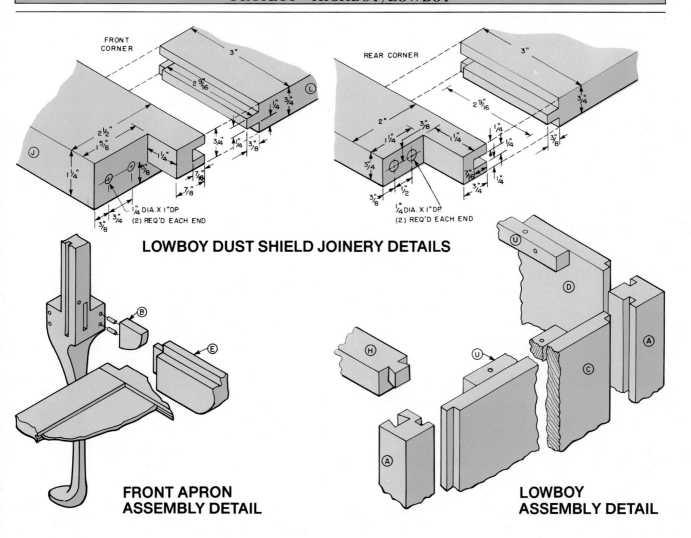

LOWBOY DUST SHIELD JOINERY DETAILS

FRONT APRON ASSEMBLY DETAIL

LOWBOY ASSEMBLY DETAIL

Joinery Details. The lowermost rail is just 3/4″ thick, while the upper rail (and all the other rails in the highboy portion) are 1-1/4″ thick.

Fitting the Parts — Dry assemble all parts first to make sure they fit. Hand fit the dovetails to their respective notches, then mark each dovetail and each notch so you can get them back together the same way you fitted them. When it comes time to glue up the parts, wipe off the excess glue with a *very* wet rag. This will raise the grain slightly, but you can sand it down again when you're doing the finish sanding.

Glue the dust shields together first. Glue the rails together, but *don't* glue the panels in place. Just let them sit loose in the grooves, so that the frames can expand and contract with changes in humidity. This will let the shields 'breathe with the weather' without warping the frame. If you glue the panels in place, the frames will warp, and the drawers will begin to stick.

Tip ◆ Before you clamp the shields up for the last time, check for squareness. *They must be square!* If they're off even a few degrees, they'll throw the rest of the joinery in this project off. Also, check that the drawer guides are perfectly square to the front rails. If not, the drawers may stick.

While the glue on the dust shields is drying, screw cleat strips to the sides and back. These strips should be drilled with holes every 2″. These holes should be slightly larger than the shanks of the screws you're using. For example, if you're using a #8 screw, drill a #12 pilot hole. This 'slop' will allow the wood in the sides and the top to expand and contract without splitting out or warping the case. Use round-head screws with washers to prevent the screw heads from going through the holes.

Glue the sides to the legs, check for squareness, and let the glue dry. Then get a helper (I repeat, get a *helper* — maybe two) to help you glue the side assemblies to the back, dust shields, top rails, and apron. These parts need to go together all at once, and you only have 15-20 minutes at the most to get everything squared and clamped before the glue starts to set. Refer to the Lowboy Assembly and Front Apron Assembly Details to see how everything goes together.

When all the glue is dry, belt sand adjoining surfaces flush, then finish sand the entire assembly. When you're sanding the veneered plywood parts be extremely careful not to sand through the veneer.

Drawers — You'll need four drawers for the lowboy — two small drawers, a medium size drawer, and a long drawer. See the Drawer Explode, Drawer Front Profile, Drawer Joinery Layout, and other related detail illustrations to see how to cut and fit the drawer parts. Notice that,

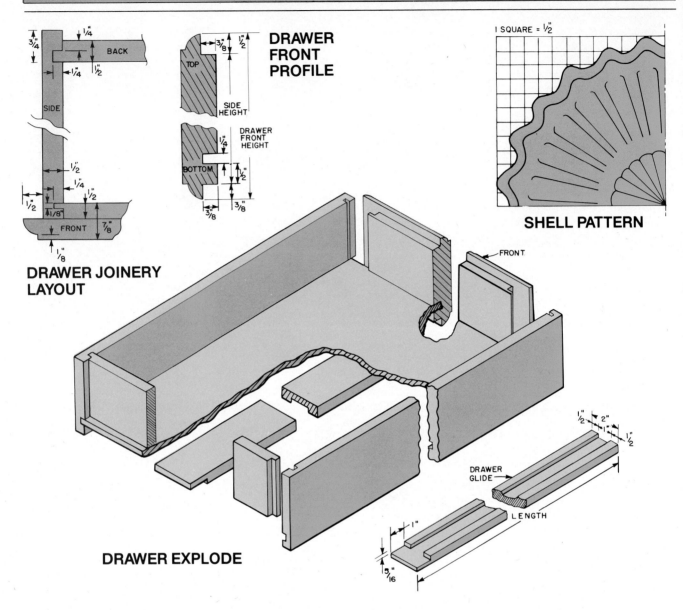

DRAWER FRONT PROFILE

DRAWER JOINERY LAYOUT

SHELL PATTERN

1 SQUARE = 1/2"

DRAWER EXPLODE

once again, there are no fancy dovetails or hard-to-cut joints. The drawers all fit together with a simple system of rabbets, grooves, and dadoes. The only shaping you need to do is on the drawer fronts, and this can be done with a quarter round bit in your router. (See Figure 5.)

Get the dimensions of the drawers and the drawer

Figure 5. Shape the drawer fronts with a quarter-round bit or shaper cutter. There should be a 1/8" step between the flat and the rounded surfaces.

parts from the Drawer Parts Chart right after the Bill of Materials. Match the drawer number on the accompanying illustration to the number in the chart, then cut all parts accordingly. Since there are so many drawers and heaven's own supply of drawer parts in this project, I provided a chart to help simplify things.

Before you assemble the drawers, carve the shell in the front of the bottom middle drawer. A shell is a traditional motif in Queen Anne furniture, and it's a lot easier to make than it looks. This one in particular is a snap, since all the rays are symmetrical. Enlarge the pattern so that the rays are about 6" long, trace it on the drawer front, and chip away anything that doesn't look like a shell. (For a more detailed explanation of how to carve shells, see the "Block-front Dresser" chapter. — Editor)

When you're ready to glue up the drawers, assemble them first *without* the drawer glides. Fit the drawers to their respective openings, shaving excess stock off the sides or bottom with a hand plane and belt sander, as needed. Then put the drawer glides in position in the case and slide the drawers in on top of them to be sure of the fit. Mark the

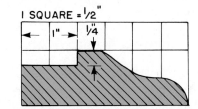

1 SQUARE = 1/2"

LOWBOY TOP EDGE PROFILE

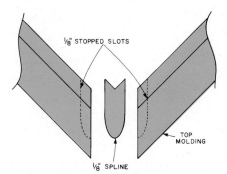

1/8" STOPPED SLOTS

TOP
MOLDING

1/8" SPLINE

**LOWBOY MOLDING FRONT CORNER
DETAIL**

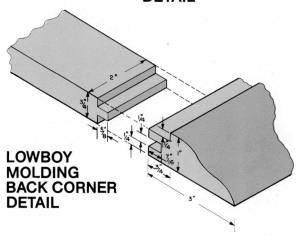

**LOWBOY
MOLDING
BACK CORNER
DETAIL**

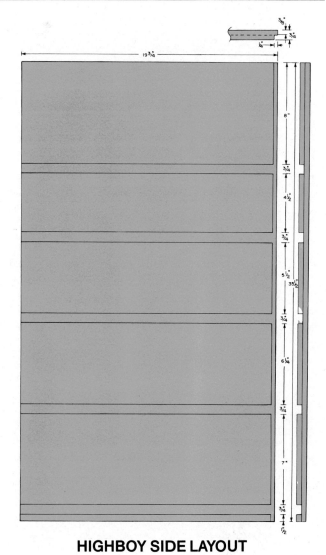

19¾"

8"

3/4

4½"

3/4

5½"

35½

3/4

6¼"

3/4

7"

3/4

½

HIGHBOY SIDE LAYOUT

position of the drawer glides, remove the drawers, and tack the glides on the drawer bottoms with brads. Once again, try the fit. If a drawer sticks, remove the glide and reposition it. Continue until each drawer fits perfectly, then glue the glides in place.

> **Tip** ◆ Rub the glides, guides, and the bottom edge of the drawer sides with paraffin wax to help the drawers slide in and out smoothly.

Topping Off — Now comes the big decision: Do you want to stop with a lowboy? Or do you want to go for the big time and make the whole highboy?

If you just want a lowboy, glue up 1" thick stock to make a board the width and length of the top. Shape the edges as shown in the Lowboy Top Edge Profile, and attach it is the lowboy assembly by driving screws up through the cleat strips into the underside of the top.

If you want to go right on to the highboy, make edge molding and a back piece. Miter the front corners of the edge molding and reinforce these miter joints with stopped splines, as shown in the Lowboy Molding Front Corner

Detail. Join the molding to the back piece with a tongue-and-*stopped*-groove joint, as shown in the Lowboy Molding Back Corner Detail. After you've glued these pieces together, screw the top molding in place on the lowboy assembly.

And you can have it *both* ways. If you want to enjoy this project as a lowboy for a little while, while you gather your resolve to make the highboy, cut rabbets in the edge of a solid panel so that it rests flush inside the molding. Screw (but *don't* glue) the panel in place so that it can be removed easily. Sand down the top surface, apply a finish to the entire project, and rest up for the Big One.

Making the Highboy

As you begin working on the highboy portion, you may be overcome by a feeling of déjà vu. "I've done all this before," I can hear you say. Well, that's right. You have done a lot of it before — I designed the highboy case so that it's very similar to the lowboy.

Case — Cut the sides, back, and the front trim to size. If you're using veneered plywood, keep the good side up on

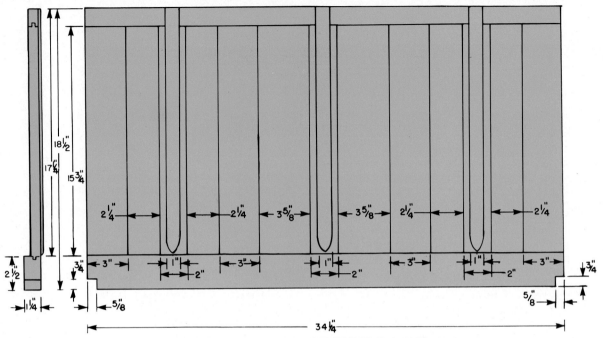

HIGHBOY UPPER DUST SHIELD LAYOUT

the table saw. Then cut the joinery, as shown in the Highboy Side Layout illustration.

Cut and assemble five dust shields in the same manner that you made the dust shields for the lowboy. The bottom four shields only have one rail in the center, the same as the topmost shield in the lowboy. For the top dust shield, follow the dimensions in the Highboy Upper Dust Shield Layout. The front rails of all the dust shields should be cut from 1-1/4″ thick stock, as shown in the Highboy Dust Shield Joinery Detail.

Cut the front stiles, and saw dovetails in both ends. Then make the dovetail slots in the top dust shield. Don't worry about fitting the stiles to the slots just yet; wait until you add the pediment.

Dry assemble the sides, front trim, shields, and back to be sure of the fit. If everything seems to go together properly, call your helpers in and glue up the case. However, leave off the front trim until *after* you build and attach the pediment. Check the case for squareness *before* the glue sets, while you still have time to adjust the clamps.

> **Tip ◆** To be absolutely sure the highboy will mate with the lowboy, temporarily remove the top molding from the lowboy. Use this molding to check the dry assembly, then glue up the case with all the parts sitting on the molding in proper alignment.

Pediment — Perhaps the most time consuming part of this project is making the 'bonnet top' pediment. This appears to be all the more difficult because this particular highboy has a *true* bonnet, not a false front. But it's really not that tricky. All the parts go together with simple butt or dowel joints. It just takes a great deal of patient hand work.

Cut out the pediment front and back, following the Pediment Pattern. Drum sand the sawn edges to remove any millmarks. Mount the finial support block to the pediment front, then drill the front and back for all dowel

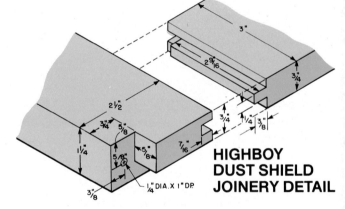

HIGHBOY DUST SHIELD JOINERY DETAIL

joints. (See the Pediment Explode.) Also, cut the dovetail slots in the bottom edge of the front part.

Temporarily assemble the pediment front, back, inner sides, cleat strip, and bottom with wood screws. Fit the pediment to the case. You may have to do a little hand work to get these assemblies to mate. Once you have a good fit, disassemble the pediment then reassemble it with glue. But don't reattach it to the case yet.

Cut the top panels from 1/4″ plywood. Make the side-to-side dimension about 1″ longer than called for in the Bill of Materials — this will give you room to custom fit the top panels to the pediment. If you use solid stock instead of plywood, be sure that the grain direction runs from side to side, not front to back. Using a table saw, cut 1/8″ wide, 3/16″ deep kerfs in the *underside* of the panels, spaced every 1/2″. These kerfs will allow you to bend the panel to the pediment top. (See Figure 6.) Fit the panels in place, cut them to the proper length, then attach them to the top edge of the pediment with glue and brads.

As an option, you may want to consider making the bonnet top from 1″ strips. This is tedious: Both edges of each strip have to be jointed at a different angle so that they

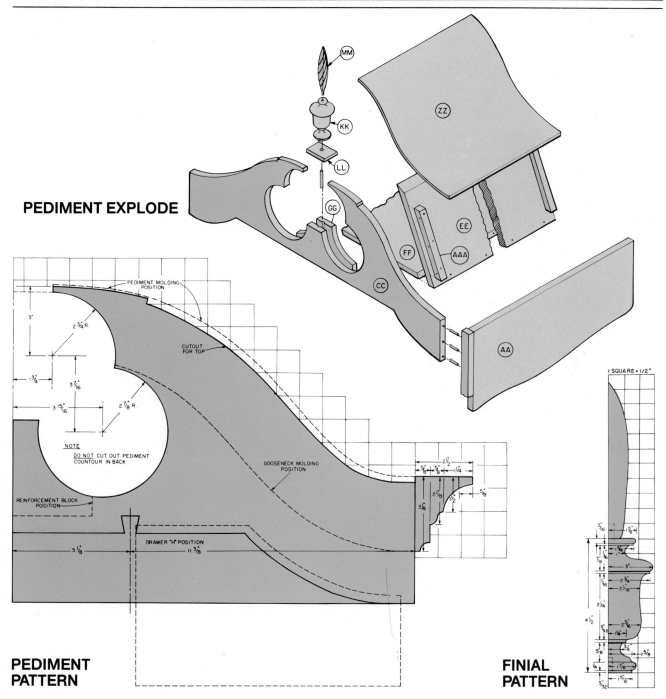

PEDIMENT EXPLODE

**PEDIMENT
PATTERN**

**FINIAL
PATTERN**

fit together. But the finished top is somewhat stronger than a kerfed panel.

Turn the finial parts on a lathe, then carve the top part to look like a flame. You can use the traditional 'urn-and-flame' design shown here, or design something to suit yourself. Finials were often the 'signature' of a colonial craftsman — every cabinetmaker had his own particular design. For this reason, you may want to design a finial that's yours and yours alone. When you finish the finial, put a base under the lower part and dowel the parts in place.

Glue and dowel the front trim to the pediment, then attach this assembly to the case. Fit the front stiles to the dovetail notches, and glue these parts in place. When the glue cures, belt sand all adjoining surfaces flush and finish sand the case.

Figure 6. Make a series of kerfs in the underside of the top panel. This will make the panel flexible enough so that you can fit it to the pediment.

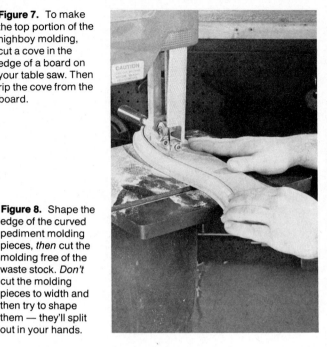

Figure 7. To make the top portion of the highboy molding, cut a cove in the edge of a board on your table saw. Then rip the cove from the board.

Figure 8. Shape the edge of the curved pediment molding pieces, *then* cut the molding free of the waste stock. *Don't* cut the molding pieces to width and then try to shape them — they'll split out in your hands.

Pediment Molding — The molding around the top edge of the pediment looks complex, but it is built up in several simple parts, as shown in the Pediment Pattern. The bottom part has a small cove cut in one bottom corner. The middle part has an ogee, and the top part has a large cove. Make the bottom and middle parts with a router or shaper. To make the top part, cut a cove in one corner of a board on your table saw. (See Figure 7.) Then rip cut the cove molding from the board.

To make the curved or 'gooseneck' molding pieces for the front of the pediment, first cut the *bottom* curve on a band saw. Drum sand to remove millmarks, then shape the bottom edge. After you've finished shaping, cut the *top* curve to separate the molding from the waste stock. (See Figure 8.) This works for every piece except the top gooseneck parts. You won't be able to cove cut these on a table saw. Instead, make several 1/8″ thick pieces of decreasing width. Stack these like stairsteps and glue them together. Then carve the cove by hand with a gouge chisel.

Miter the ends of the molding parts where needed, then glue these parts one at a time to the pediment. Let the glue dry and remove any glue beads with a scraper. True up the joined corners with carving chisels and a rabbet plane, if necessary, and finish sand.

Highboy Drawers — Use the same techniques (and the same chart) to make the drawers for the highboy as you used for the lowboy. The only difference you need to be aware of is that the upper left and upper right drawer fronts have a big bite taken out of one corner. You can get the shape of these drawer fronts from the Pediment Pattern.

Also remember that the upper middle drawer gets a shell carving. Use the same pattern as you did for the shell on the lower middle drawer, but enlarge the pattern to make a full circle. The rays should be about 3″ long — half the size of the carving on the lowboy portion.

Hardware and Finishes

Whether you make a lowboy or a highboy, you'll need to purchase hardware for the drawers and select a finish for the wood. I have a few suggestions:

Hardware — Use 'Chippendale' drawer pulls, with brass bails pivoting in pins fitted through a flat brass escutcheon. This styled brass hardware was another design element that Western cabinetmakers borrowed from the East. The elaborately shaped escutcheons were patterned after Oriental 'cloud forms'. You can buy these pulls from several hardware suppliers. Here are two:

Horton Brasses
Nooks Hill Road
P.O. Box 95F
Cromwell, CT 06416

Wolchonok & Son
155 E. 52nd Street
New York, NY 10022

Finishes — Almost any sort of finish will look good on this piece if you take your time and do it right. The most important finishing decision you'll make is how fine you want to sand the wood.

Sanding will depend on the type of stock you're using and how prominent you want to make the grain pattern. If you're using a wood with a bland grain pattern, such as maple, don't bother sanding with anything finer than 220# grit. If you want the grain to stand out slightly, take the surface down to 250# or even 320#.

You can also make the grain more prominent by using a 'penetrating' finish, such as tung oil or Danish oil. If you want the grain to show *and* a varnished look, apply a 'wash' coat of shellac and alcohol (mixed 1 to 1) over the penetrating finish after it dries. Then apply a 'building' finish like Deft. The thinned shellac will seal in the oil so that it doesn't cloud the surface layer.

Tip ◆ Apply as many coats of finish to the *inside* of the case as you do to the outside. This will help keep the case from warping.

One Last Homily

Let me wrap this up by recalling an old proverb: "A journey of a thousand miles begins with a single step." I know it's corny, but it aptly describes this project — a Queen Anne high chest begins with a single simple joint, then another, and another, and another. Not one of those joints is hard to make. You just have to keep making them until you get what you're after. — *Designed by Jim McCann, built by Jay Hedden*

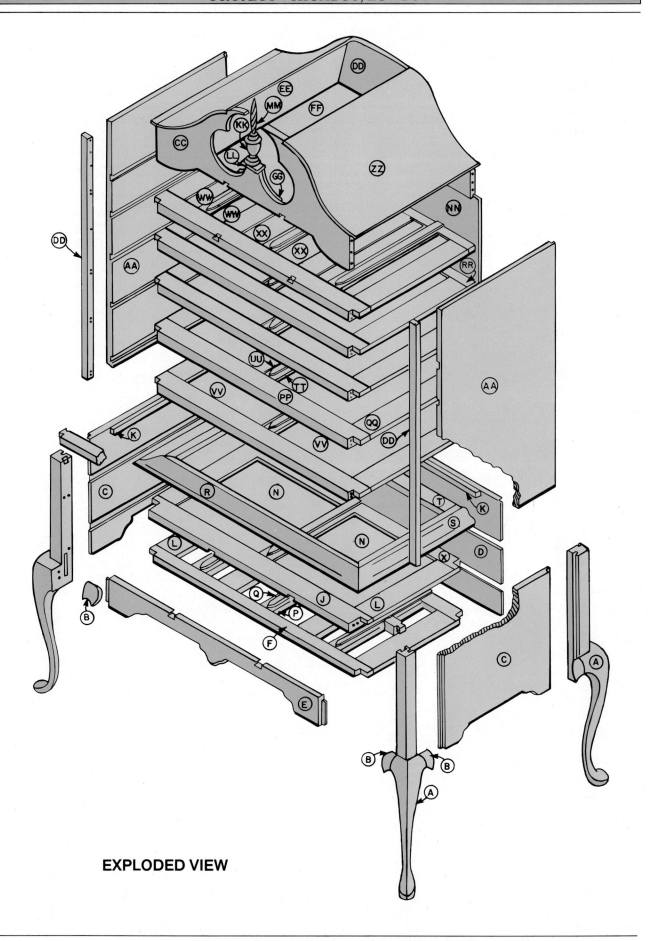

EXPLODED VIEW

BILL OF MATERIALS — Highboy/Lowboy

(Finished Dimensions in Inches)

	Lowboy Parts	Size	Material	Assembly
A.	Legs (4)	3-1/2 x 3-1/4 x 34	Hardwood	Main part of Lowboy
B.	Ears (8)	7/8 x 1-3/4 x 2-1/4	Hardwood	Doweled to Leg
C.	Sides (2)	3/4 x 18-3/4 x 17	Hw. Ply.	Rabbet & groove to Legs
D.	Back	3/4 x 17-3/8 x 35-3/4	Hw. Ply.	Rabbet & groove to Back Legs
E.	Apron	3/4 x 4 x 36-1/2	Hardwood	Mortised to Front Legs
F.	Bottom Front Rail	3/4 x 1-1/4 x 37-1/2	Utility	Doweled to Front Legs
G.	Front Stiles (2)	3/4 x 1-1/4 x 8	Hardwood	Dovetailed to Apron and Rail
H.	Top Front Rail	1-1/4 x 1-5/8 x 36	Hardwood	Dovetailed to Front Legs
J.	Center Front Rail	1-1/4 x 2-1/2 x 37-1/2	Hardwood	Doweled to Front Legs
K.	Cleat Strips (4)	3/4 x 3/4 x 12	Utility	Screwed to Sides, Molding
L.	Middle Rails (6)	3/4 x 3 x 17-1/8	Utility	Tongue & groove to other Rails
M.	Rear Rails (2)	3/4 x 2 x 37-1/2	Utility	Dadoed in Back
N.	Dust Panels (2)	1/4 x 15 x 18-1/4	Plywood	Ride in grooves in frames
P.	Guide Supports (4)	3/4 x 2 x 17-1/8	Utility	Tongue & groove to Rails
Q.	Drawer Guides (4)	1/4 x 7/8 x 18-1/8	Maple	Screwed to Supports
R.	Top Front Molding	1 x 3 x 39	Hardwood	Splined to Side Molding
S.	Top Side Molding (2)	1 x 3 x 21-5/8	Hardwood	Tongue & groove to Rail
T.	Top Rear Rail	3/4 x 2 x 33-3/4	Utility	Tongue & groove to Molding
U.	Top (Lowboy option)	1 x 21-5/8 x 39	Hardwood	Screwed to Cleat Strips

	Highboy Parts	Size	Material	Assembly
AA.	Sides (2)	3/4 x 19-3/4 x 35-3/4	Hw. Ply.	Main part of Highboy
BB.	Front Trim (2)	3/4 x 1 x 35-3/4	Hardwood	Splined to Sides
CC.	Pediment Front	3/4 x 13-3/4 x 33	Hardwood	Doweled to Front Trim
DD.	Pediment Back	3/4 x 13-3/4 x 33	Hw. Ply.	Rabbeted to Back
EE.	Inner Sides (2)	3/4 x 18-1/2 x 10-1/2	Hw. Ply.	Screwed to Cleat Strips
FF.	Pediment Bottom	3/4 x 18-1/2 x 18-1/2	Hw. Ply.	Screwed to Inner Sides
GG.	Finial Support	3/4 x 7 x 6	Hardwood	Glued to Pediment Front
HH.	Gooseneck Molding (2)	2-1/4 x 5-1/4 x 24	Hardwood	Screwed to Pediment Front
JJ.	Side Molding (2)	2-1/4 x 3-1/4 x 23	Hardwood	Screwed to Sides (from inside)
KK.	Finial Urn	2-3/4 dia. x 4-1/2	Hardwood	Doweled to Pediment
LL.	Finial Base	3/8 x 1-7/8 x 2-5/8	Hardwood	Glued to Urn
MM.	Finial Flame	1-1/4 dia. x 5-1/4	Hardwood	Doweled to Urn
NN.	Back	1/4 x 34-1/4 x 34-1/2	Plywood	Rabbeted to Sides
PP.	Front Rails (5)	1-1/4 x 2-1/2 x 34-1/4	Hardwood	Doweled to Front Trim
QQ.	Middle Rails (12)	3/4 x 3 x 17-1/4	Utility	Tongue & groove to other Rails
RR.	Back Rails (4)	3/4 x 1-1/4 x 34-1/4	Utility	Dadoed to Sides
SS.	Bottom Back Rail	1-1/4 x 1-1/4 x 34-1/4	Utility	Dadoed to Sides
TT.	Guide Supports (7)	3/4 x 2 x 17-1/4	Utility	Tongue & groove in frames
UU.	Drawer Guides (7)	1/4 x 7/8 x 18-1/8	Maple	Screwed to Supports
VV.	Dust Panels (8)	1/4 x 13-1/8 x 16-1/2	Plywood	Ride in grooves in frames
WW.	Dust Panels (4)	1/4 x 3 x 16-1/2	Plywood	Ride in grooves in frames
XX.	Dust Panels (2)	1/4 x 4-3/8 x 16-1/2	Plywood	Ride in grooves in frames
YY.	Front Stiles (2)	3/4 x 1-1/4 x 8	Hardwood	Dovetailed to Pediment, Rail
ZZ.	Top Panels	1/4 x 15 x 20-1/2	Hw. Ply.	Bradded to Pediment
AAA.	Cleat Strips (4)	3/4 x 3/4 x 8	Utility	Screwed to Ped. Front, Back

Hardware

'Chippendale' Brass Drawer Pulls (4 for Lowboy, 14 for Highboy)
Brass Ring Pulls (1 for Lowboy, 2 for Highboy)
#8 x 1-1/4" Flathead Wood Screws (2-3 dozen for Lowboy, 4-5 dozen for Highboy)
3/4" brads (5-6 dozen for Highboy only)

Drawer Parts

(Finished Dimensions in Inches)

	Front (7/8″)	Sides (1/2″)	Back (1/2″)	Bottom (1/4″)	Glides (1/4″)
A.	7-1/4 x 9-3/4	6-5/8 x 20-1/2	5-5/8 x 8-1/4	8-1/4 x 20-1/2	2 x 20-1/8
B.	7-1/4 x 15-1/4	6-3/8 x 20-1/2	5-5/8 x 13-3/4	13-3/4 x 20-1/2	2 x 20-1/8
C.	4-3/4 x 35-3/4	3-7/8 x 20-1/2	3-1/8 x 34-1/4	34-1/4 x 20-1/2	2 x 20-1/8
D.	7-1/4 x 33-3/4	6-3/8 x 20-1/4	5-5/8 x 32-1/4	32-1/4 x 20-1/4	2 x 19-7/8
E.	6-1/2 x 33-3/4	5-5/8 x 20-1/4	4-7/8 x 32-1/4	32-1/4 x 20-1/4	2 x 19-7/8
F.	5-3/4 x 33-3/4	4-7/8 x 20-1/4	4-1/8 x 32-1/4	32-1/4 x 20-1/4	2 x 19-7/8
G.	4-3/4 x 33-3/4	3-7/8 x 20-1/4	3-1/8 x 32-1/4	32-1/4 x 20-1/4	2 x 19-7/8
H.	7-1/4 x 11-1/2	6-3/8 x 20-1/4	5-5/8 x 10	10 x 20-1/4	2 x 19-7/8
J.	7-1/4 x 9-3/4	6-3/8 x 20-1/4	5-5/8 x 8-1/4	8-1/4 x 20-1/4	2 x 19-7/8

Portable Computer Desk

This ingenious desk turns into a carrying case for your printer, modem, and other peripherals — makes your entire system portable!

Early on in the computer age, I discovered the joys of having an electronic slave to do my typing, filing, and figuring. So when my business started taking me across the country, I bought a portable computer to take with me. Why resort to prehistoric pads and pencils just because I'm away from home?

However, I quickly learned that a portable computer isn't as handy as it might be — through no fault of the com-

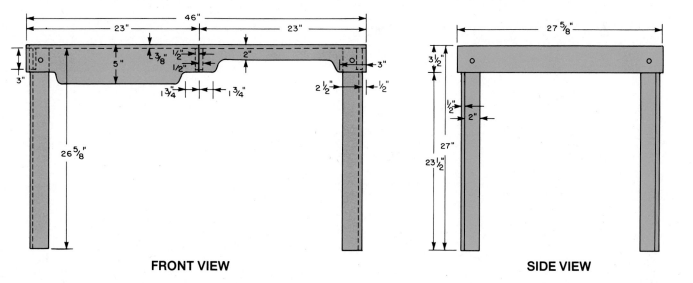

FRONT VIEW

SIDE VIEW

puter's. First of all, there's no place to put it in the average motel room. The desks aren't deep enough (the keyboard leaks over the edge and wants to drop in your lap) and the tables are too high for comfortable typing. Second, while the computer may fold up into a handy carrying case, the printer and other peripherals don't. I found myself traveling with only half a system and no place to put it.

After a few months of putting up with the problem, I hit upon the solution: A desk that doubles as a carrying case for the peripherals! The desk is really just a box that unfolds into two halves, bolted together. The legs bolt to the corners of the box. When folded up, the legs store in the box along with the printer, modem, cables, disks, manuals — even a thesaurus! (See Figure 1.) When the box is completely closed, it's about the same size as a suitcase. (See Figure 2.)

Making the Box and Legs

To make the desk, use 3/8″ cabinet grade plywood for the

desk tops, and 1/2″ thick solid stock for the sides and legs. The desk shown here is made from oak, but if I had it to do over again, I'd use basswood — it's light but strong.

Measure the height of your largest peripheral — probably your printer. Mine is 5″ tall, so I made the desk/box 7″ wide to make room for foam rubber padding. If your printer is taller (or shorter), you may wish to adjust the dimensions of the basic box somewhat.

After you've decided on the dimensions, cut all parts to size. Make a 3/16″ x 1/4″ rabbet in each edge of each desk top. Miter the corners of the sides and saw 3/16″ x 1/4″ grooves on the inside, as shown in the Desk/Box Explode. *Don't split the sides down the middle yet!*

Assemble the parts to make an enclosed box — you may have to do some hand fitting to get them all to fit just right. When you have them all fitted, disassemble the box, apply glue to all the miters and grooves, then reassemble. Clamp the parts together tightly with band clamps and let the glue cure *at least* 24 hours.

Carefully cut the box apart. Split the two long sides and one short side on a table saw, right down the middle. Split the fourth side with a sabre saw, following the pattern shown in the Front View. (See Figure 3.) When the box is

Figure 1. The computer desk knocks down into a carrying case for your printer and other peripherals. The legs fit in the back of the case behind the printer.

Figure 2. When closed, the case is about the same size as a large suitcase. Notice that the handle also serves as a latch.

Figure 3. Split three sides of the box on a table saw, right down the middle. Split the fourth side with a sabre saw, sawing a simple pattern that will serve as a kneehole on the completed desk.

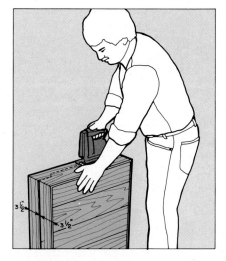

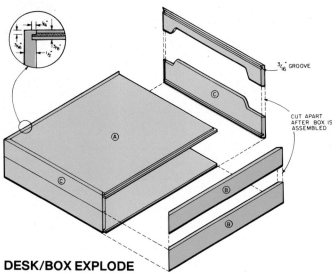

DESK/BOX EXPLODE

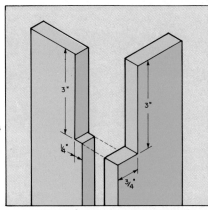

Figure 4. Notch the leg stock to fit over the corner blocks *before* you glue up the legs. Notice that one side is notched deeper than the other.

Figure 5. Rip the legs to the proper width and cut them to the proper length **after** you've glued them up.

Figure 6. Install the handle on the case with T-nuts and stove bolts. The handle must straddle the seam of the case.

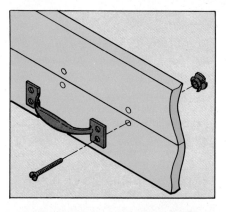

Figure 7. Bolt the legs to the inside of the desk top with carriage bolts, washers, and nuts.

unfolded into a desk, this pattern makes a 'kneehole' on one side, so that you can scoot a chair up to the desk and work comfortably. When the box is split, glue 3/4″ x 3/4″ x 3″ blocks in all eight corners of the two box halves. These corner blocks reinforce the miter joints and keep them from splitting out.

The tops of the legs must be notched to fit around these blocks. The easiest way to do this is to notch the leg stock *before* you glue it up. (See Figure 4.) You'll also find it helps to cut the leg stock a little longer and wider than needed. After you've assembled the legs, rip both sides to the proper width and cut them off at the proper length. (See Figure 5.)

Assembling the Desk

Assemble your computer desk first as a carrying case. Mortise a long side for a piano hinge and install the hinge. Close up the box and place a metal handle so that it straddles the seam on the long side opposite the hinge. This piece of hardware will serve as *both* a handle and a latch to keep the case closed. Mark the box for 3/16″ bolt holes — two holes above the seam, and two below, as shown in Figure 6.

Drill the bolt holes slightly oversize, then insert T-nuts in the holes from the inside of the case. Attach the handle to the case with flathead stove bolts screwed into the T-nuts. To open the case, simply unscrew the bolts and remove the handle. This unorthodox arrangement eliminates any dangling hardware on the sides of the project when you have it set up as a desk.

After you've fitted the case hardware, open the box all the way so that both halves butt up against one another, forming a long, flat desk top. Spread a tarp on the floor and turn the desk top upside down on it. Drill two 3/8″ bolt holes through the 'inside' long sides, just above the piano hinge. Bolt the box halves together with carriage bolts, flat washers, and hex nuts to make the desk top rigid.

Clamp the legs in place, straddling the corner blocks. Drill two 3/8″ bolt holes in each corner, one through each side of each leg. Finally bolt the legs in place with carriage bolts, washers, and nuts. (See Figure 7.)

After you've assembled this project as both a case and a desk — and made sure you can easily convert it from one to the other — disassemble it and remove all the hardware. Apply a penetrating finish, such as tung oil or Minwax. I recommend you avoid varnishes and polyurethanes. These are easily scratched — and they don't travel well.

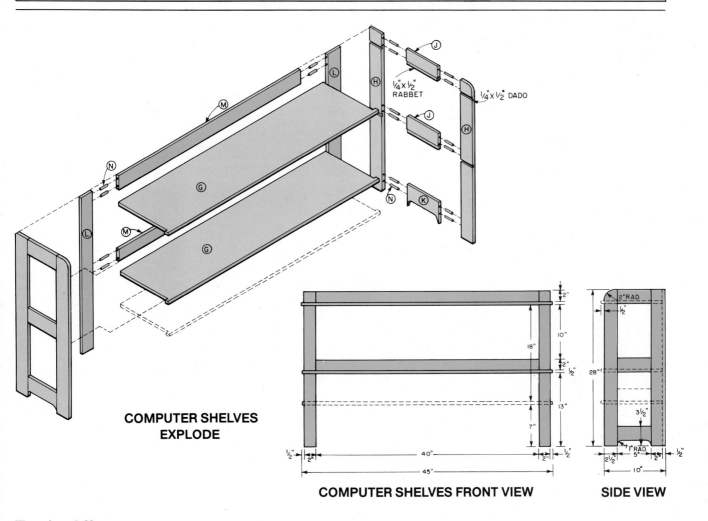

COMPUTER SHELVES EXPLODE

COMPUTER SHELVES FRONT VIEW

SIDE VIEW

Topping Off

After building this desk and using it for a short time, I grew to love it. I even set it up at home, since it turned out to be such an attractive piece of furniture. But I found it has one annoying limitation, especially if you leave it set up in one place for a long time — no storage space. So I built a set of shelves for the top.

These shelves don't travel; they don't fold up into a neat package. But they do give you a place to put manuals, disks, printouts, and paper when you're not on the go.

The shelves are made from 1/2″ thick stock (like the sides of the desk). To save wood and give the shelves the same lightweight look as the desk, the shelf supports are three simple frames doweled together. Cut the rabbets and dados in the side frame parts *after* you've glued up the frames.

Assemble the shelves to the frame with glue and screws. Depending on the type of computer you have, you may want to adjust the height of the bottom shelf. If you have a Kaypro, Compaq, TRS-80 4P, or similar portable, you can leave the shelf where I show it in solid lines on the Shelving Unit Front View.

If you have an Apple IIe, IBM PC, TRS-80 2000, or something with that same modular design, lower the bottom shelf (and the middle rails of the side frames) to where they're shown in dotted lines. Slide the computer under the shelf and set the monitor on top of it. — *Nick Engler*

BILL OF MATERIALS — Portable Computer Desk

(Finished Dimensions in Inches)

Desk

A.	Desk Tops (2)	3/8 x 22-1/2 x 27-1/8
B.	Long Sides (2)	1/2 x 7 x 27-5/8
C.	Short Sides (2)	1/2 x 7 x 23
D.	Front/Back Leg Halves (4)	1/2 x 2-1/2 x 26-5/8
E.	Side Leg Halves (4)	1/2 x 2 x 26-5/8
F.	Corner Blocks (8)	3/4 x 3/4 x 3

Hardware

1-1/2″ x 24″ Piano Hinge and Mounting Screws
4″ Metal Door Pull
3/16″ T-Nuts (4)
10-32 x 1″ Flathead Stove Bolts (4)
3/8″ x 2″ Carriage Bolts, Flat Washers, and Hex Nuts (10)

Shelves

G.	Top/Bottom Shelves (2)	1/2 x 10-1/2 x 44-1/2
H.	Side Stiles (4)	1/2 x 2-1/2 x 28
J.	Side Top/Middle Rails (4)	1/2 x 2-1/2 x 5
K.	Side Bottom Rails (2)	1/2 x 3-1/2 x 5
L.	Back Stiles (2)	1/2 x 2 x 28
M.	Back Rails (2)	1/2 x 2-1/2 x 40
N.	Dowels (32)	1/4 dia. x 1

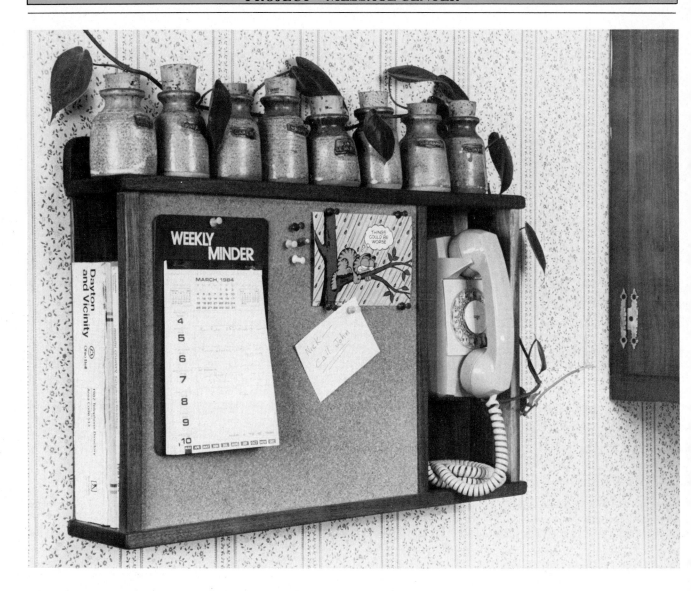

Message Center

A simple cabinet makes your phone easier to use — and more attractive.

These days a telephone can be so much more than just a telephone. You can buy phones that will automatically dial numbers, tell the time, record your calls, play music, and even let you walk and talk without tripping over a phone cord.

But with all these electronic innovations, we're still plagued with some old problems: Where do you store the phone book? How can you keep a pen and paper handy? And where do you post messages and reminders? A simple 'message center' cabinet with a cork front solves all these problems and makes the most advanced telephone easier to use.

Select a wood (or stain) that matches your telephone. Some woods look better with certain phones. For example, a black phone looks good with light woods such as beech or maple, but it gets lost on a dark background. I made the message center shown here out of walnut to set off our cream-colored phone.

Before you cut the parts, check the dimensions on my drawings to make sure your phone and phone book(s) will fit. You may want to make the phone compartment wider, narrower, shallower, or deeper to accommodate your phone. You may also want to adjust the dimensions of the book compartment, depending on your phone books (See the Front and Side Views.)

Most of the joinery in this project is simple butt joints, reinforced with glue and wood screws. The backboard and the top fit together with matching rabbets, reinforced *vertically* with screws (set in 'wells') and *horizontally* with finishing nails. (See the Exploded View.) This helps support the weight of the message center when it's hung on the wall.

The corkboard sits in several grooves routed in the top, bottom, and sides of the cabinet. (Note that the grooves in the top and bottom pieces are 'stopped' — they

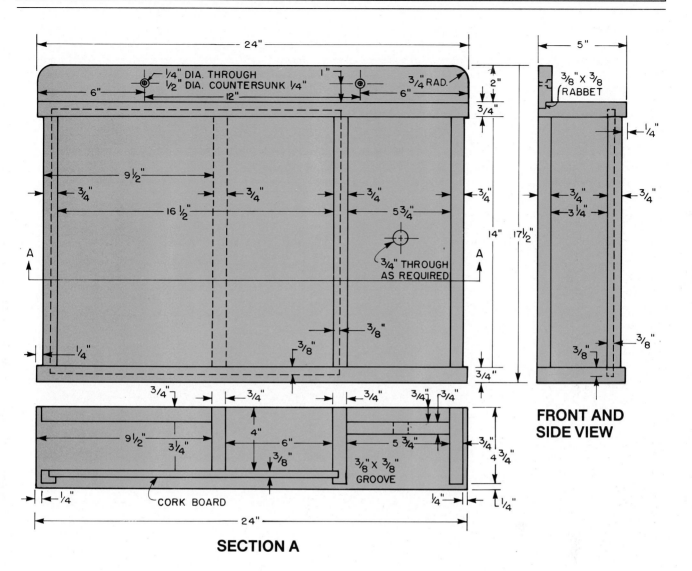

SECTION A

FRONT AND SIDE VIEW

don't run the entire length of the boards.) There are two ways to make these grooves: Perhaps the easiest is to use your drill press as an 'overarm' router, as shown in Figure 1. But this requires a special router chuck to do this safely.

If you don't have this accessory, use a hand-held router. (See Figure 2.) *Make sure* the wood is clamped securely to your workbench and make several passes — cutting 1/8″ deeper with each pass — until the grooves are 3/8″ deep.

Figure 1. There are two simple ways to make the grooves for the corkboard. (A) You can use your drill press as an 'overarm' router.

Figure 2. Or (B) you can use a hand-held router, as shown. If you use a hand-held router, *be sure* that the wood is clamped securely to your workbench.

Figure 3. To keep from splattering the corkboard, mask it off before you apply the finish.

After you've cut the joinery, finish sand all parts. Assemble the message center, being careful not to get glue on the corkboard. (It's best not to glue the cork board in the grooves — just let it 'float'.) Cover all the screw heads with plugs and sand the plugs flush. Before you apply a finish, mask the corkboard. (See Figure 3.) This will keep you from accidentally splattering the cork.

When the finish is dry, install your phone in its compartment, next to the corkboard. Thread the phone cord through the back of the compartment, through a 3/4″ hole. Hang the completed message center by its backboard, using molly anchors or toggle bolts. Put your phone books in the book compartment, paper and pens on the ledge under the phone, a few stickpins in the cork, and there you have it! An ingenious message center to enhance even the most sophisticated telephones. — *Nick Engler*

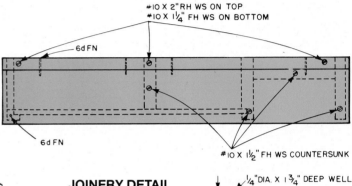

#10 X 2″ RH WS ON TOP
#10 X 1¼″ FH WS ON BOTTOM
6d FN
6d FN
#10 X 1½″ FH WS COUNTERSUNK

JOINERY DETAIL

¼″ DIA. X 1¾″ DEEP WELL
PLUG
1¾″
2″
1¾″

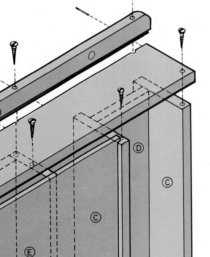

EXPLODED VIEW

BILL OF MATERIALS — Message Center

(Finished Dimensions in Inches)

A.	Backboard	3/4 x 2-3/8 x 24
B.	Top/Bottom	3/4 x 5 x 24
C.	Phone Compartment Sides (2)	3/4 x 4-3/4 x 14
D.	Phone Compartment Back	3/4 x 5-3/4 x 14
E.	Book Compartment Side	3/4 x 4 x 14
F.	Book Compartment Back	3/4 x 9-1/2 x 14
G.	Front Trim	3/4 x 3/4 x 14
H.	Corkboard	3/8 x 14-3/4 x 16-1/4

Hardware

#10 x 2″ Roundhead Wood Screws (3)
#10 x 1-1/4″ Flat Head Wood Screws (11)
6d Finishing Nails (6)
Molly Anchors or Toggle Bolts (2)
Phone

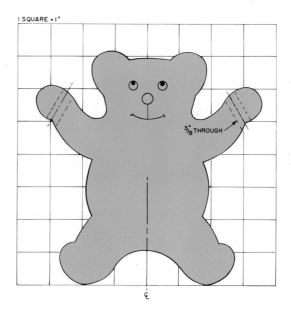

PIVOT BAR LAYOUT

1 SQUARE = 1"

3/8 THROUGH

BEAR PATTERN

Climbing Bear

A few minutes and a few scraps of wood are all it takes to make this great action toy.

Try, if you can, to figure out the physical principle that makes this toy work: Hold the ropes apart slightly and pull first on one rope, then the other. The bear will shimmy up toward the bar. Bring the ropes together and he'll slide back down. Fascinating? Your kids will think so.

The trick to making this toy work is to drill the holes in the arms *at a slight angle*. (See the Bear Pattern and Figure 1.) As you pull on a rope, it will wedge itself in its hole, allowing the slack rope to slide through the other hole. It also helps if the holes are about 1/8″ larger than the diameter of the rope. For example, if you use 1/4″ curtain cord to make this toy, drill 3/8″ holes.

Besides the bear, you'll also need to make a 'pivot bar'. This simple 3/4″ x 3/4″ x 7″ bar keeps the ropes spread at the proper distance and acts as a lever to raise one rope while lowering the other. Thread two 36″ long ropes through the arm of the bear, then through the holes near the ends of the bar. Tie simple knots in the 'up' ends to keep the ropes from pulling through. You'll also want to tie

knots or fasten beads to the 'down' ends of these ropes, to give the kids something to hang onto — and to keep the bear from sliding off the ropes.

Thread a shorter rope (about 6″ long) through the holes near the middle of the bar, and knot the ends to form a loop. Use this loop to hang the toy from a nail or hook.
— *Nick Engler*

Figure 1. Drill the holes in the bear's arms at a slight angle. It helps to clamp the bear down to your workbench while you do this.

BILL OF MATERIALS — Climbing Bear

(Finished Dimensions in Inches)

A.	Bear	3/4 x 7 x 7-1/4
B.	Pivot Bar	3/4 x 3/4 x 7
C.	Beads (2 — optional)	3/4 dia.

Hardware

1/4″ Curtain cord (7′)

Lacquered Desk

This unique desk is a work of art — in more ways than one.

In the late seventeenth and early eighteenth centuries — the William & Mary period — imported furniture from the Orient began to influence European and American cabinetmakers. Among the elements they copied was the cabriole or 'horsebone' leg as it was called back then, the ball-and-claw foot, and ornately patterned brass hardware.

But perhaps the most striking design influence was 'japanning' (named after the country), in which the surface of the furniture was first coated with a colored varnish, then

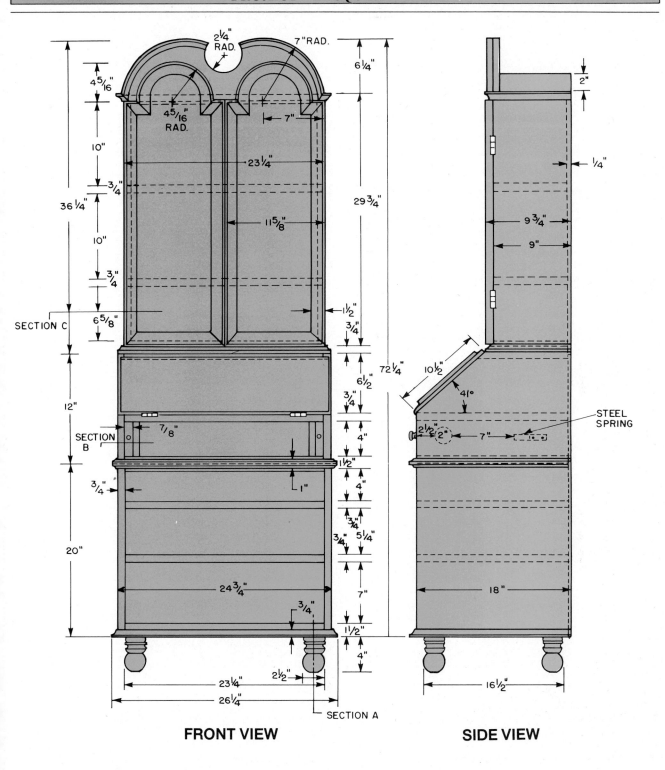

FRONT VIEW

SIDE VIEW

painted with pictures of boats, animals, mythical creatures, forests, pastoral landscapes — anything that struck the japanner's fancy. Sometimes these pictures were built up in relief; sometimes they were gilded. Always, they were finished with multiple coats of clear lacquer to make it look as if the scenes were set in glass. In fact, japanned furniture was more often called 'lacquered' furniture.

Japanning died out by the early 19th century, but interest in the technique has recently revived. Those few original examples of japanned furniture that have survived are now worth thousands of dollars. (One japanned William & Mary highboy from New England was appraised at over $100,000.) If you admire japanned furniture but don't have that kind of money, you can create the same elegant effect with modern materials — and no artistic ability!

To show you how it's done, we "japanned" a copy of a William & Mary secretary desk. The plans and instructions for the desk are reproduced here, along with the instructions for modern japanning. But you don't have to build the desk to take advantage of the technique. Japanning can be

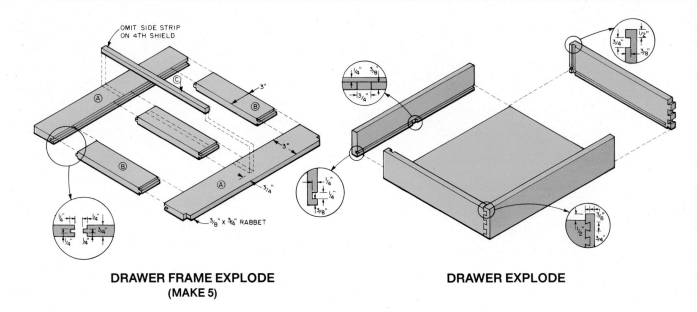

DRAWER FRAME EXPLODE
(MAKE 5)

DRAWER EXPLODE

used to adorn chests, drawer fronts, table aprons — any wooden surface that would benefit from decoration.

Making the Desk

Materials — The desk you see here is made out of many different plywoods, hardwoods, and softwoods. Because the wood is completely covered during japanning, the choice of materials is unimportant. You can use leftover scraps from several different projects; it will all end up looking the same.

However, if you want to build the secretary and leave off the japanning, select an attractive hardwood. Mahogany was the preferred wood during the William & Mary period, but American cabinetmakers often used walnut, maple and cherry.

Chest of Drawers — The secretary is built in three pieces — the chest of drawers, the desk unit, and the bookcase. The pieces come apart so that you can easily move the lacquered desk from place to place.

Begin by making four drawers and five drawer frames, as shown in the Drawer Explode and Drawer Frame Ex-

plode illustrations. The drawer sides are assembled to the drawer fronts with 'half-blind' dovetails. You can make these dovetails easily with a hand-held router and a dovetail template, as shown in Figure 1. (In fact, a template makes dovetails easier to cut than any other drawer joint!) If you don't have a router or template, you can substitute other joinery.

Notice that the bottom edge of the drawer back is notched to fit over the guides that run down the middle of the drawer frames. However, only four out of the five frames need these guides. The fourth frame from the bottom — the frame that sits on top of the chest of drawers — does not support a drawer.

Cut the joinery in the chest sides with a router, then assemble the chest case. Add cove molding to the bottom of the case, and 'double cove' molding to the top. You can cut this special top molding on a shaper or router table using a cove bit. (See Figure 2.) When you attach the top molding, remember that *half* the width protrudes above the top of the case. This forms a 'lip' around the top edge that holds the desk unit in position.

Figure 1. You can quickly cut the dovetails in the drawer sides and front with a hand-held router and dovetail template.

Figure 2. Use a shaper or router table to cut the 'double-cove' molding that masks the seam between the chest and the desk unit. You'll need to make two passes to cut both coves.

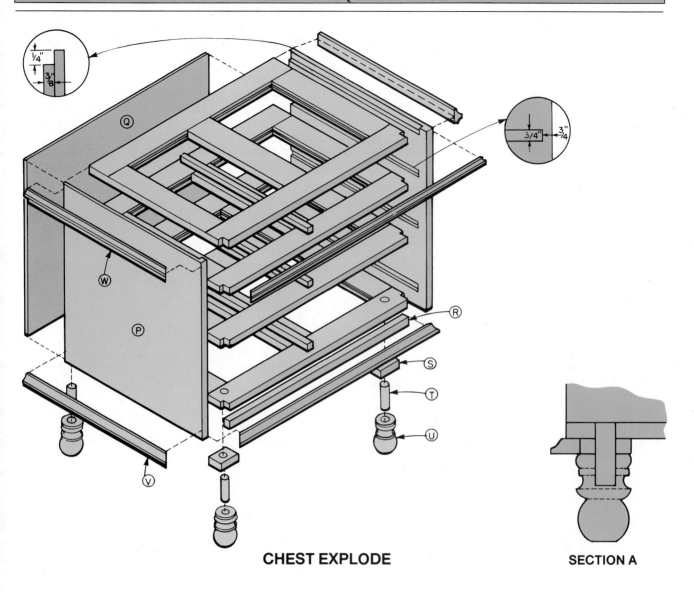

CHEST EXPLODE

SECTION A

Desk Unit — There is nothing special about making the desk unit; all the joinery is similar to the joinery on the chest of drawers with two exceptions: The hinges that hold the lid to the desk top must be carefully positioned so that the lid lays flat against the sides when the secretary is closed, and so that there is no gap between the desk top and the lid when the secretary is open.

Also, the desk drawer is narrower than the drawers in the chest, to accommodate the sliding lid supports. These supports are 'stopped' when you pull them out by a flat spring that butts against the edge of a hole in the spacers. We show the openings for the supports to be 7/8″ wide. This allows room for flat springs up to 1/16″ thick. If your springs are thicker or you have trouble fitting the supports in their openings, mortise the springs into the lid supports.

Tip ◆ To remove a lid support after you've inserted it in its opening, remove the desk drawer, then reach in through the hole in the spacer and depress the spring.

If you wish, make some 'pigeonholes' and mount them

in the back of the desk. We show one possible arrangement in our drawings with an 'In' and 'Out' set of holes separated by two small drawers for stamps, paper clips, etc. However, you may want to design something tailored to your own needs.

Bookcase — This project is designed so that you can stop with the desk unit and omit the bookcase top. But if you go on, the bookcase unit is the simplest to make. The only tricky steps are making the curved moldings for the pediment and the curved tops for the door frames. All of these parts are cut in a similar fashion: Trace the shape of the molding or frame onto a board and cut the *inside* curve on a bandsaw. Shape the inside edge as needed. (See Figure 3.) When shaping the top door frame, remember to cut an ogee in the front and a rabbet in the back. After shaping, cut the outside curve to free the molding or frame from the board. (See Figure 4.)

Warning: *Don't* try to cut the molding or frame parts from the board, then shape them. Shaping thin, curved pieces can be extremely dangerous. It's much safer (and easier) to leave the parts attached to the board while shaping the edge.

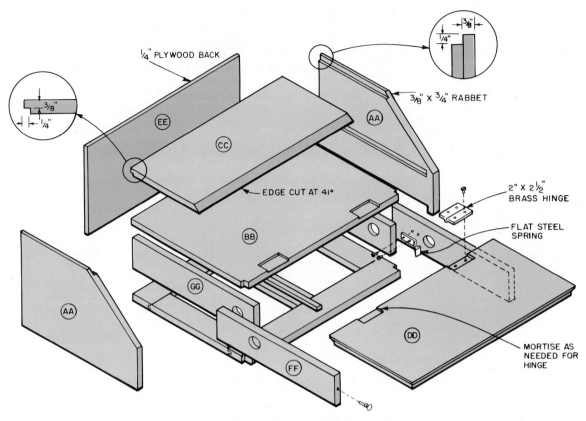

DESK UNIT EXPLODE

Labels in diagram: ¼" PLYWOOD BACK, ⅜" × ¾" RABBET, EE, AA, CC, BB, GG, AA, FF, DD, EDGE CUT AT 41°, 2" × 2½" BRASS HINGE, FLAT STEEL SPRING, MORTISE AS NEEDED FOR HINGE, ⅜", ¼"

Figure 3. To make the curved moldings or frame parts, cut the inside curve on a bandsaw. Then shape the inside edge on a shaper or router table.

Figure 4. After the molding or frame part is shaped, cut the outside curve to free the piece from the board.

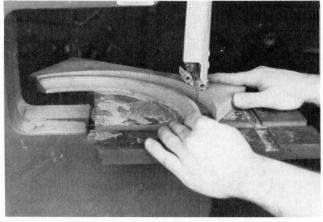

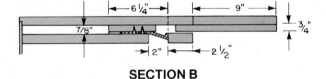

SECTION B

Labels: 6¼", 9", 7/8", 2", 2½", ¾"

Assemble the units by stacking them on top of one another. When they're properly positioned, fasten them together with wood screws. Fit the drawers and lid supports in their proper openings, and attach the doors to the bookcase. When everything is fastened and fitted to your satisfaction, disassemble the units, remove all hardware, and finish sand any parts that need it.

Japanning

True japanning, as performed by the oriental cabinetmakers who invented the technique, was a painstakingly slow and expensive process. After completing a piece of furniture, the japanner scraped the wood until it was glass-smooth. Then, over a period of months, he applied as many as thirty coats of resin from the exotic *Rhus vernicifera,* or Asian Sumac tree.

European and American woodworkers could not afford the necessary time for careful scraping and multiple coats of finish, so they developed substitutes. The wood was primed with 'whiting', a chalk-like substance, then scraped smooth. Over this primer, the Western japanner applied one or more coats of a tinted varnish or shellac. Black was the most common tint, but japanners also used white, red, yellow, green, and blue on occasion.

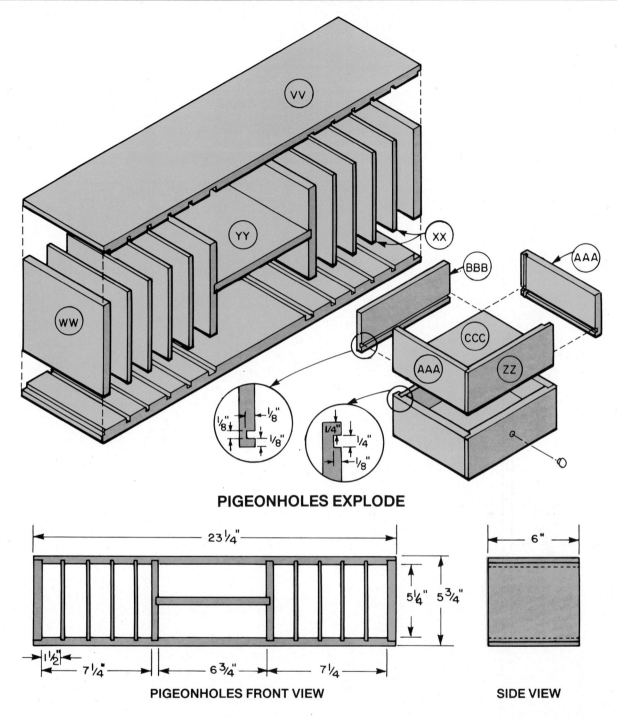

PIGEONHOLES EXPLODE

PIGEONHOLES FRONT VIEW

SIDE VIEW

The varnished surface was then covered with wonderfully bizarre interpretations of oriental designs, using oil paints and pigments. If the japanner wanted a picture or design to stand out in relief, he built up the surface with multiple coats of whiting and painted over it. Sometimes he would gild the figures with golf leaf or metal dust. The completed paintings were covered with several coats of clear varnish or shellac to protect them and make them blend in with the surface.

You may find it difficult to scrounge up the original ingredients for whiting or *Rhus vernicifera* resin from your local merchants, so we have again developed substitutes — gesso, acrylic enamel, acrylic paints, and gel medium. These

materials should be readily available from an art supply shop.

Make sure the three units — chest, desk, and bookcase — are *disassembled,* then coat the surfaces with gesso (our substitute for whiting). Gesso is a thick, white substance that will quickly fill in any imperfection in the wood or joinery. This stuff is so thick that if the units are fastened together when you apply the gesso, the gesso will crack when you try to take them apart. Apply three coats, scraping and sanding between each coat. (See Figure 5.)

After the gesso is dry, apply at least two coats of acrylic enamel — this takes the place of a tinted varnish. Enamel is available in a wide range of colors, so you

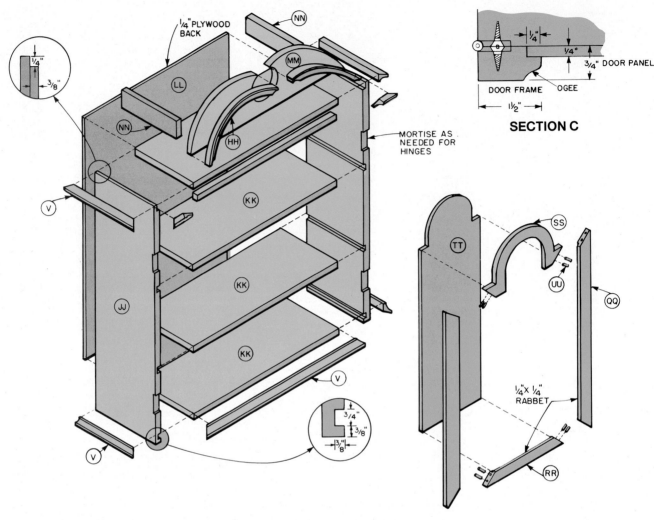

¼" PLYWOOD BACK

NN

MM

LL

NN

HH

V

KK

KK

JJ

KK

V

V

MORTISE AS NEEDED FOR HINGES

¼"

³⁄₈"

¾"

³⁄₈"

³⁄₈"

SECTION C

¼"

¼"

¾" DOOR PANEL

DOOR FRAME

OGEE

1½"

SS

TT

UU

QQ

¼" X ¼" RABBET

RR

BOOKCASE EXPLODE

Figure 5. Cover the finished desk with three coats of gesso. Scrape each coat smooth, then lightly sand the surface to remove any scraper marks.

shouldn't have any trouble finding a hue that matches the 'oriental' colors used by earlier japanners. When the enamel is dry, stack (but don't fasten) the units temporarily.

At this point you can go in one of two directions: If you're an accomplished artist (or you know an accomplished artist with time to spare), you can paint scenes and designs over the enamel with acrylic pigments. If you don't count yourself as an artist, you can resort to decoupage. Since we were a little short on artistic talent at the moment, we chose the latter alternative.

If you decide to take the same route, purchase several museum quality prints, then tape them to the desk. Shuffle them around if you have to until you find a pleasing arrangement. When you've got them where you want them, mark around them and glue a narrow 'beaded' molding to the surface to create frames for the pictures. (See Figure 6.) Remove the prints from the desk before actually gluing the molding down.

If you want, you can gild the molding to really set the prints off. Use a brush-on gold paint or — if you want to get really fancy — apply gold leaf. (We opted for the gold leaf — it took about four 'books' to cover the molding you see here.) Use gel medium thinned with water to adhere the

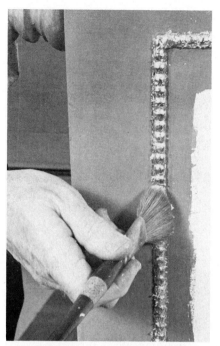

Figure 6. Tape museum-quality prints to the desk, shuffling them around until you find the arrangement you like the best. Added beaded molding to 'frame' them, if you wish.

Figure 7. Adhere gold leaf to the molding with gel medium thinned with water. You can also use gold sizing.

Figure 8. To create a gold net on the doors of the bookcase unit, stretch heavy gold thread across the surface and glue it down with gel medium.

leaf to the molding. (See Figure 7.)

Glue the prints inside the molding, once again using gel medium thinned with water as the adhesive. It's best to take the desk out of your shop and perform this step where there's no sawdust or wood chips to find their way under the prints. These will create ugly little bumps. Roll out the prints as smooth as possible and let them dry at least 24 hours. If you apply a print over the drawers, cut them apart with a razor blade after the gel has set and trim them slightly, if necessary.

To give the desk surface and prints an aged look, mix up some gel medium with a little 'burnt umber' acrylic pigment. Disassemble the units (if they aren't already) and brush this mixture over the entire surface. The gel-and-umber will slightly darken everything, giving the desk an 'antique' look.

For a special touch, you may want to create a gold net on the bookcase doors, as we did. To do this, first remove the doors and place them on a flat surface. Draw a pattern on the door surface in light pencil. Stretch heavy gold thread along the lines and glue it to the doors with gel medium. (See Figure 8.) The gel dries clear, so the gold color shines through clearly.

After you have completely 'japanned' the desk and decorated it the way you want it, coat all surfaces with urethane varnish. Take your time and apply coat after coat until the prints, molding, and threads look as if they're encased in glass.

Tip ◆ If you've applied threads to the doors, you'll find it easier to varnish them if the doors are laying flat.

Allow plenty of time between applications so that each coat dries thoroughly. Test the surface with your thumbnail before applying the next coat — if the thumbnail leaves a small indentation, the varnish isn't dry enough. When the last coat is finally dry, assemble the desk and re-attach all the hardware.

You'll quickly find that, of all the pieces of furniture you have ever built, this is a real conversation starter. More than two centuries ago, art critics extolled japanning as having "exceeded in beauty and magnificence all the pride of the Vatican . . . and the Panthenon heretofore." That may be a bit of an overstatement, but carefully done japanning can still make a good piece of furniture absolutely striking.
— *Jay Hedden*

BILL OF MATERIALS — Lacquered Desk

(Finished Dimensions in Inches)

Chest of Drawers

A.	Drawer Frame Front/Back (8)	3/4 x 3 x 24
B.	Drawer Frame Rails (12)	3/4 x 3 x 12-1/4
C.	Drawer Guides (3)	3/8 x 3/4 x 17
D.	Bottom Drawer Front	3/4 x 7 x 23-1/4
E.	Bottom Drawer Sides (2)	3/4 x 6-1/2 x 17-3/8
F.	Bottom Drawer Back	3/4 x 6-1/2 x 22-1/2
G.	Middle Drawer Front	3/4 x 5-1/4 x 23-1/4
H.	Middle Drawer Sides (2)	3/4 x 4-3/4 x 17-3/8
J.	Middle Drawer Back	3/4 x 4-3/4 x 22-1/2
K.	Top Drawer Front	3/4 x 4 x 23-1/4
L.	Top/Desk Drawer Sides (2)	3/4 x 3-1/2 x 17-3/8
M.	Top Drawer Back	3/4 x 3-1/2 x 22-1/2
N.	Drawer Bottoms (3)	1/4 x 16-1/4 x 22-1/4
P.	Chest Sides (2)	3/4 x 18 x 20
Q.	Chest Back	1/4 x 20 x 24
R.	Bottom Trim	3/4 x 3/4 x 23-1/4
S.	Foot Mounting Blocks (4)	3/4 x 2-1/4 x 3
T.	Dowels (4)	1 dia. x 3-1/2
U.	Feet (4)	2-1/2 dia. x 4
V.	Cove Molding (total)	3/4 x 3/4 x 63-3/4
W.	Double Cove Molding (total)	3/4 x 1 x 63-3/4

Desk Unit

A.	Drawer Frame Front/Back (2)	3/4 x 3 x 24
B.	Drawer Frame Raile (3)	3/4 x 3 x 12-1/4
C.	Drawer Guide	3/8 x 3/4 x 17
L.	Top/Desk Drawer Sides (2)	3/4 x 3-1/2 x 17-3/8
X.	Desk Drawer Front	3/4 x 4 x 20
Y.	Desk Drawer Back	3/4 x 3-1/2 x 19-1/4
Z.	Desk Drawer Bottom	1/4 x 16-1/4 x 19
AA.	Desk Sides (2)	3/4 x 12 x 18
BB.	Desk Top	3/4 x 17-3/4 x 24
CC.	Top Desk Shelf	3/4 x 10-1/2 x 24

DD.	Desk Lid	3/4 x 10-1/2 x 24-3/4
EE.	Desk Back	1/4 x 12-3/8 x 24
FF.	Desk Lid Supports (2)	3/4 x 3-15/16 x 17-3/4
GG.	Spacers (2)	3/4 x 4 x 17-3/4

Bookcase

V.	Cove Molding (total)	3/4 x 3/4 x 66-3/4
HH.	Curved Moldings (2)	3/4 x 3/4 x 13-3/16
JJ.	Bookcase Sides (2)	3/4 x 9 x 30-1/2
KK.	Bookcase Shelves (4)	3/4 x 8-3/4 x 22-1/2
LL.	Bookcase Back	1/4 x 22-1/2 x 30-1/2
MM.	Pediment Front	3/4 x 6-1/4 x 23-1/4
NN.	Pediment Sides (2)	3/4 x 2 x 8-1/4
PP.	Top Trim	3/4 x 3/4 x 21-3/4
QQ.	Door Stiles (4)	3/4 x 1-1/2 x 29
RR.	Bottom Door Rails (2)	3/4 x 1-1/2 x 11-5/8
SS.	Top Door Rails (2)	3/4 x 5-13/16 x 11-5/8
TT.	Door Panels (2)	1/4 x 9-1/8 x 30-13/16
UU.	Dowels (16)	3/8 dia. x 1-1/2

Pigeonholes

VV.	Top/Bottom (2)	1/2 x 6 x 23-1/4
WW.	Large Spacers (4)	1/2 x 5-1/4 x 6
XX.	Small Spacers (8)	1/4 x 5-1/4 x 6
YY.	Divider	1/2 x 6 x 7-1/4
ZZ.	Small Drawer Fronts (2)	1/4 x 2-1/8 x 6-3/4
AAA.	Small Drawer Sides (4)	1/4 x 2-1/8 x 5-7/8
BBB.	Small Drawer Backs (2)	1/4 x 2-1/8 x 6-1/2
CCC.	Small Drawer Bottoms (2)	1/8 x 5-1/2 x 6-1/2

Hardware

#8 x 1-1/4 Flathead Wood Screws (5-6 dozen)
Teardrop Drawer/Door Pulls and Mounting Screws (10)
Small Brass Pulls for Lid Supports and Lid (3)
1-1/2″ x 2-1/2″ Brass Hinges and Mounting Screws (2 pair)

TIPS
LACQUERED DESK

While the desk shown here borrows from 'William and Mary' furniture design, all the joinery is decidedly modern. Craftsmen of the William & Mary period (1690-1725) would have attached the drawer frames to the chest sides with dovetails. We suggest you use dado joints, reinforced with wood screws.

◆ It's best to put these screws *inside* a furniture case or on the *blind side* of a board where you can't see them. To do this, *toenail* the screws up through the shelf or drawer frame and into the sides of the case. (See Figure A.) Drill your pilot hole at a steep angle so that the screw won't come out the other side

when you install it. If the screw head interferes with the sliding action of the drawers — or it's seen when you open the bookcase doors — countersink the head into the shelf or drawer frame.

Figure A. To reinforce a dado joint from the *inside* of the furniture case, 'toenail' the screw at a sharp angle up through the shelf or drawer frame and into the side.

Top-Grade Workbench

All your woodworking will go faster with a hard-working workbench.

No doubt about it, the most important element of any workshop is the workbench. You can knock things together on the garage floor . . . you can tinker things apart on the kitchen table. But when the job has to be done in a hurry — or with a degree of accuracy — you need a top-grade workbench like the one shown here.

What makes a workbench top-grade? How well a workbench works for you depends on four factors: height, size, orientation, and facilities. Let's discuss these one by one:

Height

The height of your bench is determined by how high you are. Most woodworkers find that a bench about 8 inches below the elbows is about right. At this level, you'll find that the bench will put the work where you can pound on it, drive screws in it, paint it — or whatever — with a minimum of bend and stoop.

If the majority of your work is with heavy tools, you might want the bench a little lower, to give yourself more 'whap' room. On the other hand, if you do mostly fine, meticulous work, you could go a little higher — closer to your eyes. (Actually, a stool you can pull up to an average-height bench will put you comfortably close to those small jobs.)

Size

Make a bench as long or as short as your shop situation dictates. The most important size consideration is not length, but depth — front to back. For most of us, 30 inches is about right. Make it more than that, and you can't reach the other side. Make it much less and you'll find there isn't room on the bench for a lot of things you may want to work on — and the required tools to work with.

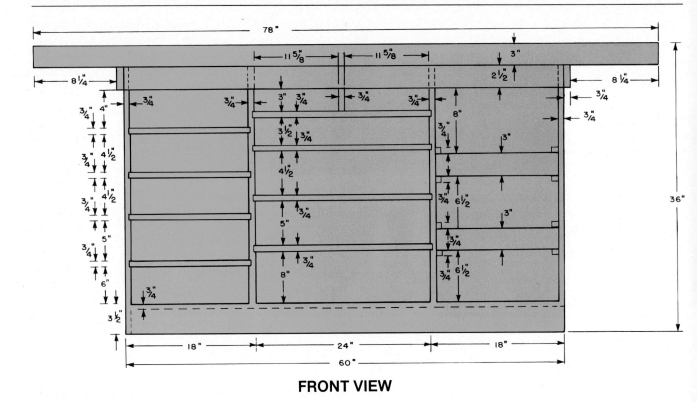

FRONT VIEW

If your bench stands with its back edge against a wall, and if you hang tools on that wall, 30 inches is an absolute maximum — and you may want to slim it down a little to make the tools easier to reach.

Orientation

The handiest workbench is an island — with all four sides open. This position multiplies the usefulness of your work-space because you can work on all sides. You can work all around a project without twisting and turning it on the bench.

Second best is the peninsula — one end against a wall, with access to two long sides and the other end. Third best is a bench with its back against the wall. You can work at either end, or all across the front. Last — and avoid this one if at all possible — is the bench in a corner.

Facilities

The biggest shortcoming on a vast majority of home work-shop benches is an inadequate vise. If you do more than piddling woodworking, you need a 10-inch woodworking vise. If you do very much of it, you'll appreciate the con-venience of a 'quick release' model, which can be pushed or pulled open or shut to accommodate different workpieces. (An example of this type of vise is the Columbian 10-RDW shown in the photos.)

A good woodworking vise will have a pop-up 'dog' to secure large workpieces on the surface of the bench. But in order to use this device, you need to make a few 'bench dogs' and drill holes in the bench top to hold them. (See Figure 1.) To clamp a large workpiece, simply pop up the vise dog, drop a bench dog into one of the holes, put your workpiece in between the two dogs, and tighten the vise.

If your shop runs heavily to metal and mechanical projects, you need a steel machinist's vise. To be equal to most tasks, it should have a jaw close to 4 inches wide, and it should open 4 inches or more. Keep in mind that a metal-working vise is, generally, unacceptable for woodworking. It mars and scratches the wood, and cannot be easily cushioned or 'cauled' to protect a wood surface. So if you do both metalworking *and* woodworking, you'll need two vises.

If you have an island workbench, you mount the

Figure 1. To clamp workpieces wider than the vise will open, bore holes every 6″ or so, in line with the pop-up dog on the vise. Use bolts or 1″ dowels for bench dogs.

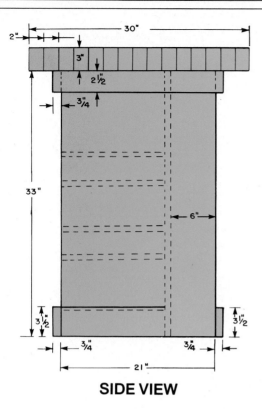

SIDE VIEW

cans, paint, enamel, and other items that must be close at hand.

How the Bench Goes Together

Basically, the workbench shown here is composed of a pair of storage cabinets tied together with a rugged top. The exact design of the cabinets depends on the kinds of work you do, the kinds of tools you use, and the amount of space you have. Ideally, they should provide access from both front and back — assuming an island or a peninsula orientation. And they should be designed to provide a variety of storage spaces on both sides. In other words, you need shelves and drawers and pull-out trays everywhere. In use, you'll soon find yourself picking one side or one end for each kind of activity, and storing the tools and materials you need for that activity within easy reach.

As drawn, the space between the cabinets is filled up with large drawers. But you can leave it open as 'knee-space' if you do much sit-down work. If you don't need the drawer space, you'll find it handy to hang tools on the sides of the cabinets.

The doors are optional. You can leave the shelves and tray open — or close them off with plywood doors. The difference? Without the doors, you'll accumulate a lot of dust and debris.

First, the Cabinets

The two cabinets that form the base are made from 3/4" thick plywood As the drawings show, the plywood parts go together to form two pedestals. Use glue and #10 x 1-1/2" wood screws for assembly.

The space between the pedestals depends on the length of the bench. Two pieces of 1x4 hold the pedestals together at the base, one in front and one in back. These 1x4's not only give the base structural strength, but also help to level the cabinet bottoms.

Fabricating the Top

There are several practical methods for putting together the top for a good workbench. Perhaps the easiest is to laminate three sheets of 3/4" thick plywood (or particleboard), using contact cement or another adhesive. Three thicknesses are essential if you want a top that will take the beating workbenches often must withstand. You can get all three layers out of two sheets of material by cutting the stock *lengthwise*. Use the two solid pieces for the top and bottom, and piece together the middle layer.

Many craftsmen prefer a bench top made from laminated 2x3's. Run one edge through a jointer, then assemble the boards into a single thick plank. There are two methods you can use. You can drill carefully spaced holes through the 2x3's, shove a threaded rod through the holes, then put drive nuts on the rods to hold things together. That's the classic method. However, with today's adhesives, there's a simpler way:

● Cut off one end of the boards true and square. Try to eliminate any faults in the wood.

● Line up the boards with the true-cut ends flush. Take the first board and smear glue on the surface that will be laminated to the next.

woodworking vise on one end, and the metalworking vise on the other. The only disadvantage you may find to this is that the surface-mounted metalworking vise will be in the way when you try to swing around a large woodworking project on the bench. If this becomes a problem, the Class-A solution is to mount the metalworking vise on a square of wood so that you can clamp it in the woodworking vise when you work with metal. (See Figure 2.)

Other facilities a good bench should have are a variety of shelf and drawer spaces for tools, nails, screws, glue, oil

Figure 2. If you work with metal now and then, bolt your metalworking vise to a block of wood and clamp it in the woodworking vise when you need to use it.

● Hold the top surfaces flush and drive 10d nails through the top 2x3 into the other. **Important:** If you have trouble keeping the top surfaces lined up, use clamps.

● Continue gluing and nailing until you have built up a plank as wide as you need.

● When the glue is dry, cut the other end square. (See Figure 3.) Remove any glue beads from the work surface and true the surface with a fore plane. (See Figure 4.)

One of the most useful features of this workbench is that the top is removable. The reason for this, born of long experience, is that over a period of time a bench top gets so beat up that you'll want a new one — without completely having to rebuild the bench.

After you've completed the top, fasten a rectangle of 1x3's on edge on the underside of the top, using lag screws. This rectangle should fit snugly over the cabinet base.

Before you flop the top over and set it in position, however, install a woodworking vise in one corner. Chisel out a mortise for the base of the vise, and bolt it to the underside of the bench top. (See Figures 5 and 6.)

Turn the top over and set it in place. Now that you have a great place to work, go ahead and build the drawers and trays that you need. — *Jackson Hand*

BILL OF MATERIALS — Workbench

(Finished Dimensions in Inches)

A.	Top Members (20)	1-1/2 x 3 x 78
B.	Front Top Mounts (2)	3/4 x 2-1/2 x 60
C.	Side Top Mounts (2)	3/4 x 2-1/2 x 22-1/2
D.	Cabinet Sides (4)	3/4 x 21 x 33
E.	Cabinet Backs (2)	3/4 x 16-1/2 x 33
F.	Bottom Trim (2)	3/4 x 3-1/2 x 60

Extras

G.	Shelves	3/4 x 6 x 17-1/4
H.	Drawer Fronts/Backs	3/4 x (Variable) x 24
J.	Drawer Sides	3/4 x (Variable) x 20-1/2
K.	Drawer Bottoms	1/4 x 20-1/4 x 23-1/4
L.	Drawer Frame Rails	3/4 x 1-1/2 x 24-3/4
M.	Drawer Frame Stiles	3/4 x 1-1/2 x 18
N.	Tray Fronts	3/4 x 4 x 16-1/2
P.	Tray Sides	3/4 x 4 x 14
Q.	Tray Backs	3/4 x 4 x 15-3/4
R.	Tray Bottoms	1/4 x 13 x 15-3/4
S.	Tray Slides	3/4 x 3/4 x 14-1/4
U.	Doors	3/4 x 18 x 27

Hardware

Vise(s) (To Suit Your Needs)
Drawer and Door Pulls
#10 x 1-1/4″ Flathead Wood Screws (5-6 dozen)

Figure 3. To make a bench top, glue and nail 2x3's flush at one end. Square-cut the other end after the glue has dried. A portable jigsaw with a long blade does the job fast.

Figure 4. Depending on how true your 2x3's are, you may need to plane the top smooth. Use a fore plane, working diagonally across the top. Finish up with a belt sander.

Figure 5. Mortise the underside of the bench top to accommodate your woodworking vise.

Figure 6. Attach the vise to the bench with lag screws (through the base) and flathead wood screws (through the face).

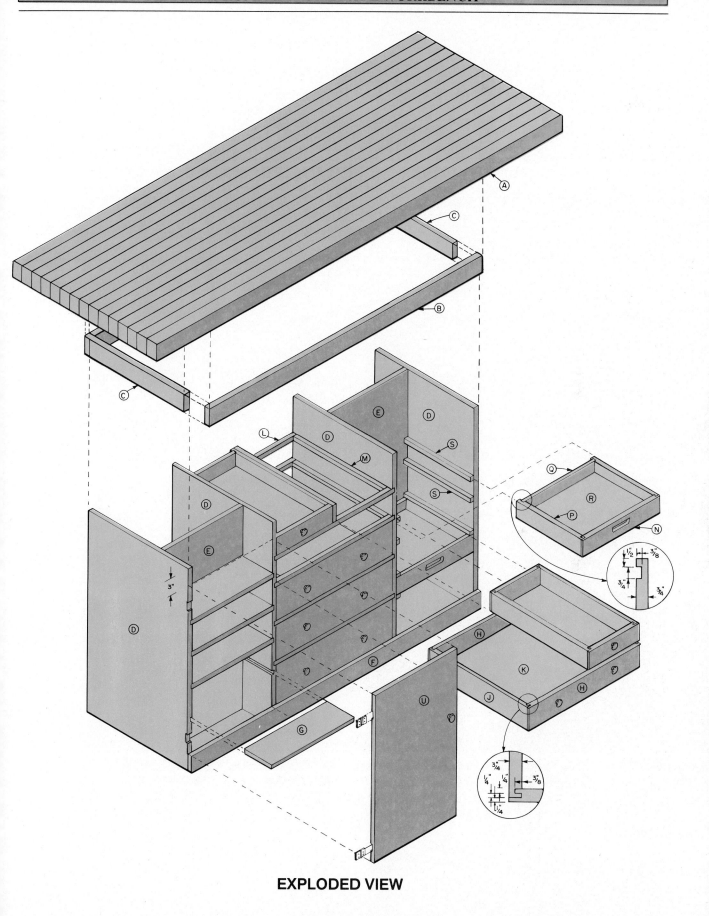

EXPLODED VIEW

Adaptable Shelves

This versatile project becomes a bookshelf, a desk, an entertainment center — or all three.

It's the age of *components*. Visit any appliance store and you'll find stereo components, television components, home computer components, video game components. All these can be plugged together in a system that adapts to

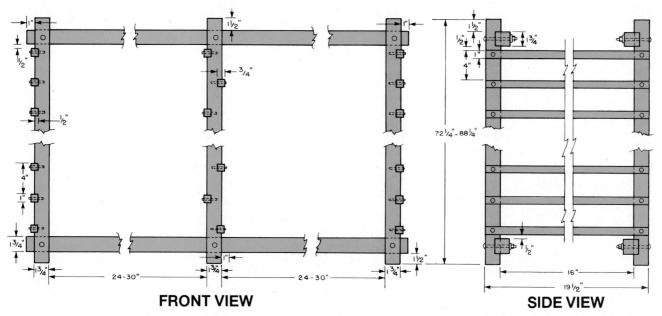

FRONT VIEW　　　　　　　　**SIDE VIEW**

your changing needs, by simply adding and subtracting components.

To hold this adaptable technology, you need an adaptable storage unit, one that can be reconfigured when you change components. By building 2-3 simple 'ladders' and laying slats across the rungs, you can have an attractive unit that lets you change *both* the height and width of the shelves at whim.

Before you begin building, measure the space where you want these 'adaptable shelves' to fit. Also measure the components (and anything else) you want to store on these shelves. You may need to adjust the width and height of the unit as shown on our drawings.

You may also wish to vary the design to blend with your furnishings. As shown, the rungs of the ladder protrude slightly from the supports, and the dowels protrude from the rungs. All the corners are rounded. This gives the finished unit a 'rustic' look, and it works well with antiques and country style furniture. (See Figure 1.) For a modern setting, set the rungs flush in the supports, sand the dowels flush with the rungs, and keep the corners 'hard.' (See Figure 2.)

As you build the shelves, a few production techniques will help you along: Rip and join all the stock, then clamp a stop block to the backstop of your radial arm saw (or the fence of your table saw) to automatically gauge the length of the rungs and the shelving slats. (See Figure 3.)

When you're ready to cut dadoes in the supports, make an L-bracket out of two pieces of scrap, as shown in Figure 4. Clamp this to the saw table, then draw lines on the bracket to indicate the desired width of the dadoes. The right line should be exactly 4″ to the left of the dado blade. Make your first dado, then slide the stock along the bracket until the dado lines up with the lines. Cut another dado and repeat. This bracket will help you accurately space all the dadoes without having to measure for every one of them.

Important Note: The rungs *alternate* from side to side on the middle ladder. (See the Front View illustration.) As you make the dadoes in the middle supports, remember to turn the stock over after each cut.

Figure 1. Protruding rungs and rounded edges give the shelves a rustic look.

Figure 2. Flush rungs and hard corners let the unit blend with contemporary furnishings.

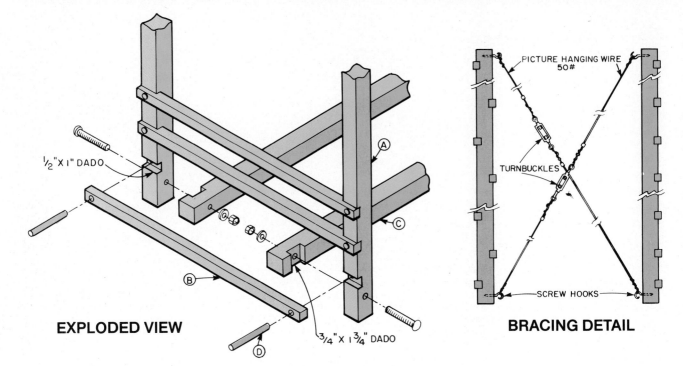

EXPLODED VIEW

½" X I" DADO

¾" X I¾" DADO

BRACING DETAIL

PICTURE HANGING WIRE 50#

TURNBUCKLES

SCREW HOOKS

Finish sand all parts, then attach the rungs to the supports with glue and dowels to make the ladders. Assemble the ladders and the stretchers with carriage bolts. Carefully stand the assembly up — you'll notice that it's pretty wobbly. To get rid of this wobble, screw hooks into the back left (or back right) and back middle supports. Run picture framing wire and turnbuckles between the hooks to form an X-brace, as shown in the Bracing Detail illustration. Tighten the wire by turning the buckles. When both wires are taut, the frame will be rigid. With the shelves in place, you'll barely notice the wires.

Tip ◆ As you turn the buckles, check the frame for squareness. The wires can pull the frame out of square if the buckles are turned unevenly.

Lay the slats in place wherever you need a shelf. Shelves can be 4", 8", 12", or 16" wide depending on how many slats you use. If you need a shelf wider than 16", or if you want to include a desk (for a home computer, perhaps), build the desk unit as shown in our drawings. This unit folds out to make a work space 28"-34" wide and 24" deep. When not in use, you can fold the desk back into the unit.

Figure 3. Use stop blocks to automatically gauge the length of each rung or shelving slat as you work.

Tip ◆ To make it easier to pull a chair up to the desk, omit the front bottom stretcher just under the desk unit. Also, pull two small dowels in the back supports to keep the desktop from tipping forward when you rest your elbows on the front edge. (See Figure 5.)

When you've completed your adaptable shelves, disassemble the unit and remove all hardware. Finish with a 'penetrating' finish such as Danish oil or tung oil. (Ours is finished with several coats of linseed oil.) Because the shelves will be moved around a lot, avoid 'building' finishes like polyurethane and varnish. These will quickly become scratched and cracked. — *Nick Engler*

Figure 4. To help accurately space the dado in the supports, make an L-bracket and clamp it to the saw table. Line up the edge of a previously-cut dado with the lines on the bracket to position the next dado.

Figure 5. Insert small dowels in the back supports to keep the desk unit from tipping forward.

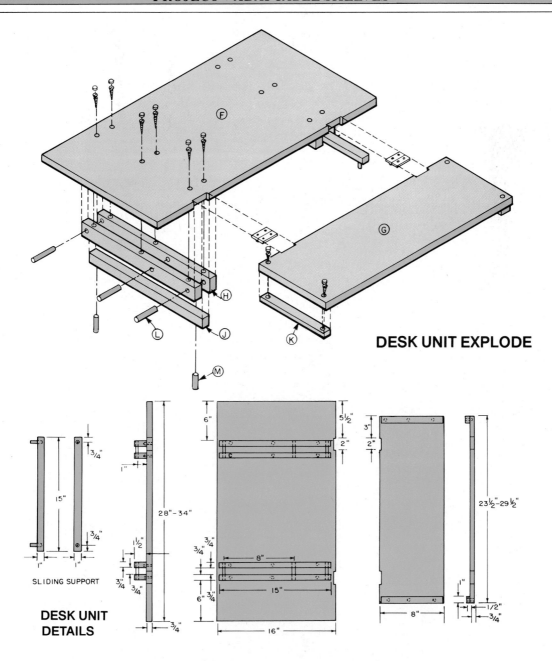

DESK UNIT EXPLODE

DESK UNIT DETAILS

SLIDING SUPPORT

BILL OF MATERIALS — Adaptable Shelves

(Finished Dimensions in Inches)

Shelving Unit

A.	Supports (4-6)	1-3/4 x 1-3/4 x (Variable)
B.	Rungs (36-63)	3/4 x 1 x 19-1/2
C.	Stretchers (4)	1-3/4 x 1-3/4 x (Variable)
D.	Dowels (72-126)	3/8 dia. x 1-1/2
E.	Slats (45-70)	3/4 x 4 x (Variable)

Hardware

3/8" x 3-1/2" Carriage Bolts, Nuts, and Washers (8-12)
50# Picture Hanging Wire (16")
3" Turnbuckles (2)
2-1/2" Screw Hooks (4)

Desk Unit

F.	Fixed Desktop	3/4 x 16 x (Variable)
G.	Folding Desktop	3/4 x 8 x (Variable)
H.	Support Brackets (4)	3/4 x 1-1/2 x 15
J.	Sliding Supports (2)	3/4 x 1 x 15
K.	Stiffeners (2)	1/2 x 3/4 x 8
L.	Dowels (6)	3/8 dia. x 2-1/4
M.	Stops (4)	1/4 dia. x 1
N.	Plugs (12)	3/8 dia. x 1/4

Hardware

1-1/2" x 2" Hinges and Mounting Screws (1 pair)
#10 x 1-1/4" Flathead Wood Screws (12)
#10 x 1" Flathead Wood Screws (4)

Firewood Box

This old-timey box stores a day's firewood — and keeps the sawdust from spreading all over the house.

There's nothing quite so cozy and comforting as a hot stove on a chilly day. Nothing looks so inviting, nothing smells so good, and nothing helps out with the winter fuel bills like a blazing fire. And — let's face it — nothing's quite so messy as firewood.

A wood box won't eliminate the mess, but it will confine it to one place and keep it out of sight. The box shown here will hold a day's and a night's firewood (depending on your wood stove) — and who knows how much bark, leaves, and sawdust.

Build the front, back, and sides of the box from 3/4" thick stock, using box joints (as shown in the photo) or lap-

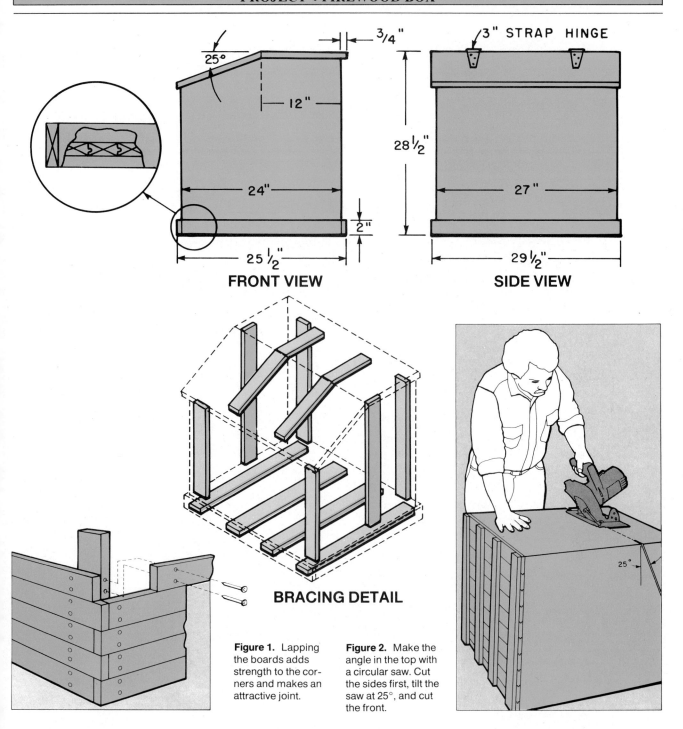

FRONT VIEW

SIDE VIEW

3" STRAP HINGE

3/4"

25°

12"

24"

25 1/2"

2"

28 1/2"

27"

29 1/2"

BRACING DETAIL

Figure 1. Lapping the boards adds strength to the corners and makes an attractive joint.

Figure 2. Make the angle in the top with a circular saw. Cut the sides first, tilt the saw at 25°, and cut the front.

25°

ping the boards at the corners (as shown in Figure 1). Make the bottom from tongue-and-groove flooring, then attach the side and bottom braces shown in the Bracing Detail. This bracework is important! A wood box takes a beating every time you dump a load of firewood in it. In order for the box to hold together, the joints must be reinforced.

It's easier to cut the angle in the top *after* you've built the box. Cut the sides first, using a circular saw. Then tilt the saw blade at 25° and cut the front. (See Figure 2.) Finally, attach the top, lid, and bottom molding. Finish with linseed oil. — *Nick Engler*

BILL OF MATERIALS — Firewood Box

(Finished Dimensions in Inches)

A.	Side Planks (18)	3/4 x 3 x 23-1/4
B.	Front and Back Planks (18)	3/4 x 3 x 26-1/4
C.	Lid	3/4 x 13-3/8 x 29-1/2
D.	Top	3/4 x 12-3/4 x 29-1/2
E.	Bottom Planks (6)	3/4 x 4 x 24
F.	Braces and Molding (total)	3/4 x 2 x 29-1/2

Hardware

8d Box Nails (1/2 lb.)
3" Strap Hinges (1 pair) and Screws

Multi-Table

No matter what kind of table you need, here it is!

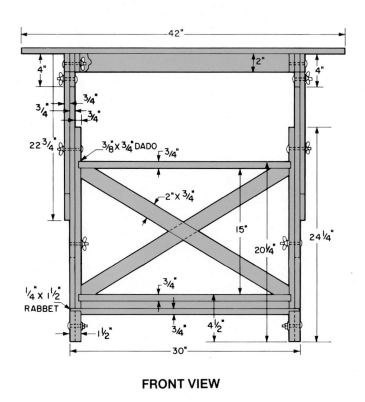

FRONT VIEW

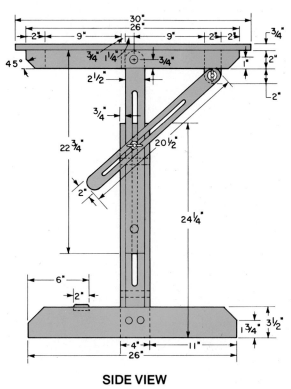

SIDE VIEW

There's no good reason for a table to be fixed at one height, rigidly horizontal. Free the top so that you can adjust it to different levels and angles, and you've increased its usefulness many times over! Better yet, you've created a piece of furniture that helps conserve valuable living space by serving several functions.

Our 'multi-table' adjusts from 27″ to 40″ above the floor, and the top tilts 45° or more in both directions, to serve as many functions as possible. At 27″, it's a typing table or computer stand. At 30″, it becomes a breakfast table or desk. At 36″, you can use it as a workbench or 'floating' counter space in your kitchen. Extend the multi-table all the way to 40″, tilt the top, and it becomes a drafting board or art easel. The key to all this versatility is a simple system of slotted boards that slide together and can be locked in place with carriage bolts and wing nuts.

Making and Machining the Parts

As you begin, give careful consideration to the stock you use to make this project. The wood must be clear, straight-grained, and **kiln-dried** (7%-8% moisture content). This reduces the chance that the wood will warp or cup after the table is built, causing the moving parts to 'hang-up'. You should also use very hard lumber, since there are metal parts that will rub against the wood. We recommend cabinet-grade cherry, rock maple, or oak. We also recommend you make the top out of veneered plywood and trim the edges with hardwood, particularly if you are going to use the multi-table as a drafting board. (See the Table Top Exploded View.) Plywood remains much flatter through changes in weather and humidity.

Plan out the machining steps carefully. The multi-table consists of several different sub-assemblies, as shown in our drawings. But rather than build one piece at a time, you can save yourself some work by making all the dadoes, then all the holes, then all the stop grooves, and so on. The machine setups to make each joint, hole, or groove are similar from part to part, no matter which sub-assembly they belong to.

Cut all parts to size and round the ends of the risers and braces. It's important that these ends be as symmetrical and as perfectly round as you can make them. To achieve this, tape each pair of parts together and 'pad saw' them on a bandsaw, staying just outside the scribed line. Then 'pad sand' them on a disc sander, sanding on the line. (See Figure 1.)

Figure 1. To make the supports, risers, and table braces perfectly symmetrical, tape these parts together in pairs. Then 'pad' saw, sand, and drill them.

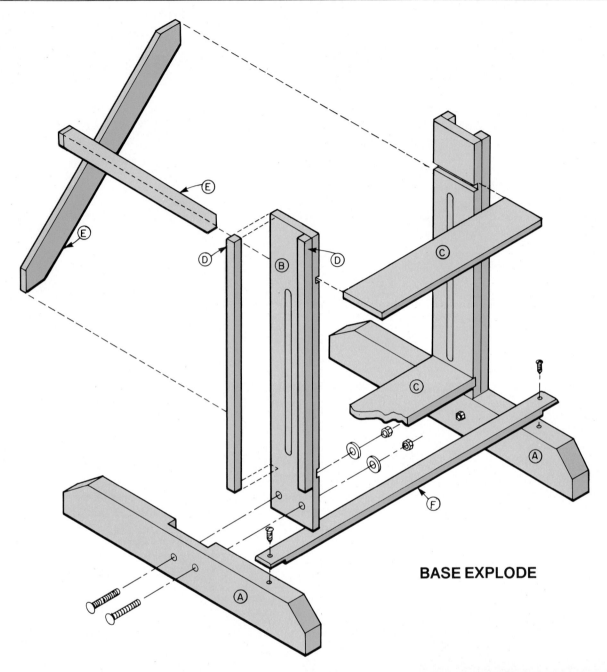

BASE EXPLODE

After cutting the parts, make the dadoes and the rabbets. Cut the rabbets in the edge of the table top on a table saw, then make all the other joints on a radial arm saw. It's easier to position a dado or a rabbet in a small board on a radial arm saw. But if you must use a table saw to cut the joinery in the small parts, here's a tip to help you accurately position your cuts:

First, find out where your saw kerf begins and ends. Position a scrap board in your miter gauge, pass it over the blade, then pull it back towards you. Turn off the table saw but *keep the board firmly gripped in the miter gauge.* With a pencil, mark the right and left sides of the kerf on the saw table. (See Figure 2.) These marks will serve as a temporary guide.

Place the board you want to dado (or rabbet) in the miter gauge. Line up the right side of the joint with the right

Figure 2. To accurately position dados and rabbets on a table saw, first mark (in pencil) the right and left sides of the kerf on the worktable.

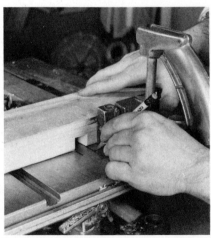

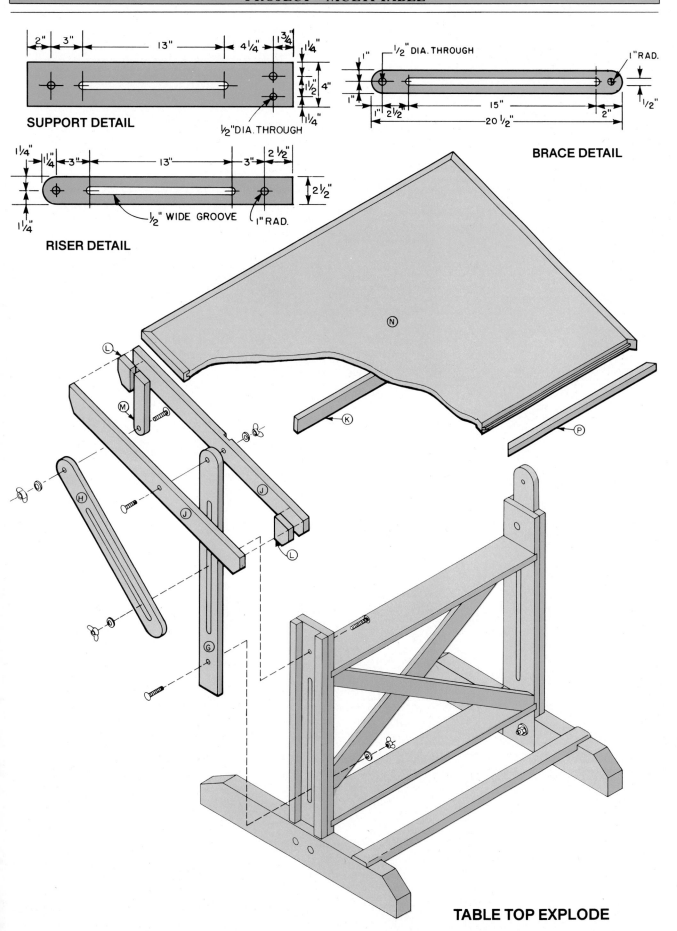

SUPPORT DETAIL

RISER DETAIL

½" WIDE GROOVE

1"RAD.

BRACE DETAIL

½" DIA. THROUGH

½"DIA. THROUGH

TABLE TOP EXPLODE

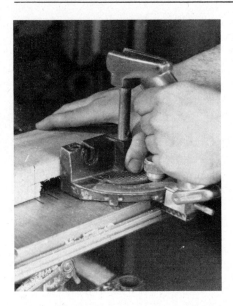

Figure 3. To gauge where to start and stop cutting, line up the sides of the dado (as marked on the board) with the corresponding kerf marks on the table.

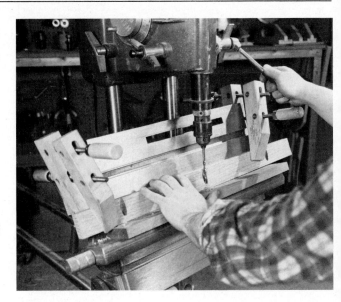

Figure 4. Drill screw pockets in the table stretcher and table mounts by tilting the drill press table (or the boards) at 15°.

kerf mark and make your first pass. Move the board to the right the width of one kerf and make another pass. (See Figure 3.) Continue until the left side of the joint lines up with the left kerf mark, then make your last pass. When you've made all the dadoes and rabbets, erase the marks on the saw table.

Drill all the 1/2″ holes in the risers, supports, braces, and legs. To make sure that the bolt holes in the supports

and the legs line up, temporarily clamp these parts together, then make the holes. Also, drill 1/2″ holes to mark each end of the stop grooves in the supports, risers, and braces. These holes should be 13″ apart on center in the supports and risers, and 15″ apart on center in the braces. (See the Support, Riser, and Brace Details.) To make sure that these parts are symmetrical, 'pad drill' them.

Also drill screw pockets in the table mounts and table

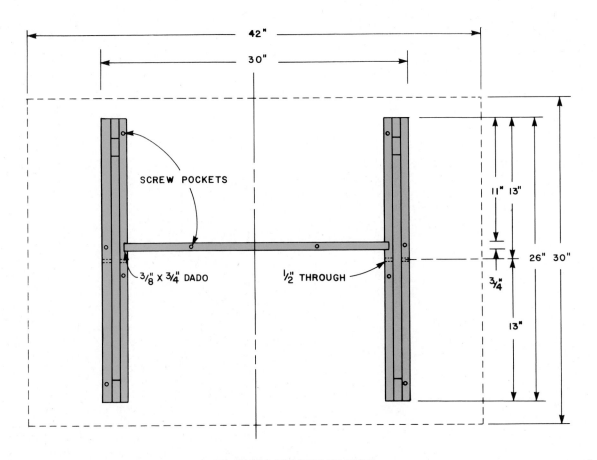

TABLE MOUNT DETAIL

Figure 5. If you're making a solid wood table top, the pilot holes in the screw pockets should be slightly larger than the shanks of the screws. This will allow the wood to move slightly with changes in humidity.

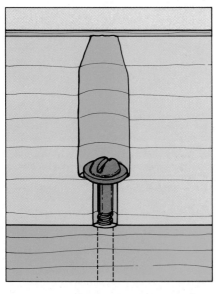

Figure 6. The easiest way to make the stop-grooves in the supports, risers, and braces is to use your drill press as an 'overarm' router. Take small bits, routing 1/8″ deeper with each pass.

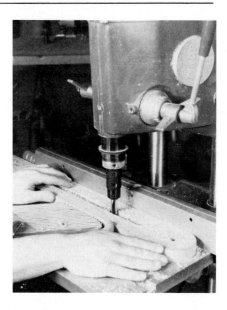

stretcher, where shown on the Table Mount Detail. If you've elected to make a solid wood top, the pilot holes for these screw pockets should be slightly larger than the screw shanks. For example, if you use #10 screws to attach the top to the table mount sub-assembly, drill 1/4″ pilot holes. (See Figures 4 and 5.)

If you have a routing chuck for your drill press or an 'overarm' router, use this to cut the grooves. Make several passes, routing 1/8″ deeper with each pass until the groove is all the way through the board. (See Figure 6.) You can also use a hand-held router, but *be sure* that the board is clamped *securely* to your workbench. (See Figure 7.)

Figure 7. If you use a hand-held router to make the stop-grooves, *be sure* that the stock is clamped securely to your worktable.

Figure 8. If you make a solid wood table top, arrange the boards so that the annual rings are all curved in the same direction. This way, a few well placed screws will hold the top flat. If you alternate the direction of the annual rings, the top may become 'wavy.'

Assembly

Finish sand all parts **before** assembly. There are so many nooks and crannies in the assembled table that it will be next to impossible to sand them. Glue the trim strips to the plywood table top. Or, if you're making a solid wood top, join the boards and glue them edge to edge.

> **Tip** ◆ As you glue up the boards for a solid top, pay attention to the edge grain. the conventional wisdom is to alternate the direction of the rings, but this is a misconception — in a few years, after the wood cups slightly, you'll have a 'wavy' table top. Instead, make sure all the annual rings curve in the same direction. The wood will still want to cup, but a few screws in the table mounts will hold it flat. (See Figure 8.)

While the glue cures on the table top, attach the table stretcher to the inside table mounts with glue and screws, then laminate the spacers, brace pivot, and outside mounts to the inside mounts. Set this sub-assembly aside and attach the trestle stretchers to the supports with glue and screws. Make sure these pieces are square to each other, then mark and miter the trestle braces as shown in the Side View. Mount these braces in the trestle with glue and screws, glue the guides to the supports, and set the trestle sub-assembly aside for the glue to cure.

When the glue dries, trim any excess off the wood with a chisel and do any necessary 'touch up' sanding. Check that the risers slide freely in between the guides on the

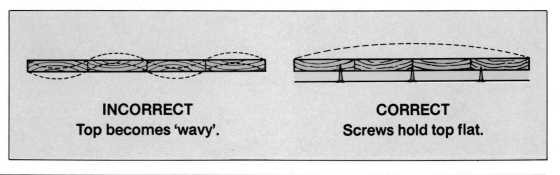

INCORRECT
Top becomes 'wavy'.

CORRECT
Screws hold top flat.

trestle. If they bind, remove a small amount of stock from the edges with a jointer or plane. Then finish all parts and sub-assemblies with a penetrating finish such as Danish oil or tung oil. *Don't* use a building finish (varnish or polyurethane); it will just gum up the moving parts.

Position the table mount sub-assembly on the table top, clamp it in place, then attach the two pieces using roundhead wood screws and washers. Put the supports in place in the trestle, and pass the bolts through the supports and risers as shown in the Table Top Explode. Put the washers and wing nuts on the lower bolts and turn them 'thumb tight.'

Turn the table top upside down on the floor, with the mounts facing up. (You may want to spread out an old blanket or tarp to protect the finish.) Turn the trestle upside down, and insert the rounded ends of the supports between the table mounts. Line up the bolt holes and bolt the trestle to the top. Have a helper hold the trestle upright while you attach the braces. Thumb tighten all wing nuts, bolt the legs to the trestle, then turn the whole assembly upright.

And there you have it — a table for all purposes! To adjust the table top to the height and tilt you require, just loosen the wing nuts and slide the risers and the braces to the necessary position, then tighten the wing nuts again. To keep the top from 'creeping' (particularly if you've put something heavy on it) use pliers to tighten the nuts. — *Nick Engler*

BILL OF MATERIALS — Multi-Table

(Finished Dimensions in Inches)

A.	Legs (2)	1-1/2 x 3-1/2 x 26
B.	Supports (2)	3/4 x 4 x 24-1/4
C.	Trestle Stretchers (2)	3/4 x 4 x 27-3/4
D.	Guides (4)	3/4 x 3/4 x 20-3/4
E.	Trestle Braces (2)	3/4 x 2 x 30-7/8
F.	Footrest (Optional)	3/4 x 2 x 30
G.	Risers (2)	3/4 x 2-1/2 x 22-3/4
H.	Table Braces (2)	3/4 x 2 x 20-1/2
J.	Outside/Inside Mounts (4)	3/4 x 2 x 26
K.	Table Stretcher	3/4 x 2 x 27-3/4
L.	Spacers (4)	3/4 x 2 x 2
M.	Brace Pivots	3/4 x 2 x 4
N.	Table Top	3/4 x 28-1/2 x 40-1/2
P.	Trim (total)	3/4 x 3/4 x 144

Hardware

1/2" x 2-1/2" Carriage Bolts (8)
1/2" x 3-1/2" Carriage Bolts (4)
1/2" Washers (12)
1/2" Hex Nuts (4)
1/2" Wing Nuts (8)
#10 x 1-1/4" Flathead Wood Screws (12-14)
#10 x 1-1/4" Roundhead Wood Screws and Washers (8)

TIPS
MULTI-TABLE

Some routing operations — such as cutting stop-grooves — can be performed much easier on an 'overarm' router, where the router is fixed in place and you slide the work underneath it. The trouble is, overarm routers are generally pretty expensive for the average home shop.

◆ Some woodworkers jerry-rig an overarm router by simply mounting ordinary router bits in their drill presses. Unfortunately, this is unsafe. A router bit must be mounted in a special chuck that reinforces the shank against sideways thrust. Otherwise, it may bend or break and fly out of your drill press at a tremendous speed.

◆ However, there are several ways to safely use your drill press as an overarm router. Several manufacturers offer special 'routing chucks' for their presses. You can also buy router bits with beefed-up shanks and 4-8 cutting edges, especially designed to be used in drills and drill presses. (See Figure A.) Or you can make your own router chuck from a standard 1/4" I.D. — 1/2" O.D. motor bushing. Just cut a slot lengthwise in the bushing with a hacksaw. Slide the shank of the router bit into the bushing, then mount the bushing *tightly* in your drill chuck. (See Figure B.)

Figure A. Several manufacturers make router bits designed to be mounted in drill chucks. These have beefed up shanks and 4-8 cutting edges.

Figure B. To make your own drill press 'routing chuck' for ordinary router bits, cut a slot lengthwise in a motor bushing. This arrangement cuts slowly, so take shallow cuts and don't force the work.

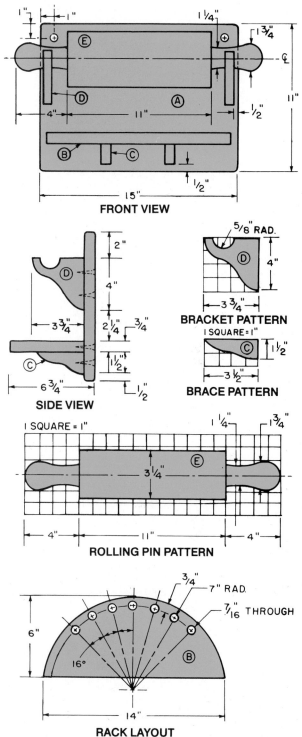

FRONT VIEW

SIDE VIEW

BRACKET PATTERN
I SQUARE = 1"

BRACE PATTERN

ROLLING PIN PATTERN
I SQUARE = 1"

RACK LAYOUT

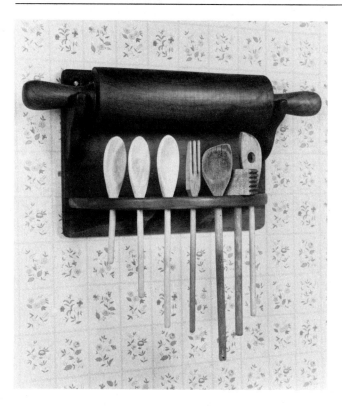

Spoon Rack

Put your wooden kitchen utensils on display.

Most cooks have a dozen wooden cooking utensils kicking around a drawer somewhere that don't get used as much as they should because they're out of sight! This rack will put those utensils out where you can see them, enjoy them — and use them.

Cut all pieces from 3/4" thick stock. Drill 7/16" holes through the rack where you want to hang the spoons. (Most wooden spoons have 1/2" handles. However, if you have some utensils with fatter handles, you may want to drill a few larger holes.)

Glue the braces to the rack, then glue *and* screw the rack to the backboard. Put the screws in from the back side, as shown in the Side View.

The rolling pin is optional, but it adds to the good looks and usefulness of this rack. You can turn a pin on your lathe using our dimensions, or purchase one from a store. (If you use a store-bought rolling pin, you may have to adjust the design and the position of the brackets.) Glue and screw the brackets to the backboard as you did the rack.

Round all the hard edges with a rasp and sandpaper, then finish the completed spoon rack with a non-toxic finish, such as mineral oil or 'salad bowl' finish. You can also use Danish oil — this oil becomes non-toxic after it cures for a few weeks. — *Nick Engler*

BILL OF MATERIALS — Spoon Rack	
(Finished Dimensions in Inches)	
A. Backboard	3/4 x 11 x 15
B. Rack	3/4 x 6 x 14
C. Braces (2)	3/4 x 1-1/2 x 3-3/4
D. Brackets (2)	3/4 x 3-3/4 x 4
E. Rolling Pin	3-1/2 dia. x 19

Hardware

(8) #10 x 1-1/2 F.H. Woodscrews

(Your-Name-Here) Mobile

It's easy to tell who this toy belongs to!

Every kid loves a toy, but a toy takes on a new attraction when it's personalized. A Petemobile or a Marymobile is a lot more fun than a generic push-car or puzzle.

To make a personalized namemobile, first write out your child's name in 'balloon' letters 3″ tall. (See our examples.) Keep the name to five letters or less, if you can. The reason? A Popular Science survey of four-year olds named 'Alexander' showed that they preferred Alexmobiles to Alexandermobiles 1 to 0. Alexandermobiles are cumbersome and confusing; while Alexmobiles are just right.

Glue up a block for the body of the namemobile — this block should be 10″ longer than the name. While the glue is setting up, cut out the front and back fenders, and round the 'outboard' edges with a rasp.

Trace the name, front contour, and back contour onto the car body. Temporarily, put the fenders in place and check that they don't overlap the name. Drill the 'inside' holes of the letters, then cut out the letters and the contours with a jigsaw or scroll saw. (See Figure 1.)

The wheels of a toy have to absorb more punishment than any other part. To make durable wheels, laminate two pieces of 3/8″ thick stock together so that the grain directions are perpendicular. Then cut out the wheels with a 2-1/4″ hole saw. You can also buy hardwood wheels through most wood supply stores. (See Figure 2.)

Figure 1. After you've drilled out the inside of the letters, cut the outside with a jigsaw. Take it slow and easy so that the blade doesn't 'cup'.

Figure 2. You can buy hardwood wheels (left), or make your own with a holesaw (right). To make your home-made wheels stronger, laminate the wheel stock.

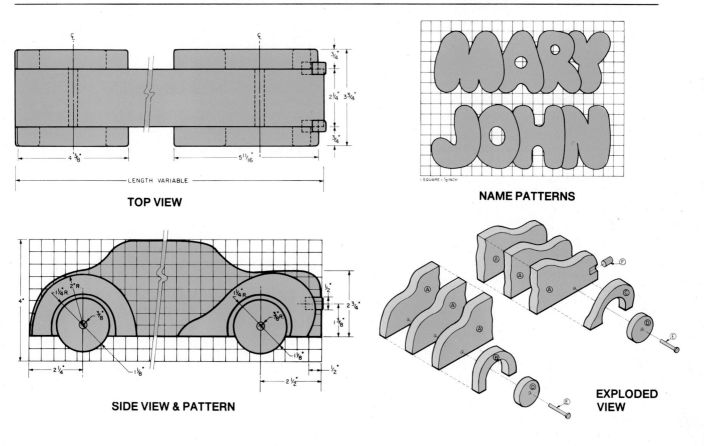

TOP VIEW

NAME PATTERNS

SIDE VIEW & PATTERN

EXPLODED VIEW

Before assembly, sand all the pieces smooth, removing all millmarks and sharp edges. Two sanding tools will help this chore go quicker: Small *drum sanders* (1/2" in diameter) will quickly remove the millmarks from the tight spots in the letters. (See Figure 3.) And *flutter sheets* will round the edges and smooth the irregular surfaces. (See Figure 4.)

Lay the fenders and the wheels in place, and mark the body where you want the axles. Drill the axle holes, then glue the fenders to the body. When the glue is set, drill 1/2" holes in the front of the car and set the headlights in place. Finally, attach the axles and wheels.

Tip ◆ The wheels will roll smoother if you coat the axles with paraffin.

The finish you put on this toy must be *non-toxic,* since the namemobile will probably be chewed on. Color the letters by painting them with food dye, full strength. Let the dye dry at least 24 hours, then apply 3 coats of mineral oil or 'salad bowl' finish. — *Nick Engler*

BILL OF MATERIALS — (Your Name Here) Mobile

(Finished Dimensions in Inches)

A.	Car Body (3)	3/4 x 4 x (Variable)
B.	Back Fenders (2)	3/4 x 2-1/2 x 4-3/8
C.	Front Fenders (2)	3/4 x 2-1/2 x 5-11/16
D.	Wheels (4)	2-1/4 dia. x 3/4
E.	Axles (4)	3/8 dia. x 2-1/16
F.	Headlights (2)	1/2 dia. x 1

Figure 3. A small drum sander will quickly remove the millmarks from the letters.

Figure 4. Use flutter sheets to round the hard edges and sand the irregular surfaces of the letters, fenders, and car body.

Chippendale Dollhouse

**Open, it's a three-story dollhouse.
Closed, it's a classic cabinet.**

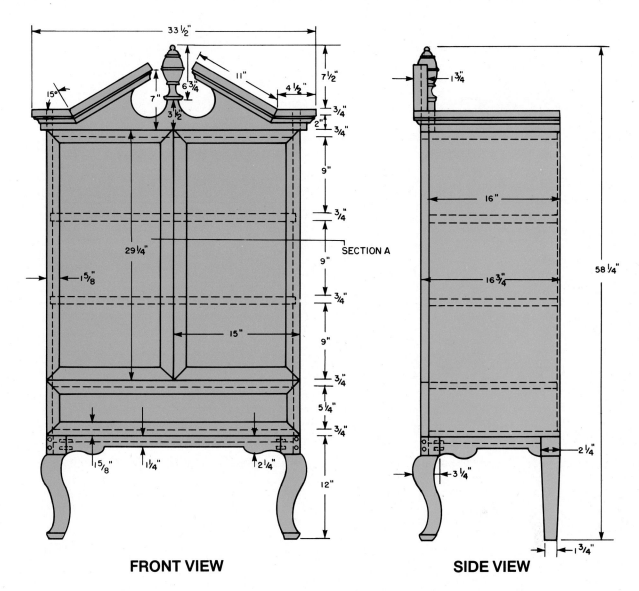

FRONT VIEW   **SIDE VIEW**

Collecting and building miniature furniture is one of the fastest growing hobbies in the country. Unfortunately, most dollhouses make poor display cases. And a dollhouse large enough to hold even a modest collection looks a bit obtrusive in a normal living room.

So here's a project that will solve both problems: On the inside, it's a three-story dollhouse that opens from the front for easy viewing. On the outside, it's a handsome Chippendale cabinet. And if Chippendale doesn't match your taste in furniture, the pediment and the legs can be easily altered to blend with more modern decors.

Building the House

When building any house, you start with the foundation. This cabinet/dollhouse is no different. The case sits on four short legs joined by a frame. (See the Base Exploded View.) As drawn, there are two cabriole legs in the front, and two tapered legs in the back. If you want to preserve the classic lines of the cabinet, make the legs that we show. If you want something more modern, make tapered or straight legs all the way around.

Cut the aprons out with a bandsaw, then glue cleats to the inside of each apron. (The cleats are needed to attach the case to the base.) Bore the legs and aprons for dowels, and dry assemble the base to make sure that all the parts line up properly. If they do, glue up the base and clamp it with one or two band clamps.

While the glue is curing on the base, build the case. As you can see from the case exploded view, this is just a basic box with several shelves dadoed into the sides and a hardboard back. You can use solid stock for the larger pieces,

Figure 1. If you make the cabinet sides and shelves from plywood, 'tape' the front edges with veneer to hide the end grain. Veneer tape is available from some lumberyards and most woodworking tool supply companies.

I SQUARE = I"

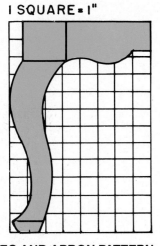

LEG AND APRON PATTERN

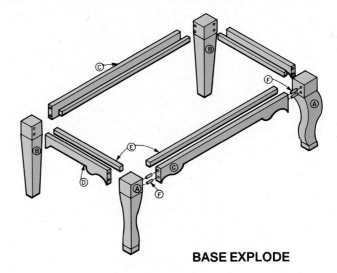

BASE EXPLODE

glued edge-to-edge to make up the required width. Or use cabinet-grade 3/4″ thick plywood and 'tape' the front edge to hide the end grain. (See Figure 1.)

The shelves in the cabinet become the floors and ceilings of the dollhouse. You can add interior walls by simply gluing 3/4″ x 9″ x 15-7/8″ boards horizontally between the shelves wherever you want them. Some dollhouse designers make 'hollow core' floors, ceilings and walls by laminating two sheets of 1/8″ hardboard to a wooden frame. (See Figure 2.) This makes it simpler to run low-voltage wiring to miniature ceiling fixtures, lamps and other electrical accessories. If you want to electrify your dollhouse/cabinet in this manner, carefully plan your wiring scheme and put the wiring in place *before* you glue up the case.

> **Tip ◆** Dollhouse suppliers offer flat, tape-like conductors for dollhouse wiring. This stuff is so flat you can apply it to a floor or wall, cover it with a felt 'carpet' or wallpaper, and you'll never know it's there. If you want an electric dollhouse, the tape conductor will save you the time and the hassle of making hollow floors, ceilings, and walls.

To attach the case and base, drill holes in the cleats slightly larger than the screws you will use to hold these two assemblies together. For example, if you use #10 screws, drill 1/4″ holes. Using roundhead wood screws and washers, screw — but *don't* glue — up through the cleats into the bottom of the case. (See Figure 3.) The oversize holes will let the wood expand and contract as the humidity changes without distorting the cabinet.

If you've elected to build a Chippendale cabinet, make a pediment out of 3/4″ stock and cove molding as shown in the Pediment Exploded View. This pediment is attached to the case in exactly the same manner as the base: Drill oversize holes in the cleats, then screw (but don't glue) the pediment to the top. If you want the cabinet to have a modern appearance, you can substitute a simple crown or cove molding for the Chippendale pediment.

Build the doors and drawer after you completed the case. These 'raised panel' parts look good with either classic or modern cabinet design, and the panels can be easily made on a table saw with a hollow-ground blade. (See Figure 4.) Our dimensions will probably be a little tight, but that's okay. You want to build doors and drawers slightly oversize, then plane them down just a little at a time until you get a perfect fit.

Use "self-latching" cabinet hinges when you install the doors. These special hinges are spring-loaded to hold the doors closed *without* catches or latches. Magnetic catches and similar hardware look fine in an ordinary cabinet when you open the doors, but they look quite out of place in the middle of a dollhouse ceiling. — *Jay Hedden*

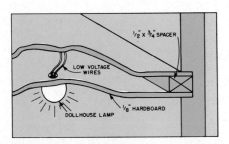

Figure 2. If you want to electrify your dollhouse, make hollow floors, ceilings, and walls to hide the wires.

Figure 3. To attach the case to the base (or the pediment to the case), drill holes in the cleats slightly larger than the screws. This lets the wood 'breathe' with the weather without distorting the case.

Figure 4. To make a raised panel, adjust your table saw to 15° and saw the edge of the board as shown. Use a hollow-ground planer blade for a smooth cut.

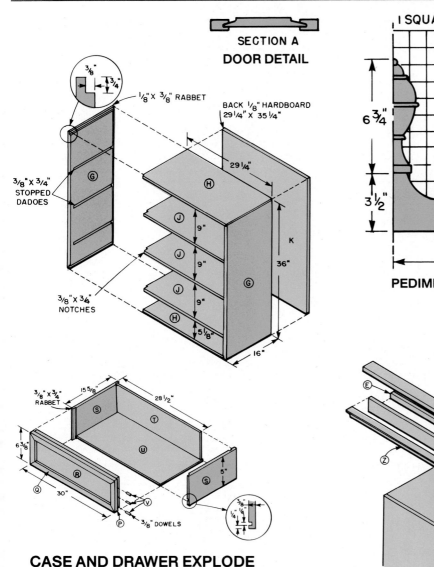

SECTION A
DOOR DETAIL

3/8" x 3/4" STOPPED DADOES

1/8" x 3/8" RABBET

BACK 1/8" HARDBOARD 29 1/4" x 35 1/4"

29 1/4"

3/8" x 3/4" NOTCHES

9"

9"

9"

5 1/8"

16"

36"

CASE AND DRAWER EXPLODE

3/8" x 3/4" RABBET

15 5/8"

28 1/2"

6 3/8"

30"

5"

3/8" DOWELS

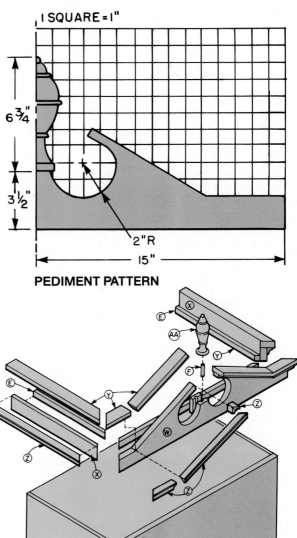

I SQUARE = 1"

6 3/4"

3 1/2"

2"R

15"

PEDIMENT PATTERN

PEDIMENT EXPLODE

BILL OF MATERIALS — Chippendale Dollhouse

(Finished Dimensions in Inches)

Base

A.	Front Legs (2)	3-1/4 x 3-1/4 x 12
B.	Back Legs (2)	2-1/4 x 2-1/4 x 12
C.	Front/Back Aprons (2)	3/4 x 2-1/4 x 25-1/2
D.	Side Aprons (2)	3/4 x 2-1/4 x 12-1/4
E.	Cleats (total)	3/4 x 3/4 x 75-1/2
F.	Dowels (16)	3/8 dia. x 2

Case

G.	Sides (2)	3/4 x 16 x 36
H.	Top/Bottom Shelves (2)	3/4 x 16 x 29-1/4
J.	Middle Shelves (3)	3/4 x 15-7/8 x 29-1/4
K.	Back	1/8 x 29-1/4 x 35-1/4
L.	Door Stiles (4)	3/4 x 1-5/8 x 29-1/4
M.	Door Rails (4)	3/4 x 1-5/8 x 15
N.	Door Panels (2)	3/4 x 12-1/4 x 26-1/2
P.	Drawer Stiles (2)	3/4 x 1-5/8 x 6-3/4
Q.	Drawer Rails (2)	3/4 x 1-5/8 x 30
R.	Drawer Panel	3/4 x 4 x 27-1/4

S.	Drawer Sides (2)	3/4 x 5 x 16
T.	Drawer Back/Front (2)	3/4 x 5 x 27-5/8
U.	Drawer Bottom	1/4 x 15-1/4 x 27-5/8
V.	Dowels (6)	3/8 dia. x 1-1/2

Pediment

E.	Cleats (total)	3/4 x 3/4 x 60-1/2
F.	Dowel	3/8 dia. x 2
W.	Pediment Front	3/4 x 5 x 30
X.	Pediment Sides	3/4 x 2 x 16-3/4
Y.	Trim (total)	3/4 x 1-3/4 x 68-1/4
Z.	Crown Molding (total)	3/4 x 3/4 x 68-1/4
AA.	Turning	2-3/4 dia. x 6-3/4

Hardware

#10 x 1-1/4 Flathead Wood Screws (3-4 dozen)
Self-Latching Cabinet Hinges (2 pair)
Door Pulls (2)
Drawer Pull

I SQUARE = I"

TOP IS REVERSE OF BOTTOM

8⅞"

ONE SIDE IS ¼" NARROWER

SHELF

SHELF APRON

SHELF (2)

5⅜"

SHELF APRON

CORNER SHELVES PATTERN

Corner Shelves

Fancy fretwork makes an attractive display for your whatnots.

Do you own a scroll saw or jigsaw? Here's a project that makes the most of those tools — 'Carpenter Gothic' shelves to display your curios. In fact, the shelves themselves make an attractive curio!

First, pick out some clear, knot-free 1/4″ thick stock. *Don't* use plywood; it tends to chip and splinter whenever the saw blade hits a void. We recommend a medium-hard, close-grained wood such as basswood or poplar. If you don't have a planer, you can have the stock planed at most lumberyards.

Tip ◆ Have the yardman plane it to 5/16″, then take the last 1/16″ off yourself with a belt sander to remove the millmarks.

Cut the back pieces to size. Remember that one back piece is 1/4″ wider than the other to allow for the overlap at the corner joint. Enlarge the pattern, and glue or trace it onto the smaller back piece. Then fasten the two pieces to-

Figure 1. 'Pad saw' the back pieces to save time and to insure that they match.

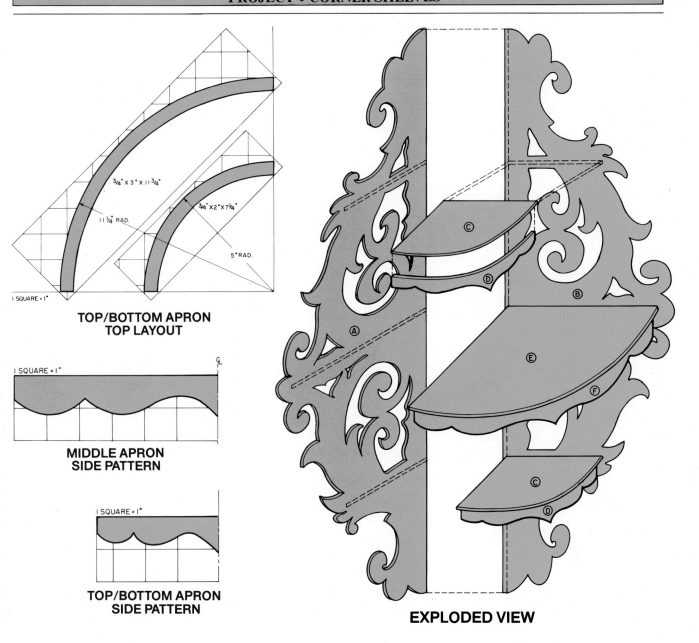

3/4" X 3" X 11 3/4"

11 1/4" RAD.

3/4" X 2" X 7 1/4"

5" RAD.

I SQUARE = 1"

TOP/BOTTOM APRON
TOP LAYOUT

I SQUARE = 1"

MIDDLE APRON
SIDE PATTERN

I SQUARE = 1"

TOP/BOTTOM APRON
SIDE PATTERN

EXPLODED VIEW

gether with brads, smaller piece on top, and 'pad saw' the pattern. (See Figure 1.) By cutting both pieces at once, you save time and insure that each back piece is a mirror image of the other.

Make the aprons on a bandsaw with a 'compound

cut'. First, cut the bottom edge pattern in the apron stock. Tape the scrap back onto the block, turn the stock 90°, and cut the curve. (See Figure 2.) When you remove all the scrap, you'll have a curved, scalloped apron.

Sand all the pieces to remove the saw marks, then assemble them with glue and brads. Finish the shelving unit, and hang it in a corner from two small nails in the topmost cutouts. — *Bob Gould*

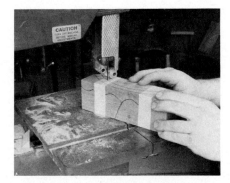

Figure 2. To make the aprons, first cut the bottom edge on a bandsaw. Tape the scrap back to the stock, turn the stock 90°, and cut the curve.

BILL OF MATERIALS — Corner Shelf

(Finished Dimensions in Inches)

A.	Left Side	1/4 x 9-1/2 x 33-3/4
B.	Right Side	1/4 x 9-3/4 x 33-3/4
C.	Small Shelves (2)	1/4 x 5-3/8 x 5-3/8
D.	Small Aprons (2)	1-1/8 x 2 x 7-1/4
E.	Large Shelf	1/4 x 8-7/8 x 8-7/8
F.	Large Apron	1-1/4 x 3 x 11-3/4

Bookcase Headboard

This handsome headboard does triple duty.

Do you like to read in bed? Need a convenient place to plug in your reading lamps, clock radio, tape deck, telephone, or what have you? How about a place to store pillow cases, sheets, and blankets? This headboard does it all!

Below mattress level, a hidden cedar chest stores your linens and keeps them smelling fresh. The lids to this chest are canted a comfortable angle to serve as backrests when you want to read or watch television in bed. Several shelves hold books, lamps, clocks and anything else you want to have with you at bedtime. These shelves are drilled so that you can run power cords behind the headboard, out of sight. Just inside the chest, there's a plug strip so you only have to run one power cord to a nearby outlet. And to top it all off, an architectural mirror adds light and the illusion of space to your bedroom. What more could you ask from a headboard?

Making the Sides and Frames

Before making that first cut, carefully measure your mattress and mattress frame. The dimensions shown in our drawings will fit a standard 'queen-size' bed. If you have any other size, you'll need to adjust the width of the headboard.

Once you've decided on the dimensions, cut all pieces to size *except* for the backrest frame stiles and the lids. These parts must be sized *after* the headboard is partially assembled to get them to fit properly. The measurements you see in the Front View are correct for the headboard that we built, but they probably will change slightly when you put yours together.

Bore 1″ holes in the top rail of the top frame, the stiles, and the bottom shelf, as shown in the drawings. These holes allow you to pass electrical cords through the headboard and behind it. Also cut the rabbets in the top frame parts and the chest bottom.

Drill the top and bottom frame pieces for dowels, then glue them up. (Don't worry about the backrest frame for

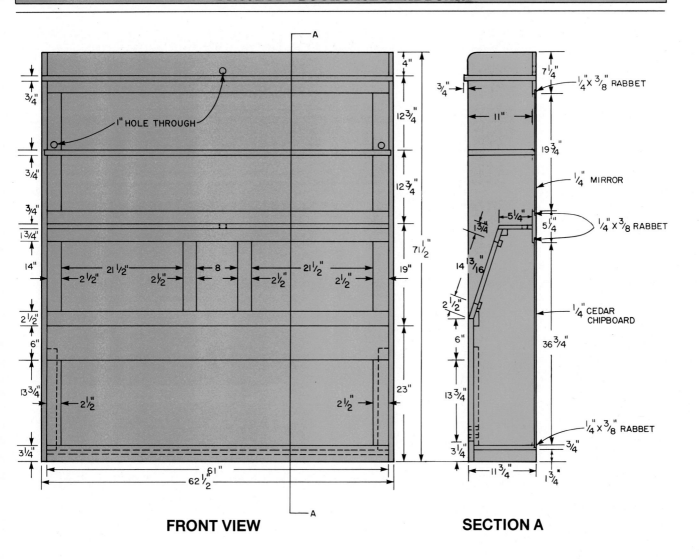

FRONT VIEW　　　　　**SECTION A**

now.) These frames are rather large, and even some better-equipped workshops may not include bar clamps long enough to secure these assemblies while the glue dries. If your shop is short on long clamps, here's a tip to get around the dilemma: Use two short clamps, and turn the sliding faces so that they 'hook' over one another, as shown in Figure 1.

While the glue on the frames is drying, cut the dadoes in the sides. The two lower dadoes on each side are 'stop-dadoes' — they don't go all the way through to the front edge. To make a stop-dado, first cut the dado part way on a table saw or radial arm saw. (See Figure 2.) Then use a chisel to 'square off' the rounded end of the dado, where the blade didn't cut deep enough. (See Figure 3.)

Saw and joint the front edge of the bottom shelf at 19°, and cut notches in the two front corners, as shown in the Top and Bottom Frames Exploded View. Finish sand all parts, then assemble the bottom shelf, top frame, and bottom frame to the sides with glue and wood screws. (Tip: Assemble the parts with the sides lying on their front edges. Attach the bottom frame first, then slide the bottom shelf

Figure 1. To make one long bar clamp out of two short ones, hook the sliding faces together as shown.

into place, then attach the top frame.) Check that all parts are in square, and leave the headboard lying on the floor while the glue cures.

Assembling the Shelves and Backrest

While the glue is drying, notch the top and middle shelves as shown in the Backrest Exploded View. Cut the top edge

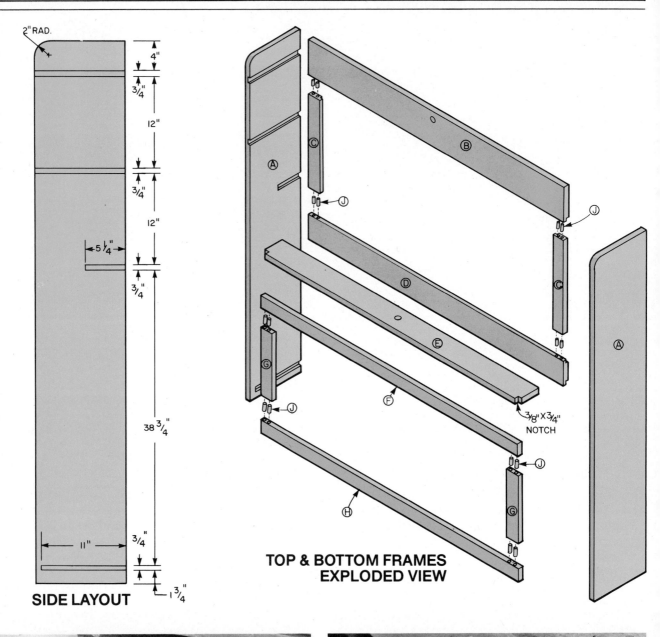

SIDE LAYOUT

2" RAD.

4"
3/4"
12"
3/4"
12"
5 1/4"
3/4"
38 3/4"
11"
3/4"
1 3/4"

**TOP & BOTTOM FRAMES
EXPLODED VIEW**

3/8" X 3/4"
NOTCH

Figure 2. When making a stop-dado, stop cutting with your dado blade just before you get to the stop mark.

Figure 3. Finish the stop-dado by squaring off the stopped end with a chisel.

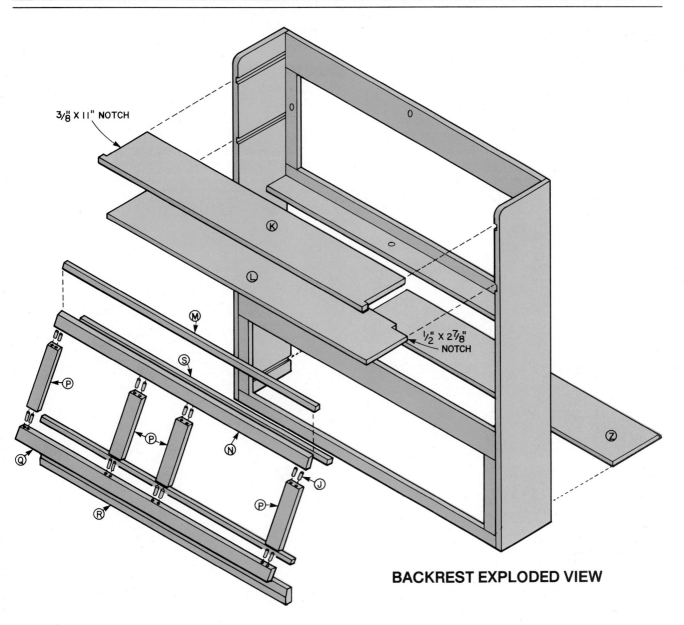

3/8" X 11" NOTCH

1/2" X 2 7/8" NOTCH

BACKREST EXPLODED VIEW

of the backrest top rail, the bottom edge of the bottom rail, and the front edge of the top and bottom cleats at 19°.

Set the headboard upright. Attach the top and bottom cleats with screws and glue, then *temporarily* clamp the top and bottom rails in place. Measure in between the rails to get the true measurements for the backrest stiles and lids. (See Figure 4.) Disassemble the rails from the headboard.

Cut the stiles, drill both rails and stiles for dowels, then glue up the backrest frame. Clamping the backrest frame will present a problem because neither of the top or bottom edges are square. The jaws of the bar clamps will mash the corners of the rails. To prevent this, make wooden cauls as shown in Figure 5 and slip them over the edges of the rails before clamping the frame.

After the glue has dried on the frame, attach the lid stops to the back side. Finish sand all parts, then assemble the backrest frame, top shelf, middle shelf, and chest bottom to the headboard with glue and screws.

Figure 4. To get an accurate measurement to the backrest stiles, clamp the rails to the partially completed headboard and measure in between them.

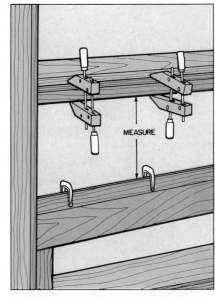

MEASURE

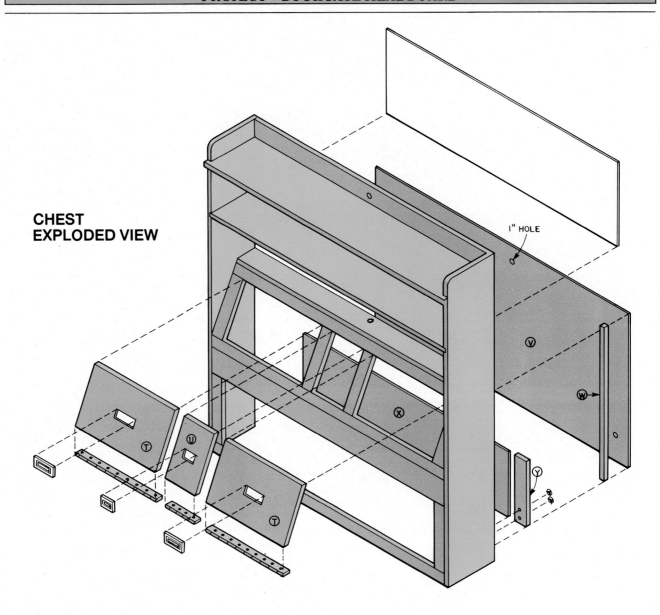

CHEST
EXPLODED VIEW

1" HOLE

Figure 5. Make wooden cauls on your bandsaw to prevent the bar clamps from mashing the beveled edges of the backrest frame.

Making the Chest

Attach the braces to the inside of the bottom frame. These braces should be made out of a very hard wood such as oak or maple. They strengthen the bottom frame and its dowel joints against any tendency for the headboard to tip over. Also attach the side cleats to the sides.

Cut the lids to size, allowing room for piano hinges on the bottom edges. Install a handle in the middle of each lid — we used 3″ and 4″ 'campaign chest' handles because they lie flat when not in use and won't stick you in the back. (See Figure 6.) These handles are available from several hardware supply companies, such as:

Wolchonok & Son   Hunrath Company
155 E. 52nd Street   153 E. 57th Street
New York, NY 10022   New York, NY 10022

Temporarily attach the lids to the headboard to make sure they fit, then disassemble the lids and remove all hardware. Remove any glue beads with a chisel, and finish sand any parts that still need it. Apply whatever stain or finish seems appropriate — we used several coats of tung oil. On the last coat, we mixed a couple of tablespoons of spar varnish in with the oil to give the final finish a light sheen.

After finishing, re-attach the lids and hardware. Mount a 'plug strip' (available in most hardware stores) on the inside of the right or left side — whichever is closest to the outlet you'll be using — where you can reach the strip easily. (See Figure 8.)

Drill two 1″ holes in the back panel, one near the top center and the other near bottom on either the right or left side (wherever you mounted the plug strip). Install the back and front panels with small (3/4″ long) screws. We recommend that these panels be made of cedar chipboard (sometimes called "cedar closet liner"). The aromatic cedar keeps your linens smelling fresh, and discourages moths and other insects. However, some folks may find the cedar just a little too aromatic — the smell can be overpowering when you're trying to get to sleep. If this is your case, coat the panels with a wash coat of shellac and alcohol mixed 1:1. The thin shellac will take the aroma down a notch.

Finally, install a 1/4″ mirror in the top frame, using mirror clips or turn buttons to hold it in place. Since this is an 'architectural' mirror (intended for its visual effects rather than dressing), you don't have to use an ordinary silvered mirror. We used a mirror with a bronze tint to match the mahogany in the headboard. Most local glass companies will special order tinted and 'veined' mirrors. They don't cost too much more than the regular variety.

Attaching Your Mattress Frame

Place the finished headboard in the bedroom where you want to use it. Butt the mattress frame up against it and mark where you should drill holes to bolt the frame to the headboard. (Most mattress frames have an end with plates and slotted holes, made especially to attach headboards.)

Drill the holes slightly oversize, through the bottom frame and the hardwood braces. Reach in through the chest openings and install T-nuts in the holes. Insert stove bolts through the mattress frame, into the holes in the head-

board, and thread them through the T-nuts. Tighten the bolts as tight as they will go with a screwdriver. (See Figure 8.)

Place the box springs and mattress on the frame, fill up the shelves of the headboard with all your favorite books and electronic gear, run the cords in and out of the 1″ holes, plug in the plug strip, and make the bed. Just remember to vacuum out the sawdust (from drilling the holes) in the chest cavity before you store your linens. — *Nick Engler*

Figure 7. Mount a plug strip on the inside of the chest cavity to organize the power cords for reading lamps, clocks, radios, and any other electronic gizmos you desire *without* overloading the rated amperage of the strip.

Figure 8. Attach the bed frame to the headboard with stove bolts. T-nuts on the inside of the chest cavity hold the metal frame tightly against the wood.

Figure 6. To install campaign chest handles, first rout a mortise. Then clean up the edges with a small chisel.

BILL OF MATERIALS — Bookcase Headboard
(Finished Dimensions in Inches)

A.	Sides (2)	3/4 x 11-3/4 x 71-1/2
B.	Top Frame Top Rail	3/4 x 7-1/4 x 61
C.	Top Frame Stiles (2)	3/4 x 2-1/2 x 19-3/4
D.	Top Frame Bottom Rail	3/4 x 5-1/4 x 61
E.	Bottom Shelf	3/4 x 5-1/4 x 61-3/4
F.	Bottom Frame Top Rail	3/4 x 6 x 61
G.	Bottom Frame Stiles (2)	3/4 x 2-1/2 x 13-3/4
H.	Bottom Frame Bottom Rail	3/4 x 3-1/4 x 61
J.	Dowels (32)	3/8 dia. x 1-1/2
K.	Top Shelf	3/4 x 11-3/4 x 62-1/2
L.	Middle Shelf	3/4 x 11-1/2 x 61-3/4
M.	Top Cleat	3/4 x 3/4 x 61
N.	Backrest Frame Top Rail	3/4 x 1-3/4 x 61
P.	Backrest Frame Stiles (4)	3/4 x 2-1/2 x 14-13/16
Q.	Backrest Frame Bottom Rail	3/4 x 2-1/2 x 61
R.	Bottom Cleat	3/4 x 2 x 61
S.	Lid Stops	3/4 x 1-1/2 x 61
T.	Left/Right Lids (2)	3/4 x 14-5/8 x 21-3/8
U.	Middle Lid	3/4 x 7-7/8 x 14-5/8
V.	Back Panel	1/4 x 37-1/2 x 61
W.	Side Cleats	1/2 x 3/4 x 36-3/4
X.	Front Panel	1/4 x 15-1/4 x 57-1/2
Y.	Braces (2)	3/4 x 1-3/4 x 16
Z.	Chest Bottom	3/4 x 11 x 61-3/4

Hardware

#8 x 1-1/4 Flathead Wood Screws (5-6 dozen)
#8 x 3/4 Flathead Wood Screws (2-3 dozen)
3″ Campaign Chest Handle and Mounting Screws
4″ Campaign Chest Handles and Mounting Screws (2)
1-1/2″ x 51″ Piano Hinge and Mounting Screws (total)
5/16″ x 2-1/2″ Stove Bolts (4)
5/16″ T-Nuts (4)

TIPS
BOOKCASE HEADBOARD

Nothing holds wood together quite so well as a wood screw. And nothing's quite so ugly as the uncovered head of a screw. You couldn't build the Bookcase Headboard without wood screws; but if you don't carefully cover up the screw heads, the appearance of the project will be ruined.

◆ There are several different ways to cover screw heads, as shown in Figure A. The most common is wood dough. Some woodworkers mix fine sawdust (from sanding the project) with model glue. You can also buy commercially-made dowels and buttons. But the most effective, least visible method of covering screws is with wooden plugs, cut from the same wood as the project itself.

◆ Make your own plugs with a *plug cutter* mounted in your drill press. Bore part way through a scrap of wood (as shown in Figure B), then cut the plugs free from the scrap on a bandsaw (as shown in Figure C). To install a plug, first countersink the screw 1/8″-1/4″ below the wood surface. Dip the plug in glue and tap it into the hole left by the screw drill. When the glue dries, sand off the plug flush with the surface.

Figure B. To make your own plugs, first bore part way through a scrap of wood with a *plug cutter*.

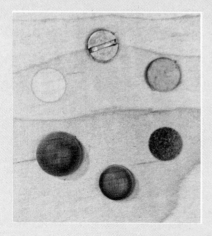

Figure A. Shown here are several ways to disguise screw heads. Clockwise from the top: Countersunk (but uncovered) screw, wood dough, sawdust mixed with model glue, dowel, button, and plug.

Figure C. Then cut the plugs free from the scrap on a bandsaw.

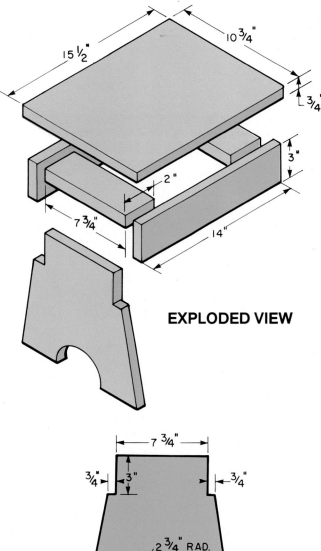

EXPLODED VIEW

Five-Board Bench

When you need a little bit more than you've got, this'll come in handy.

Made in a variety of sizes and styles, the five-board bench gets its name from the number of pieces generally used to make it. (We've added two cleats for strength, so this is actually a seven-board bench.) However many boards yours ends up to be, you can cut all the parts from ordinary 1 x 12 shelving.

Glue and screw the cleats to the underside of the top, after you first dry assemble the bench to determine their proper locations. Set the top assembly aside; attach the side braces to the legs. Finally, center the top assembly on the leg assembly and attach the two assemblies by nailing through the legs into the cleats. (This eliminates the need to put nails or screws in the top.)

If you want a handhold, bore two 1″ holes, 3″ apart on center. With a sabre saw, cut out the stock between them to make a 1″ x 3″ opening. (See Figure 1.) Round the edges of the handhold (both topside and underside) to prevent splinters and make it fit the hand comfortably. Also, round all four corners on top to keep people from barking their shins on the finished bench. — *Jay Hedden*

LEG LAYOUT

Figure 1. To make a handhold, drill two 1″ diameter holes, 3″ apart on center. Then saw out the stock between them and round the edges.

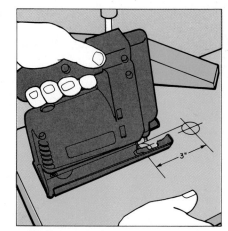

BILL OF MATERIALS — Five-Board Bench
(Finished Dimensions in Inches)

A.	Top	3/4 x 10-3/4 x 15
B.	Cleats (2)	3/4 x 3 x 7-3/4
C.	Side Braces (2)	3/4 x 3 x 13-1/2
D.	Legs (2)	3/4 x 10 x 11-1/4

Hardware

(4) #10 x 1-1/4 F.H. Woodscrews
(22) #6 Finishing Nails

Rolling Cart

Here's a quick project with a dozen different uses.

Need more bench space in your shop or kitchen? A stand for your microwave or television? A taboret, a serving cart, or an end table? This versatile cart can do it all! Better yet, you can put it together in a weekend.

Cut all parts to size and glue up the top and shelf. (You can add more than one shelf, if you need to.) Pay close

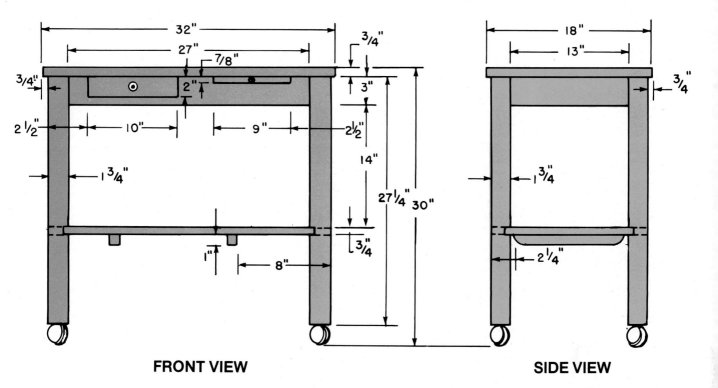

FRONT VIEW   **SIDE VIEW**

attention to the end grain of the boards when you edge-glue them. Be sure that the annual rings are all curved in the same direction.

Cut V-shaped grooves inside all four aprons with a dado blade, as shown in the Construction Details drawing. (See Figure 1.) These grooves serve as 'screw pockets' to attach the top to the table assembly. (If you don't have a dado blade, make ordinary screw pockets.) Drill oversize pilot holes, slightly larger than the screw shanks, where shown. (These oversize holes will let the top expand and contract with changes in humidity *without* stressing the table frame.)

Cut out the front apron for the drawer and cutting board. Using a router, make a 1/4″ x 1/4″ x 1″ stop-groove, 1/4″ below each cut-out. Make corresponding grooves on the back apron, then cut rabbets in the end of each guide to form 1/4″ x 1/4″ tenons. These tenons must fit the grooves snugly. When installed, the top of each guide should be flush with the bottom of the cut-out.

Cut dadoes in the legs to hold the shelf. Each leg gets two dadoes, 90° apart and the same distance from the top and bottom of the leg. If you're using a table saw to make these joints, clamp a stop block to your rip fence to help position the dados accurately. (See Figure 2.) If you're using a radial arm saw, clamp a stop block to the backboard.

Drill 3/8″ holes, 3/4″ deep in the legs and aprons so that you can dowel them together, as shown in the Construction Details drawing. Make the holes in the ends of the aprons first, then use dowel centers to mark the holes in the legs. When doweled together, the aprons should be inset 1/4″ from the outside edge of the legs.

Assembly can be tricky, since all these parts have to go together at once. However, this step shouldn't require more than three arms if you follow this procedure:

Figure 1. If you have a dado blade, you can cut the 'screw pocket' grooves in the aprons in 1-2 passes with the tilt adjusted to 15° as shown. This is a lot quicker than making 10 or more individual screw pockets on a drill press.

Figure 2. To position the dados in the legs exactly the same distance from each end, clamp a stop block to the rip fence 2″ or more in front of the blade. Be careful the leg doesn't touch the block as it passes over the blade.

Glue the back legs, back apron, and side aprons together, then set this sub-assembly down on your workbench with the side aprons sticking up in the air. Glue the front legs and front apron together, insert the guides in the back apron, then glue the front leg sub-assembly to the back leg sub-assembly. Put a band clamp around the legs and aprons, then flip the completed table and frame so the legs are in the air.

While the glue is still wet, gently spread the legs so that you can slide the shelf in place. Glue the shelf at each corner, and reinforce these joints with flathead wood screws 'toe-nailed' through the shelf and into the legs from underneath. (See the Construction Details drawing and Figure 3.) Screw (but *don't* glue) the braces to the underside of the shelf. Position the table frame on the table top, and attach these pieces with roundhead wood screws (but no glue) through the pilot holes in the "screw pockets."

Make a simple drawer and cutting board for the completed cart. Insert them in the proper cut-outs, then screw the stops on the underside of these pieces, straddling the guides. Finally, bore the ends of the legs for ball casters, if you so desire.

Figure 3. Attach the shelf to the legs with wood screws 'toe-nailed' from underneath. Drill the pilot holes with a hand-held drill.

The finish you put on your cart will be partially determined by how you intend to use it. Almost any finish will look just fine, but if you intend to use this cart mostly in your kitchen, we recommend a water resistant finish such as tung oil, spar varnish, or polyurethane. — *Nick Engler*

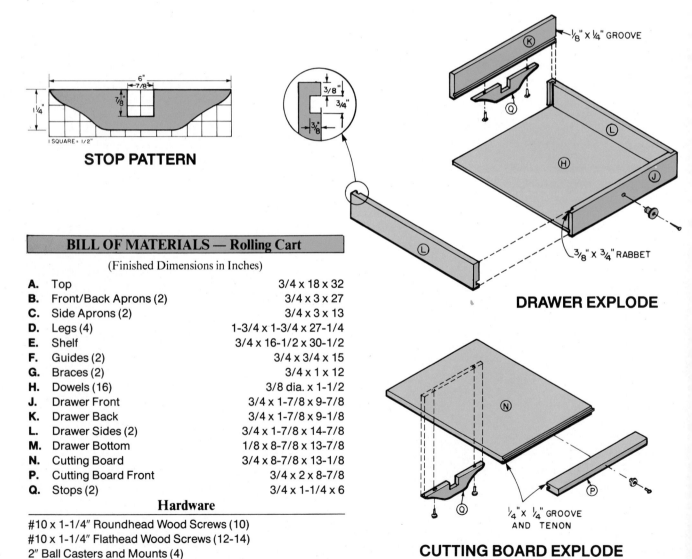

STOP PATTERN

I SQUARE = 1/2"

1/8" x 1/4" GROOVE

3/8" x 3/4" RABBET

DRAWER EXPLODE

1/4" x 1/4" GROOVE AND TENON

CUTTING BOARD EXPLODE

BILL OF MATERIALS — Rolling Cart

(Finished Dimensions in Inches)

A.	Top	3/4 x 18 x 32
B.	Front/Back Aprons (2)	3/4 x 3 x 27
C.	Side Aprons (2)	3/4 x 3 x 13
D.	Legs (4)	1-3/4 x 1-3/4 x 27-1/4
E.	Shelf	3/4 x 16-1/2 x 30-1/2
F.	Guides (2)	3/4 x 3/4 x 15
G.	Braces (2)	3/4 x 1 x 12
H.	Dowels (16)	3/8 dia. x 1-1/2
J.	Drawer Front	3/4 x 1-7/8 x 9-7/8
K.	Drawer Back	3/4 x 1-7/8 x 9-1/8
L.	Drawer Sides (2)	3/4 x 1-7/8 x 14-7/8
M.	Drawer Bottom	1/8 x 8-7/8 x 13-7/8
N.	Cutting Board	3/4 x 8-7/8 x 13-1/8
P.	Cutting Board Front	3/4 x 2 x 8-7/8
Q.	Stops (2)	3/4 x 1-1/4 x 6

Hardware

#10 x 1-1/4" Roundhead Wood Screws (10)
#10 x 1-1/4" Flathead Wood Screws (12-14)
2" Ball Casters and Mounts (4)
Drawer Pulls (2)

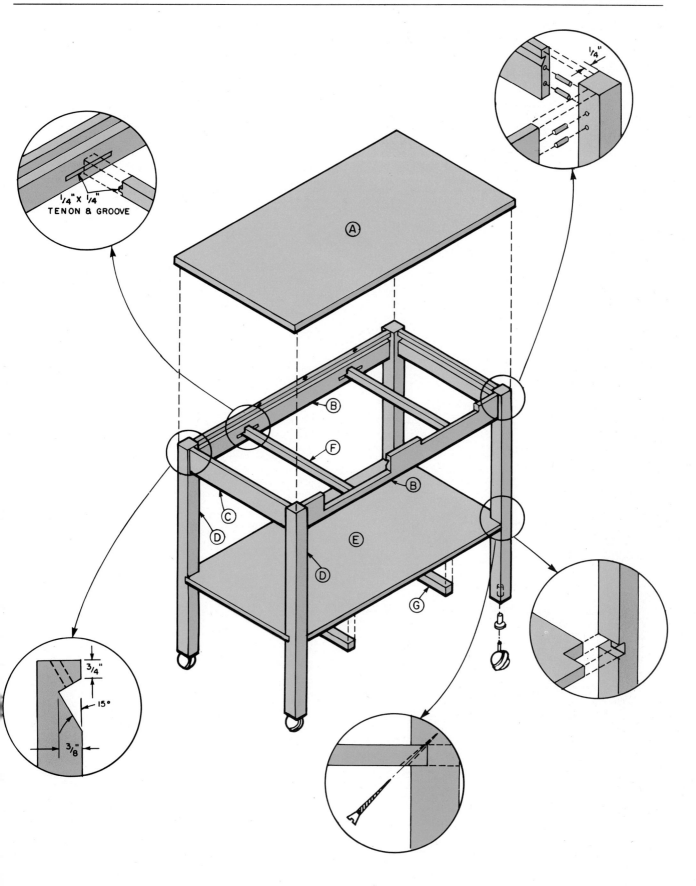

1/4" X 1/4"
TENON & GROOVE

1/4"

3/4"
15°
3/8"

A

B

F

B

C

D

D

E

G

CONSTRUCTION DETAILS

Dry Sink

This eighteenth century dry sink hides a twentieth century stereo system.

I f you love classic music *and* classic furniture, you may be caught in a dilemma. Most entertainment centers and stereo racks are contemporary in style. They look every bit as modern as the audio equipment they are designed to hold — and way out of place in a room full of period furniture.

But who says audio equipment racks have to look like audio equipment? With a little ingenuity, you can modify a period furniture design to hold a state-of-the-art stereo sys-

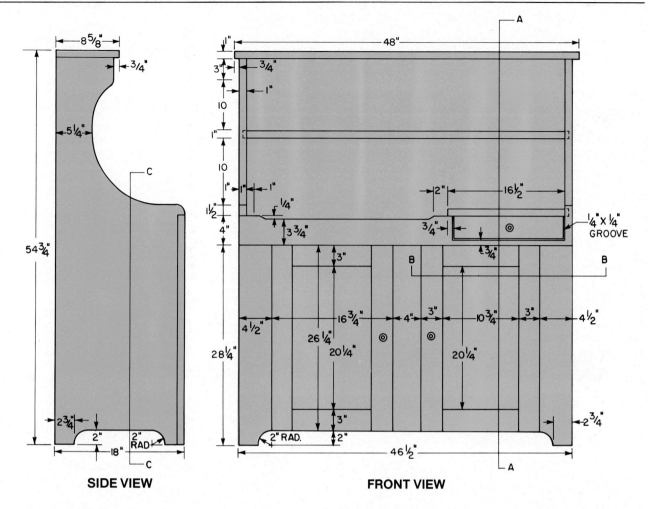

SIDE VIEW

FRONT VIEW

tem without changing the classic lines. Our dry sink looks like a Colonial Period antique, but it holds a receiver/amplifier, record player, tape deck, and large LP collection with room for more!

Making the Parts

Before you cut any wood — or even purchase the lumber — measure your stereo system to see if it will fit our dry sink. As designed, the record player sits in the 'well,' behind

a false door. (See Figure 1.) The amplifier rests on a shelf underneath the sink. (See Figure 2.) There is room for a record library under the amp, and you can stack a tape deck and several other pieces of equipment under the well. If your equipment won't fit, you may have to rearrange the location of the components, adjust the dimensions of the project, or both.

While you're looking over the dimensions, notice that the dry sink is made from 1″ thick stock, for the most part.

Figure 1. Behind the false drawer front on this dry sink, there is a well that holds a record player.

Figure 2. A stereo amplifier rests on a shelf underneath the sink. Beneath the amp, there's room for a large record collection.

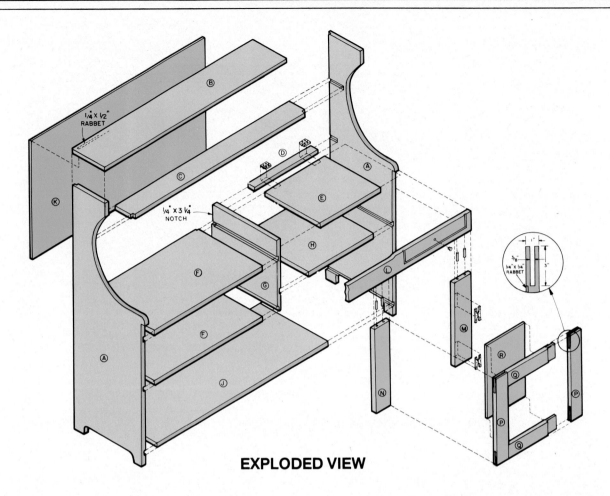

1/4" X 1/2"
RABBET

1/4" X 3 1/4"
NOTCH

3/8"
1"
1/4" X 1/4"
RABBET
3"

EXPLODED VIEW

This adds to the project's authenticity: Country and Colonial period cabinets and cupboards were often made from '4/4' and '5/4' boards. Some lumberyards still carry 1" thick lumber, or they will make it up for you on special order. But if you can't get it, adjust the dimensions shown for 3/4" thick stock.

Glue up 17" wide stock for the sides, shelves and other wide parts, then cut all parts to size. Using a sabre saw, cut the slight 'dip' in the apron and the large half-circle in the sides. (See Figure 3.) To make the long notch in the front of the sides, glue a 1" x 2" x 1-1/2" block to the front edge, let the glue cure, then round the top corner of the block.

Most of the joinery can be cut with a hand-held router. You can also do the 'detailing' on the dry sink with a router. After you've cut the joinery, change to a 1/4" veining bit. Rout a 1/4" deep groove in the apron top (as shown on the Front View), outlining the front of a phony drawer. Once again, use long straight boards clamped to the stock as a guide.

The back gets 6-7 vertical 1/4" wide x 1/8" deep grooves, cut at random intervals to make the panel look as if it were made from several different boards. You may also want to cut two 1/4" x 1/4" grooves in the upper shelf, 1" and 1-1/2" from the back edge. (See Figure 4.) These grooves serve as 'dish stops' so that you can display plates on the shelf.

Figure 3. Cut the large half circles in the sides with a sabre saw. The stock is kept up off the workbench by 2x2 blocks.

Figure 4. The 1/4" wide, 1/4" deep grooves in the upper shelf make it possible to display plates and other flatware.

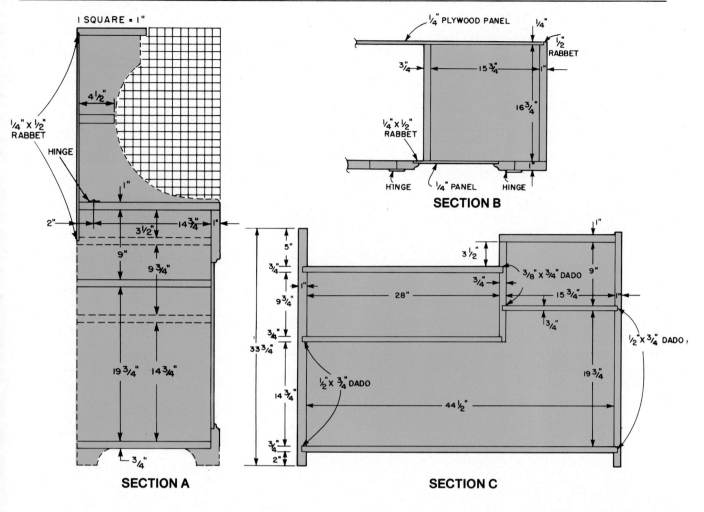

1 SQUARE = 1"

1/4" X 1/2" RABBET

HINGE

4 1/2"

1"

2"

3 1/2"

14 3/4"

1"

9"

9 3/4"

19 3/4" 14 3/4"

3/4"

SECTION A

1/4" PLYWOOD PANEL

1/4"

1/2" RABBET

3/4"

15 3/4"

1"

16 3/4"

1/4" X 1/2" RABBET

HINGE

1/4" PANEL

HINGE

SECTION B

5"

3/4"

1"

9 3/4"

3/4"

33 3/4"

14 3/4"

3/4"

2"

1/2" X 3/4" DADO

28"

3 1/2"

3/4"

3/8" X 3/4" DADO

1"

9"

15 3/4"

1"

3/4"

44 1/2"

1/2" X 3/4" DADO

19 3/4"

SECTION C

Put aside your router and bore the apron top and stiles for dowels. With a bandsaw, cut the notch in the back edge of the well side, then finish sand all parts.

Assembling the Case

Begin assembly by laying the sides on their back edges and attaching the bottom and upper shelves. Make sure the shelves are square to the sides, then attach the top, the middle shelf and sink bottom, well side, and well bottom. When these parts are in place, add the apron. Continue to work with the dry sink lying on its back.

Glue all the joints, then reinforce these joints with screws or nails. Use screws on the inside of the case, where they won't be seen. To attach shelves and other parts to the sides, 'toenail' the screw up through the bottom of the shelf and into the side. (See Figure 5.) On the outside of the case, use *cut nails* to fasten parts. (See Figure 6.) These special nails are available at most hardware stores, and have an antique look to them. You may also wish to purchase hand-forged or square nails from a specialty hardware supplier.

Stand the dry sink up, and install the back, well cover and lid. Notice that the back does not come down past the sink bottom. There's a reason for this: The cabinet under the sink has an open back so that you can easily run power cords, patch cords, and speaker wires behind the dry sink. The open back also helps ventilate the stereo components so they don't overheat.

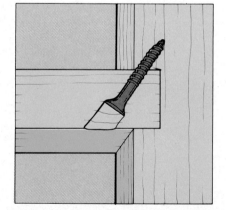

Figure 5. Attach the bottom and middle shelves to the sides with #10 x 1" wood screws 'toenailed' up through the bottom of the shelf and into the side.

Figure 6. On the outside of the dry sink, fasten parts together with cut nails. These square-shanked nails give the project an antique look.

Making and Installing the Doors

Choose some very straight, very clear boards to make the door frame parts. Since these doors will be flush-mounted, it's important that all parts are straight and flat so that the completed doors fit properly.

Cut the mortises and tenons with a bandsaw. To saw the bottom of the narrow mortises, 'nibble' the stock away with the bandsaw blade. (See Figure 7.) You can also dowel the rails and stiles together, if you wish. However, a mortise-and-tenon joint is much stronger — and strength may be a critical factor on a door that you use frequently.

Assemble the door frames with glue and let the glue cure for *at least* 24 hours, until it reaches maximum strength. Then rout a rabbet in the backside of the frames for the door panel, and square the corners with a chisel. Install the door panels using 'turn buttons' to hold them in place, but *don't* glue the panels to the door frame. Wood panels should 'float' in a frame, expanding and contracting with changes in humidity.

If you wish, install molding around the inside edges of the frame, making the edges looked shaped. Plane down the outside edges, if necessary, so that the doors are 1/8″ narrower than the door openings in the dry sink.

Install pulls on the doors and false drawer, then install the doors on the apron with wrought iron 3″ H-hinges. Many hardware suppliers carry these hinges, but two good sources are:

Renovator's Supply   Wolchonok & Son
Renovator's Old Mill   155 E. 52nd Street
Miller's Falls, MA 01349 New York, NY 10022

When everything is fitted and installed to your satisfaction, remove the doors, lid, and hardware from the dry sink. Sand all cut nails flush with the wood surface, and do any touch-up sanding that needs to be done. Apply a penetrating finish for a traditional 'hand-rubbed oil' look. Let the finish dry for at least 48 hours, so that none of the vapors from the evaporating finish foul your expensive electronic equipment.

Figure 7. Use a bandsaw to cut the narrow mortises in the door frame stiles. 'Nibble' away the excess stock at the bottom of the mortise with the bandsaw blade.

Put your stereo system in place and wire it up. On our system, we ran the speaker wires out of the back of the dry sink and under the rug to speakers in other parts of the room. With the speakers placed unobtrusively, you wouldn't even know there was a stereo in the room — until you turn on the music! — *Nick Engler*

BILL OF MATERIALS — Dry Sink

(Finished Dimensions in Inches)

A.	Sides (2)	1 x 18 x 53-3/4
B.	Top	1 x 8-5/8 x 48
C.	Upper Shelf	1 x 4-1/2 x 45-1/2
D.	Back Well Cover	1 x 2 x 17
E.	Lid	1 x 15-3/4 x 16-1/2
F.	Sink Bottom/Middle Shelf (2)	3/4 x 17 x 28-7/8
G.	Well Side	3/4 x 16-1/4 x 17
H.	Well Bottom	3/4 x 16-1/2 x 17
J.	Bottom Shelf	3/4 x 17 x 45-1/2
K.	Back Panel	1/4 x 30 x 45-1/2
L.	Apron Top	1 x 4 x 46-1/2
M.	Left/Right Apron Stiles (2)	1 x 4-1/2 x 28-1/4
N.	Middle Apron Stile	1 x 4 x 26-1/4
P.	Door Stiles (4)	1 x 3 x 26-1/4
Q.	Door Rails (4)	1 x 3 x 16-3/4
R.	Door Panels (2)	1/4 x 11-3/4 x 21-1/4

Hardware

6d Cut Nails (1/4-1/2 lb.)
#10 x 1″ Flathead Wood Screws (2 dozen)
Door/Drawer Pulls and Mounting Screws (3)
1-1/2″ x 3″ Butt Hinges and Screws (1 pair)
Adjustable Lid Support and Mounting Screws
3″ 'H' Hinges and Screws (2 pair)
Magnetic Cabinet Door Catches and Mounting Screws (2)

TIPS
DRY SINK

Cutting dadoes and rabbets in large cabinet parts can present a problem. It would be difficult (at best) to hoist the dry sink sides up on your table saw and cut the necessary joinery with any accuracy. And it would be impossible on most radial arm saws — you just don't have the 'throw' you need.

◆ For this reason, we suggest you use a hand-held router. Clamp a long, straight board to the part to serve as a guide. Use a straight bit and hold the router firmly against the board. Make several passes, cutting 1/8″ deeper with each pass until the dado or rabbet reaches the proper depth.

◆ If you need to perform this operation very often, you may want to make yourself a "dado jig" for your router, as shown in Figure A. This jig can be adjusted for both the length and width of the dado by loosening a few bolts. Once adjusted, it clamps to the cabinet part and creates a 'fence' for your router.

Figure A. Use a hand-held router to cut dadoes and rabbets in large cabinet parts. A simple jig speeds the chore and helps make it more accurate.

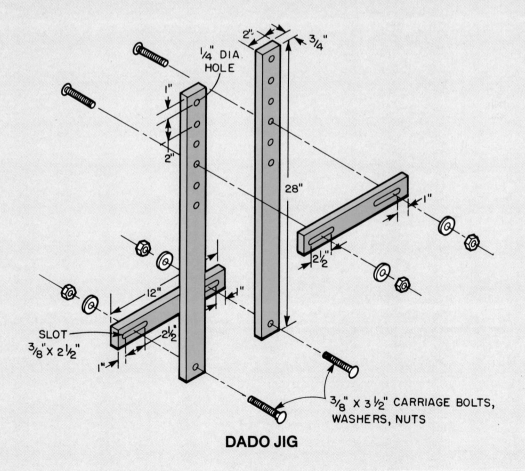

DADO JIG

Quilt Rack

Why hide your elegant quilts and afghans in a chest? Put them on display!

Here's an easy weekend project for your bedroom or guest room: A colonial "quilt rack" to hold your blankets, quilts, afghans, and comforters. It also makes an attractive towel rack in your bathroom.

Turn the two support columns from 1-3/4″ square stock, and the bottom stretcher from 1-1/4″ square stock. Be careful that the stretcher doesn't start to bend or 'whip'

on the lathe while you're turning it. The slender stock could easily break and fly out of the lathe. If you have trouble with whipping, you may want to use a 'steadyrest' to stabilize the stock. (See Figure 1.) The upper stretchers can be turned, or you can simply round the edges with a rasp or shaper. Or you can make them from 3/4″ dowel stock, particularly if you're working with a light hardwood such as beech or maple.

Cut out the feet and wings from 3/4″ thick stock with a bandsaw or jigsaw. Pay particular attention to the grain direction, as marked on the patterns. There must be as much 'long grain' as possible in these parts if they are to have any strength.

When you've made all the parts, bore them for dowels. Most holes are bored only 3/8″ or 3/4″ deep, but the holes in the support columns where the wings and feet are attached can be bored completely through the columns. To

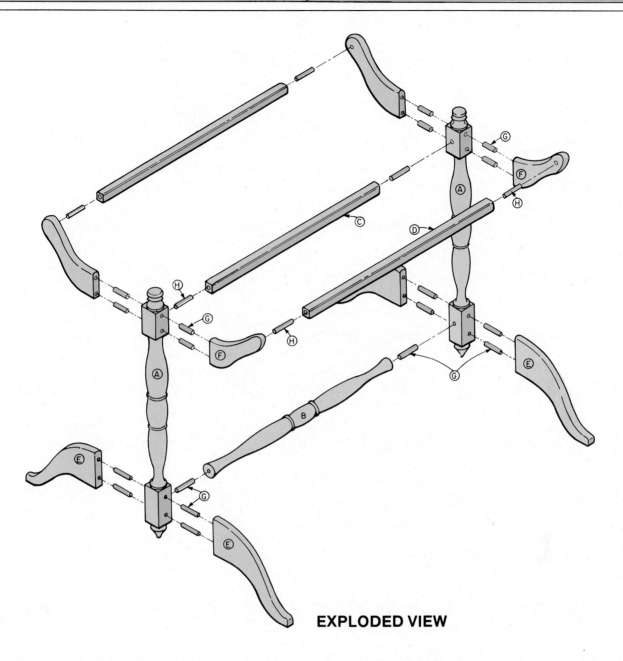

EXPLODED VIEW

accurately position these holes, bore the wings and feet first, then use 'dowel centers' to mark the support columns. (See Figure 2.) Dowel centers are available from some hardware stores and most tool supply companies.

Dry assemble the quilt rack to check that all parts are properly aligned. Then take it apart and finish sand all parts. Gluing up may pose a problem since the wings and feet are such odd shapes. However, the problem is simply

Figure 1. When turning slender pieces, use a 'steadyrest' so that they don't bend or break on the lathe.

Figure 2. Use dowel centers to help position the holes in the support columns.

solved if you have a few hardwood clamps, as shown in Figure 3. Glue the wings and feet to the columns first, let the glue set, then glue the stretchers between the two columns. Place the entire assembly on a flat surface and clamp it with bar clamps so that the rack is square. — *Bob Gould*

Figure 3. To clamp the wings or feet to the support columns, use several hardwood clamps as shown.

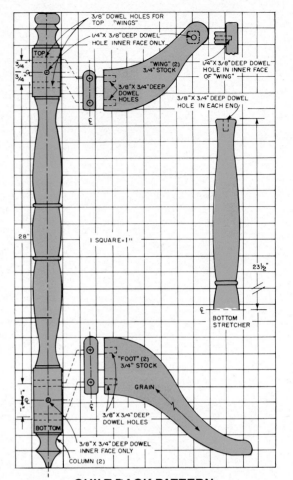

QUILT RACK PATTERN

BILL OF MATERIALS — Quilt Rack

(Finished Dimensions in Inches)

A.	Support Columns (2)	1-3/4 x 1-3/4 x 28
B.	Bottom Stretcher	1-1/4 dia. x 23
C.	Upper Center Stretcher	3/4 x 3/4 x 23
D.	Upper Outer Stretchers (2)	3/4 x 3/4 x 24
E.	Feet (4)	3/4 x 3-1/2 x 11-1/2
F.	Wings (4)	3/4 x 3-1/2 x 8-1/2
G.	Dowels (18)	3/8 dia. x 1-1/2
H.	Dowels (6)	1/4 dia. x 1-1/8

TIPS

QUILT RACK

To safely turn a spindle on a lathe, you have to clamp it tightly between the centers. But when you try to turn long, slender spindles under this pressure, they tend to bow in the middle. As the spinning stock bows, it starts to 'whip' and vibrate on the lathe. If you don't stop the lathe, the spindle will soon break.

◆ If you're having trouble with whipping — and you might, when you turn the bottom stretcher — make a 'steadyrest' or 'backrest' to stabilize the turning in the middle. For very long or very slender turnings, you might need two or more steadyrests.

◆ A steadyrest can be made quickly from some casters and scrap wood, as shown in the diagram. (You may have to modify our design for your lathe.) To use this jig, clamp it to the lathe bed and adjust the position of the casters so that they just touch the stock when it's *not* spinning.

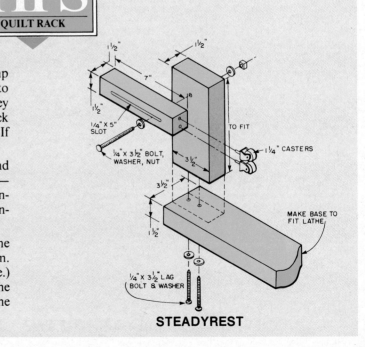

STEADYREST

Studio Tables

If you think these beauties are just sticks and glass, look closer!

The most recent movement in furniture design is the *Studio* movement (so called because many woodworkers in this movement work out of small art studios). Studio furniture borrows heavily from other schools of design, such as Modern, Mission, Art Deco, and even Shaker! But it has several distinguishing features all its own. Perhaps the most striking feature is the way studio woodworkers use joinery. There is usually no attempt to hide the joints. Instead, the dadoes, rabbets, dovetails, and box joints all become part of the overall design.

These living room tables are an excellent example of what I'm talking about. At first glance, they look as if they're patterned after a simple modern design — just some 2x2's and glass glued together to form rectangles of differ-

ent sizes. But look closely at the corners. The 2x2's are double mitered, then assembled with a three-way 'butterfly' joint. (See Figure 1.) This visible joint enhances the design of the project and emphasizes the craftsmanship that went into making it.

Figure 1. Three-way butterfly joints at each corner enhance the overall design of the tables.

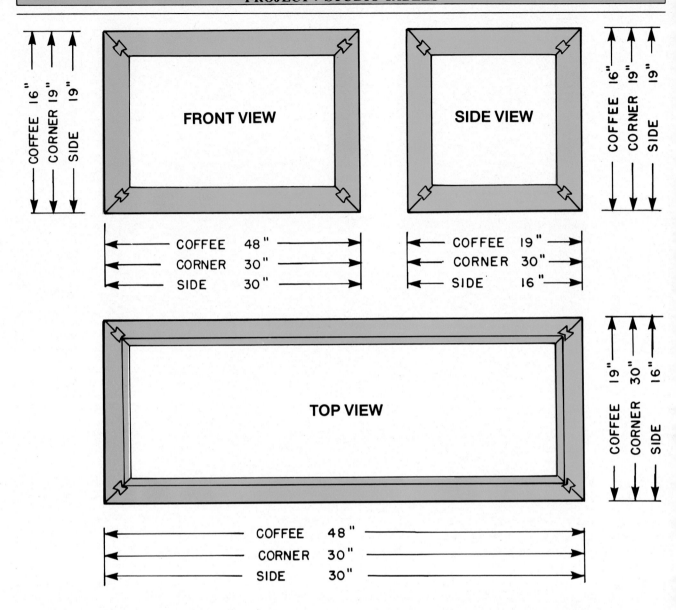

FRONT VIEW

COFFEE 16"
CORNER 19"
SIDE 19"

COFFEE 48"
CORNER 30"
SIDE 30"

SIDE VIEW

COFFEE 16"
CORNER 19"
SIDE 19"

COFFEE 19"
CORNER 30"
SIDE 16"

TOP VIEW

COFFEE 19"
CORNER 30"
SIDE 16"

COFFEE 48"
CORNER 30"
SIDE 30"

What makes this particular joint so intriguing is that it's difficult to visualize just how it goes together. I wanted to draw an exploded view for this chapter, but I found it impossible to do so. The best I could come up with was the photo you see in Figure 2. This isn't a true explode; rather, the joint has been sort of 'peeled back'. But it does show you the relationship of all the parts in the three-way joint.

Figure 2. Each frame part is double mitered on the ends, and each mitered face is routed with a dovetail groove. Butterfly keys — three to a corner — fit in the grooves and hold the frame together.

Some Tips on Mass Production

To make the three tables, you'll need to cut 72 butterfly joints — or 144 miters, 144 routed dovetail grooves, and 72 butterfly keys. What I'm getting at is this is a piece of *production* woodworking. Set up your tools carefully to make one part of the joint, then cut all like pieces.

Accuracy is extremely important in production woodworking. Check and doublecheck your setups before you start cutting good stock. Make sure that all clamps, set screws, and adjusting knobs are tight. You don't want any part of a machine setup to creep out of alignment while you're working. If this happens, the last butterfly joint you cut won't match the first, and you'll have to begin again.

On the other hand, there is some room for slop. I found through experience that if you make the butterfly joints too snug, you'll have a bear of a time assembling the tables. Set up your tools to cut the dovetail grooves 1/64"-1/32" larger than the keys. The joints will wobble when you dry assemble the tables, but the glue will fill in the cracks and take out the slop.

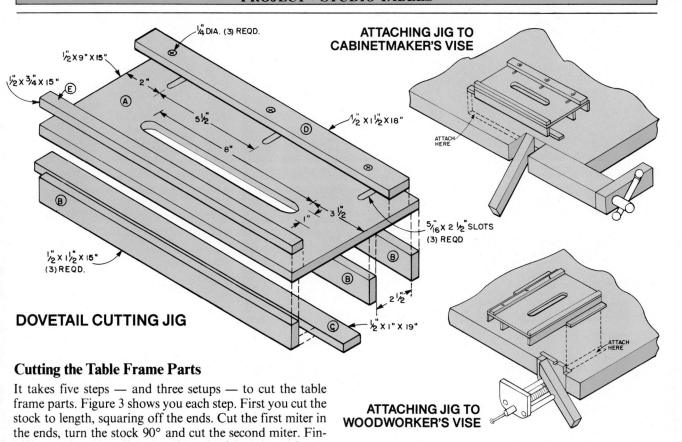

ATTACHING JIG TO
CABINETMAKER'S VISE

DOVETAIL CUTTING JIG

ATTACHING JIG TO
WOODWORKER'S VISE

Cutting the Table Frame Parts

It takes five steps — and three setups — to cut the table frame parts. Figure 3 shows you each step. First you cut the stock to length, squaring off the ends. Cut the first miter in the ends, turn the stock 90° and cut the second miter. Finish by routing dovetail grooves in each of the mitered faces.

Let me walk you through these steps and discuss the setups in greater detail: Start by cutting all the 2x2's to length. To make sure that these pieces are *exactly* the same length, use stop blocks clamped to the fence of your saw.

When you've cut the stock to length, put a piece of scrap in your table saw miter gauge. Clamp it to the face of the gauge so the wood won't move. Cut the scrap, turn off the saw, and pull the miter gauge (with the scrap) back towards you. With a fine-tipped pen, draw a line on the saw table using the cut edge of the scrap as a straightedge. This line will show you *exactly* where the kerf of your saw begins.

Discard the scrap and angle your miter gauge at 45°. Put good stock against the miter gauge and line up the corner of the board with the line on the saw table. (See Figure 4.) Cut the first miter, then turn the wood 90°. Once again, line up the corner with the line and cut the second miter. (See Figure 5.) Repeat this procedure for both ends of all the table frame parts.

Warning: I removed the saw guard for clarity to take these photos. In actual practice, always use a saw guard.

To rout the dovetail grooves in the mitered faces, you need to make a special jig, as shown in the illustration. This

Figure 3. There are five steps to machining the frame parts: (1) Cut the stock to length, (2) cut the first miter, then (3) cut the second, (4) rout a dovetail groove in the first mitered face, then (5) rout the second.

Figure 4. Before cutting the miters, mark your saw table so you know precisely where the saw kerf begins. Then line up the corner of the stock with the kerf mark and cut the first miter.

Figure 5. Finish cutting the ends by turning the stock 90°, lining up the corner with the kerf mark, and cutting a second miter. *Note: The saw guard is removed for photography. Always use a saw guard in actual practice.*

jig serves two purposes. First, it holds the table frame parts at a 45° angle so the mitered faces are square with the router. Second, it serves as an adjustable guide for the router. The back fence moves so that you can control the width of the routed groove.

Clamp or screw this jig to your workbench right over your wood vise, as shown in Figure 6. Insert a table frame part up through the vise and into the jig as far as it will go. Make sure that the mitered face that you are routing rests flush against the underside of the jig, then clamp the vise shut.

When you rout the groove, watch for splintering. As the bit spins, it cuts smoothly into the stock on one side and tears out on the other. To reduce this tear-out, take your time, especially when you're entering and exiting the stock. Getting the smoothest possible cut requires a bit of practice, so I suggest you practice on a few scraps first. When you've got the hang of it, cut the first mitered face, turn the stock 90°, and cut the second. (See Figure 7.) Repeat this procedure for all the mitered faces of all the table frame parts.

> **Tip** ◆ Routing 144 dovetail grooves can be real hard on your back and your ears. I suggest you arrange the jig and the stock so you can sit down comfortably on a stool. And wear ear plugs or hearing protectors to screen out the router noise.

Figure 6. Clamp the routing jig to your workbench so that it straddles the wood vise. The jig lines up the stock at the proper angle to the router, while the vise actually holds it in place.

Figure 7. Rout the dovetail grooves slowly and carefully so that you don't tear out the wood.

Cutting the Butterfly Keys

The butterfly keys are cut with the same router bit that you used to cut the dovetail grooves. But you'll need a router table or a similar jig to hold your router while you cut these pieces.

Adjust the height of the router so the top of the bit cuts the key stock precisely in the middle. Arrange a few featherboards to help hold the stock against the fence, then slowly feed the stock into the bit. (See Figure 8.) Pay close attention to the rotation of the bit; you want to feed the wood *against* the rotation. After you've made your first pass, turn the stock over and make a second. (See Figure 9.) Repeat this procedure for the other side of the stock. You need to make four passes in all to cut the key stock.

Once you've cut the stock, cut the keys from the stock on a bandsaw. Each key is about 1-3/8″ long (a little longer than you'll actually need). One end is square, and the other is mitered at 53°. (See Figure 10.) You'll need three keys for each corner — 24 per table or 72 for the whole set, as I mentioned before.

Figure 8. Cut the butterfly key stock with the same dovetail bit you used to rout the grooves. Cut against the rotation of the bit.

Figure 9. After you've made one pass, turn the key stock over and make another. Repeat for the other side. It will take four passes to completely shape the key stock.

Figure 10. Cut 1-3/8″ long keys from the key stock. One end is square, and the other is mitered at 53°.

Assembly and Finishing

Assembling these tables is a bear; there's no two ways about it. You'll need all the help you can get — spouses, neighbors, relatives, anybody who's handy and isn't afraid to get covered in glue. I had three helpers and could have used four. As it was, we all did enough swearing for a dozen people.

What makes this project so hard to assemble is that each table — all 12 frame parts and 24 keys — has to go together all at once. You have just fifteen minutes, maybe less, to assemble all the parts, clamp them together, check for squareness, and adjust the clamps before the glue starts to set.

To aid this process, make a couple of dry runs first. You need to dry assemble the tables anyway to make sure all the joints fit. But go so far as to actually clamp and square up the parts. This way you can iron out any problems before it's too late.

When you're ready for the glue, don't be afraid to use lots of it. I mean *lots*. I'm ashamed to show you the photos from the assembly procedure; my shop looks like an explosion in a glue factory. But you need all this glue to insure a strong joint at every corner.

And don't wipe off the excess glue before it dries. You want enough glue to take up any slop in the joints, remember? And glue shrinks when it cures. If you wipe off the excess, the remaining glue will shrink back into the joints and leave cracks.

After the glue is dry, carefully remove the surface glue with a scraper. Belt sand table frames, sanding the keys flush with the table frame parts. Choose the best-looking side of the frames for the top, then glue 3/8" x 1-1/2" strips on the inside face of the top frame to create a ledge for the glass table tops. (See the Glass Ledge Detail.) Miter these strips at the corners to make a 'frame inside a frame'.

After you've added the strips, decide how you want to treat the corners and edges of the table. I rounded my tables off with a hand-held router. But you could also chamfer the edges with a hand plane, or leave them 'hard'. (Think twice about leaving hard edges on these tables, especially if you have small children — or sensitive shins.) When you've

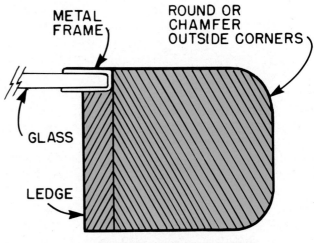

GLASS LEDGE DETAIL

shaped the corners and edges, finish sand the tables and apply a finish to all surfaces.

When you add the glass, you may want to put a polished or brushed metal frame around each piece. I found this really sets the glass off from the wood. These frames are available from most art suppliers and picture framing shops. But if you use the frames, remember to adjust the dimensions of the glass (as given in the Bill of Materials) for the width of the frame stock.

> **Tip ◆** Consider using safety glass for the table tops — especially if you have small children. Most glass shops can special order 'smoky' or tinted safety glass for you. They may also try to talk you into using acrylic plastic, but I would avoid this. Plastic scratches too easily.

These studio tables will cost you some time and trouble. But when you finally get them out of your shop and into your living room, it will all seem worth it. The three-way butterfly joints really are intriguing. Each time I look at them I wonder, "How did I do that?" — *Jim McCann*

BILL OF MATERIALS — Studio Tables

(Finished Dimensions in Inches)

Coffee Table

A.	Top-to-Bottom Frame Parts (4)	1-3/4 x 1-3/4 x 16
B.	Side-to-Side Frame Parts (4)	1-3/4 x 1-3/4 x 19
C.	Front-to-Back Frame Parts (4)	1-3/4 x 1-3/4 x 48
D.	Glass Ledge Strip (total)	3/8 x 1-1/2 x 127
E.	Butterfly Keys (24)	9/16 x 9/16 x 1-3/8

Corner Table

A.	Top-to-Bottom Frame Parts (4)	1-3/4 x 1-3/4 x 19
B.	Side-to-Side Frame Parts (4)	1-3/4 x 1-3/4 x 30
C.	Front-to-Back Frame Parts (4)	1-3/4 x 1-3/4 x 30
D.	Glass Ledge Strip (total)	3/8 x 1-1/2 x 113
E.	Butterfly Keys (24)	9/16 x 9/16 x 1-3/8

Side Table

A.	Top-to-Bottom Frame Parts (4)	1-3/4 x 1-3/4 x 19
B.	Side-to-Side Frame Parts (4)	1-3/4 x 1-3/4 x 16
C.	Front-to-Back Frame Parts (4)	1-3/4 x 1-3/4 x 30
D.	Glass Ledge Strip (total)	3/8 x 1-1/2 x 85
E.	Butterfly Keys (24)	9/16 x 9/16 x 1-3/8

Hardware

1/4" x 15-3/8" x 44-3/8" Glass (for Coffee Table)
1/4" x 26-3/8" x 26-3/8" Glass (for Corner Table)
1/4" x 12-3/8" x 26-3/8" Glass (for Side Table)
Metal Frames for Glass (optional)

Craftsman's Tool Chest

Why should all your best projects end up in the house? Why not make something for your workshop to remind you just what a fine woodworker you are!

You know that feeling of satisfaction you get when you take time to straighten up your shop? When all your tools are organized — up on the pegboard or in the drawers where they belong — the shop just *feels* better.

The trouble with most home shops (mine included) is that the smaller tools never really get organized. Even when I cleaned the shop, they usually ended up in a jumble in one or two drawers. But not any more. This two-part, nine-drawer tool box keeps all my small and medium-sized hand tools neatly arranged, right down to the last little allen wrench.

I designed this project in two parts so that you can easily adapt it to your own shop needs. You can build just the box, the box and the base together, or the box and as many separate bases as you like.

Preparing the Stock

To make the box and base, I used birch, birch veneer plywood, and, for the 'utility' woods, poplar and pegboard. All the parts that show are birch and birch veneer; parts such as drawer backs and drawer bottoms are poplar or pegboard. However, you can use any other combination of materials you like. Just be sure to use hardwoods for the drawer glides and drawer sides, since these parts will constantly rub together.

Figure 1. To joint the end grain of a board, set your jointer to remove 1/32" or less. Joint in approximately 1", as shown.

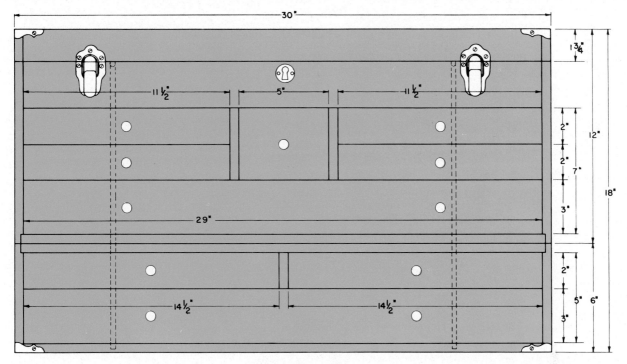

FRONT VIEW

If you have a thickness planer, glue up stock 42″ long and 12-1/2″ wide for the sides. The extra width and length allows for saw kerfs and squaring up the stock. Be sure to scrub off all excess glue to minimize the chance of nicking the planer knives. Rip and joint the stock to exactly 12″ wide, then plane it down to 1/2″ thick on your planer. Also plane the remaining hardwood and utility stock to the required thicknesses.

If you don't have a thickness planer, resaw three 4-1/2″ wide boards to 9/16″ thick on a bandsaw. Joint the edges, glue them up, then sand the surface smooth with a belt sander. Resaw and sand any other stock you need to the proper thickness.

Cutting the Parts and Joinery

Cut all parts to size, according to the Bill of Materials. Rip the stock to width first, then cut to length.

Tip ◆ When you cut the sides to length, cut them an extra 1/16″ long. Then joint 1/32″ from each end to remove any millmarks and make them perfectly true. (See Figures 1 and 2.)

Rout stop dadoes, stop grooves and rabbets in the sides, partitions, and compartment bottom, to join drawer glides and other parts. (See Figure 3.) You may want to use a saw blade with a 1/8″ kerf to make some of the 1/8″ wide dadoes and grooves. You'll also want to use a chisel to make the rabbets in the lower front corner of the sides. Using a dado blade, cut 1/8″ x 1/8″ tongues in the faces, tops, bottoms, and backs to fit in the smaller grooves and dadoes. (See Figure 4.)

Drill the box bottom and the base top, then counterbore for T-nut fasteners, as shown in the Box-to-Base Con-

Figure 3. You can make most of the joinery needed to assemble the box and base with a router.

Figure 2. To finish up, remove the board from the jointer, turn it around, and complete the pass. This procedure prevents 'tear-out' at the end of a pass.

Figure 4. Cut the small lips on the box and base parts with a dado blade. Protect your rip fence by bolting a scrap of wood to it.

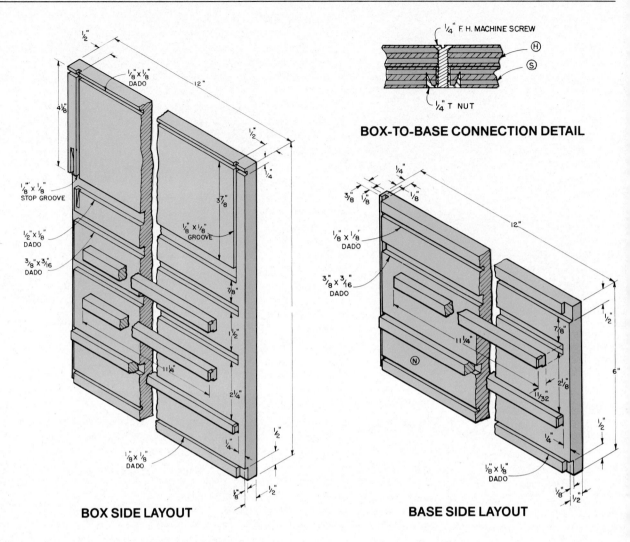

BOX-TO-BASE CONNECTION DETAIL

BOX SIDE LAYOUT

BASE SIDE LAYOUT

nection illustration. If you're making a second base, drill one base bottom, then both base tops at this time. Clamp or tack these pieces together and 'pad drill' them so all the holes line up exactly.

When you're finished making the Box-to-Base holes, drill 1/4″ diameter holes for the locking rods, 2-3/4″ deep, up through the bottom of the front face. Also drill 1/4″ diameter, 1/4″ deep holes in the bottom-most front trim. Drill 1/4″ diameter holes all the way through the other front trim pieces. Location of these holes is critical; they must align vertically.

When you have cut all the joinery, finish sand all parts. Since this tool box has so many surfaces, nooks, and crannies, it would be extremely frustrating if you tried to sand it *after* assembly.

Assembling the Box and Base

Glue all trim pieces to the fronts of the partitions, box bottom, base top, and base bottom. Sand these pieces flush to the plywood, but be careful not to sand off the veneer. Then glue the drawer glides into the partitions and sides. Carefully scrape or chisel off all excess glue.

Chisel the notches for the partitions in the backside of the front face and the front trim, as shown in the Partition Assembly illustration. Then attach the partition assemblies

to the compartment bottom and base top with glue and #8 x 1-1/4″ flathead wood screws.

'Dry assemble' the box to make sure that the sides, faces, tops, bottoms, and back fit properly. Working with the box upside down, clamp the front and back faces to the top, then clamp the box sides to this assembly. Slide the compartment bottom in from the back, and slide the box bottom in from the front. Insert the back from the bottom. (Was this as confusing to read as it was to write? Don't worry — it's simpler than it sounds.)

Turn the box right side up and check all the joints for squareness. Then dry assemble the base in a similar manner and check it.

Figure 5. Cut the lid from the box on your table saw. Set the depth of cut to 9/16″. At this depth, the blade won't go all the way through the glue blocks, so you'll have to finish cutting these blocks with a coping saw.

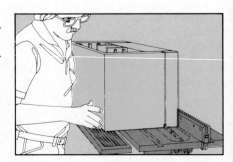

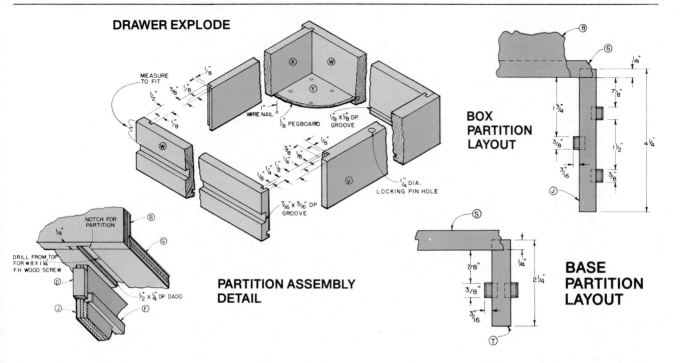

DRAWER EXPLODE

BOX PARTITION LAYOUT

PARTITION ASSEMBLY DETAIL

BASE PARTITION LAYOUT

When you're sure that all parts fit correctly, disassemble the box and base. Glue all four glue blocks to the inside of the front and back faces so that they will reinforce the corners of the top compartment. (See the Exploded View.) Also, install T-nuts in the holes in the base top.

For final assembly of the base, glue the front and back faces to the box top. Allow the glue to set, then glue the sides and the bottom to the top assembly. Attach the back with glue and brads to the partition and bottom. This will keep the box and partitions rigid. Assemble the base in the same manner, omitting the first step in which you glue the faces to the top.

When the glue is dried, cut the lid from the box on your table saw, using a hollow ground planer blade. (See Figure 5.) Set the depth of cut for 9/16″, so that the blade doesn't quite slice through the corner blocks. This will leave the top rigidly attached while you cut all four sides. Smooth the sawn surfaces with a block plane or sanding block.

Making and Fitting the Drawers

You can cut all the locking tongue-and-dado drawer joinery using a table saw blade with a 1/8″ kerf. Start by setting the depth of cut to 3/8″, then cut the ends on all the drawer fronts. (See Figure 6.) Use a wooden push stick as a backup to prevent chipping and a featherboard for control.

Reset the depth of cut to 1/8″ and cut the tongues on the drawer fronts to length. (See Figure 7.) Also cut the dadoes in the drawer sides (to attach the fronts and backs), and the grooves in the fronts, backs, and sides (to hold the drawer bottoms). Reset the depth of cut again to 1/4″ and cut the rabbets in the drawer backs.

Rout 3/8″ wide, 3/16″ deep grooves in the drawer sides to fit the glides. You may want to make these grooves 1/32″ wider and deeper than the glides, so that the parts don't bind when you pull the drawers in and out.

When you've cut all the drawer joinery, dry assemble the drawers and check for squareness. If all the joints fit properly, reassemble the drawer parts with glue, and tack the bottom in place with 1″ wire nails.

After the glue is dry, hand fit the drawers to the box and base. No matter how careful you are, you'll find that the drawers and the drawer openings vary slightly, so you'll have to sand the drawers to fit on a belt sander, and widen or deepen the grooves for the drawer glides with a small chisel. After you fit each drawer, mark it for location so you won't accidently switch it with another.

Figure 6. To make a locking tongue-and-dado joint, first cut a dado in the end of the board.

Figure 7. Finish the tongue-and-dado joint by cutting the tongue to length.

Finishing Up

Remove the drawers and set them aside. Belt sand the top of the base and the bottom of the box, then fasten the box and the base together with T-nut fasteners. Hinge the top to the box. Replace the drawers, then belt sand the front of the tool chest so that all drawers and other parts are flush. Remove the drawers again and disassemble the box and base.

Carefully mark and drill 1/4″ holes in the drawer front for the locking rods. These steel rods will slip into the holes, holding the drawers shut. Cut 3/16″ diameter rods so they protrude 1/2″ from the front face, when you slip them in place. Bend this extra 1/2″ over and cut notches on the inside of the front faces to receive the bent rods.

Install all the other hardware — lock, lock plate, latches, pulls, and chain to keep the compartment top from flopping all the way back and springing the hinges. Then remove all hardware and finish sand where needed. Apply the finish of your choice to all parts, inside and out.

That's it. There's nothing left to do but assign your tools to their proper drawer or compartment. Of course, my small tools still get tossed in, so the drawers are still in a jumble — but it's a better organized jumble. — *Jim McCann*

This project first appeared in HANDS ON! *magazine. Thanks to Shopsmith, Inc. for their permission to publish it here.*

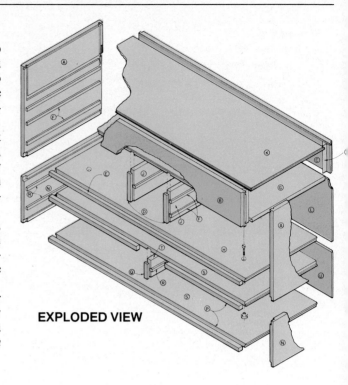

EXPLODED VIEW

BILL OF MATERIALS — Craftsman's Tool Chest

(Finished Dimensions in Inches)

Box

A.	Sides (2)	1/2 x 12 x 12-1/8
B.	Front Face	1/2 x 4-5/8 x 29-1/4
C.	Back Face	1/2 x 4-1/8 x 29-1/4
D.	Box Partition Trim (2)	1/4 x 1/2 x 4
E.	Front Trim	1/2 x 1/2 x 29-1/4
F.	Drawer Glides (12)	3/8 x 3/8 x 11-1/4
G.	Compartment Bottom	1/2 x 11-3/8 x 29-1/4
H.	Top/Bottom	1/2 x 11-1/4 x 29-1/4
J.	Box Partitions (2)	1/2 x 4-1/4 x 11-1/2
K.	Box Top	1/4 x 11-1/4 x 29-1/4
L.	Box Back	1/4 x 8-1/8 x 29-1/4
M.	Glue Blocks (4)	1/2 x 1/2 x 3-7/8

Base

E.	Front Trim (2)	1/2 x 1/2 x 29-1/4
F.	Drawer Glides (6)	3/8 x 3/8 x 11-1/4
H.	Top/Bottom (2)	1/2 x 11-1/4 x 29-1/4
N.	Sides (2)	1/2 x 6 x 12
P.	Base Partition Trim (2)	1/4 x 1/2 x 2
Q.	Base Partitions (2)	1/2 x 2-1/4 x 11-1/2
R.	Base Back	1/4 x 6 x 29-1/4

Drawer 1

S.	Drawer 1 Fronts (4)	1/2 x 2 x 11-1/2
T.	Drawer Sides (8)	3/8 x 2 x 11-1/2
U.	Drawer 1 Backs (4)	3/8 x 1-3/4 x 11
V.	Drawer 1 Bottoms (4)	1/8 x 11 x 11-1/4

Drawer 2

W.	Drawer 2 Front	1/2 x 4 x 5
X.	Drawer 2 Sides (2)	3/8 x 4 x 11-1/2
Y.	Drawer 2 Back	3/8 x 3-3/4 x 4-1/2
Z.	Drawer 2 Bottom	1/8 x 4-1/2 x 11-1/4

Drawer 3

T.	Drawer Sides (4)	3/8 x 2 x 11-1/2
AA.	Drawer 3 Fronts (2)	1/2 x 2 x 14-1/4
BB.	Drawer 3 Backs (2)	3/8 x 1-3/4 x 13-3/4
CC.	Drawer 3 Bottoms (2)	1/8 x 11-1/4 x 13-3/4

Drawer 4

DD.	Drawer 4 Fronts (2)	1/2 x 3 x 29
EE.	Drawer 4 Sides (4)	3/8 x 3 x 11-1/2
FF.	Drawer 4 Backs (2)	3/8 x 2-3/4 x 28-1/2
GG.	Drawer 4 Bottoms (2)	1/8 x 11-1/4 x 28-1/2

Hardware

1/2″ dia. Brass Drawer Pulls (11)
Brass Corner Caps and Mounting Screws (8)
Brass Drawbolt Latches and Mounting Screws (1 pair)
Box Lock with Mounting Screws and Brass Lock Plate
14″ Chains (2)
#8 x 1/2″ Roundhead Wood Screws (4)
1/4″ x 3/4″ Flathead Machine Screws (4)
1/4″ T-nuts (4)
1″ x 2″ Brass Hinges (1 pair)
Brass Box Handles (2 pair)
3/16″ dia. x 36″ Steel Rod
5/8″ Brads (2 dozen)
1″ Wire Nails (1 dozen)
#8 x 1-1/4″ Flathead Wood Screws (1 dozen)

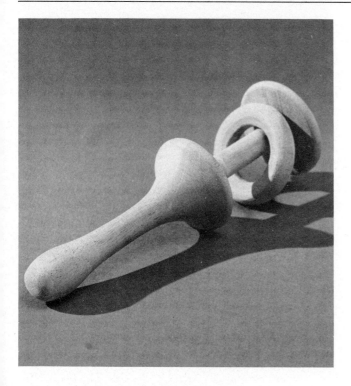

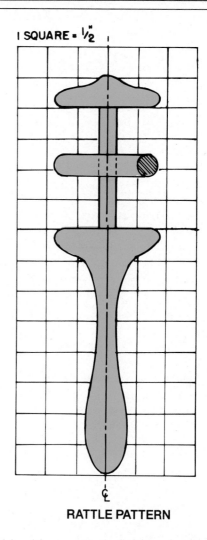

I SQUARE = 1/2"

RATTLE PATTERN

Turned Rattle

A simple lathe technique produces a fascinating toy.

It would seem that the easy way to make this rattle is to turn the handle, turn the top, make the ring, then dowel them all together. But most experienced turners know there's a much easier way! This rattle can be made from *one* piece of wood in a few minutes on your lathe.

You can probably guess how to make the handle and the top, even the shaft. But how do you separate the ring from the shaft? And how do you turn the *inside* of the ring? Just use an old turner's trick called 'undercutting'.

Rough out the shape of the rattle from a 1-3/4″ x 1-3/4″ x 6-1/2″ block, leaving the ring attached to the shaft. Finish sand the entire rattle, including the outside of the ring. After sanding, take the point of your skew chisel and very carefully undercut the ring. (See Figure 1.) Cut in a little from one side, then the other until the ring separates from the shaft.

Smooth the middle of the shaft, turn off the lathe, and tape a piece of 80# sandpaper to the shaft. (See Figure 2.) Grasp the ring lightly, then turn the lathe back on. Tilt and 'roll' the ring back and forth, using the sandpaper to shape the inside surface. Finish sand the inside surface by taping progressively finer pieces of sandpaper to the shaft.

Tip ◆ Carefully round and smooth all surfaces on this rattle. Remember, the infant you give it to will be chewing on it as well as shaking it.

Finish with a non-toxic finish such as mineral oil or 'salad-bowl dressing'. If the infant isn't due for a month or more, you can also use Danish oil — this becomes non-toxic after it sets up for 30 days. — *Nick Engler*

Figure 1. To separate the ring from the shaft, 'undercut' the ring with the point of your skew chisel. Work carefully from both sides of the ring until it comes loose.

Figure 2. Tape sandpaper to the shaft to shape and finish the inside surface of the ring.

Wall Cabinet

It stores just as much stuff as a floor model and it saves space!

There's an unwritten law that afflicts all home-owners: "Stuff — dishes, books, clothes — expands to fill all available storage space." Consequently, while you always seem to have an abundance of stuff, you never have enough storage. And even if you have a spare bookcase or storage cabinet kicking around, chances are you're short on floor space and don't have any place to put it.

A wall cabinet solves both problems. It creates more storage space *without* taking up valuable floor space. Your stuff has more room to expand, and you still have room enough to stretch out.

Before you begin making this project, think about the stuff you want to store in it — that will dictate the dimen-sions. Kitchen or utility cabinets should be 15"-21" deep, bookshelves 11"-15" deep, and curio or display cabinets 6"-11" deep. Adjust the dimensions on our drawings to fit your stuff.

Also think about where you will put this cabinet. The cabinet is hung by bolting it directly to the studs in the wall. The 'stringers' in the back of the cabinet line up with the studs, then they're fastened to the studs with lag bolts. Find out where the studs are in your wall, measure where you

Figure 1. Make a simple jig that rides along your rip fence to make the mortises and tenons. This jig keeps the board straight up and down, while the dado blade cuts a joint in the end.

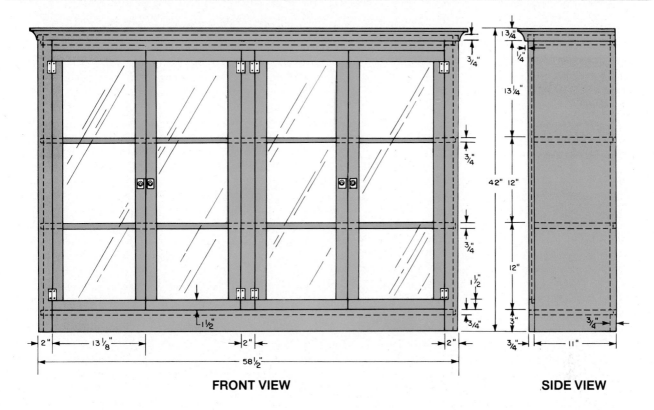

FRONT VIEW

SIDE VIEW

want to put the cabinet, then adjust the position of the stringers accordingly.

To make the case, cut dados in the sides and stringers, and rabbets in the back edge of the shelves. Finish sand these parts, then assemble them with wood screws and glue. Bore the frame rails and stiles for dowels, and glue up the frame. Check both sub-assemblies before the glue dries to make sure they are perfectly square.

While the glue is drying on the frame, make the doors. Because these doors are flush mounted, it's extremely important to use absolutely straight, absolutely clear wood for the rails and stiles. If there is even the slightest warp or bow in one of the pieces, the door will not fit properly.

The door frame parts are joined by slot mortise-and-tenons. Cut this joint on a table saw with a dado blade and a homemade jig. This jig rides along your rip fence and keeps the board straight up and down, while the blade cuts the joint. (See Figure 1.) Adjust the position of the rip fence so the blade saws out the middle of the rails (for a mortise in one pass), or rabbets the sides of the stiles (for a tenon in

two passes). Assemble the door frames with glue, check for squareness, and let the glue cure.

Make the cove molding in two steps: First, cut a cove on the face of the board on the table saw. Clamp a board to the worktable at 23° to the blade. This board serves as a fence while you pass the stock over the blade. (See Figure 2.) Make several passes cutting 1/8″ deeper each time, until you've cut a cove 1/2″ deep and 2″ wide in the molding.

Second, adjust the fence of your jointer to 45°, leaning in toward the knives. Also adjust the depth of cut to 5/32″. Chamfer all four corners, making *two* passes over the knives to cut the *front* corners, and *four* passes to cut the *back* corners. (See Figure 3.)

Attach the frame to the front of the shelving sub-assembly with glue and wood screws. Attach the cove molding to the top of the case, as shown in Figure 4. Notice that the screws that hold the molding in place go through the case from the *backside*. This way, you won't ever see them, or have to worry about covering them up.

Figure 2. To make the cove molding, first cut a cove in the face of the stock. Pass the wood over a saw blade at 23°.

Figure 3. Finish the molding by chamfering the corners at 45° on a jointer.

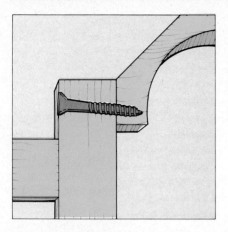

Figure 4. Attach the cove molding to the case with glue and screws. Pass the screws through the case and into the molding from the *backside,* so they don't show.

BILL OF MATERIALS — Wall Cabinet

(Finished Dimensions in Inches)

A.	Sides (2)	3/4 x 11″ x 41
B.	Shelves (4)	3/4 x 11″ x 57-3/4
C.	Left/Right Frame Stiles (2)	3/4 x 2 x 41
D.	Middle Frame Stile	3/4 x 2 x 35-1/4
E.	Top Frame Rail	3/4 x 2-3/4 x 54-1/2
F.	Bottom Frame Rail	3/4 x 3 x 54-1/2
G.	Door Stiles (8)	3/4 x 1-1/2 x 35-1/4
H.	Door Rails (8)	3/4 x 1-1/2 x 13-1/8
J.	Stringers (2)	3/4 x 2 x 38
K.	Cove Molding (total)	3/4 x 2-5/8 x 89-1/2
L.	Dowels (12)	3/8 dia. x 1-1/2

Hardware

2″ x 3″ Butt Hinges and Screws (4 pair)
Door Pulls and Mounting Screws (4)
Cabinet Door Latches (4)
3/8″ x 4″ Lag Bolts (4-6)

Rabbet the back of the door frames for 1/8″ glass panels (if you want to see your stuff) or 1/4″ wood panels (if you don't). Fit the door frames to the case, planing them down until there's a 1/16″ gap all the way around them as they sit in the openings. Mortise for hinges and install the doors. Wait until *after* you've hung the cabinet on the wall to install the panels, especially if you're using glass.

Disassemble the doors and hardware from the case, finish sand all parts that still need it, and apply your favorite finish. Re-assemble, bolt the cabinet to the wall, and watch it fill up with stuff. — *Nick Engler*

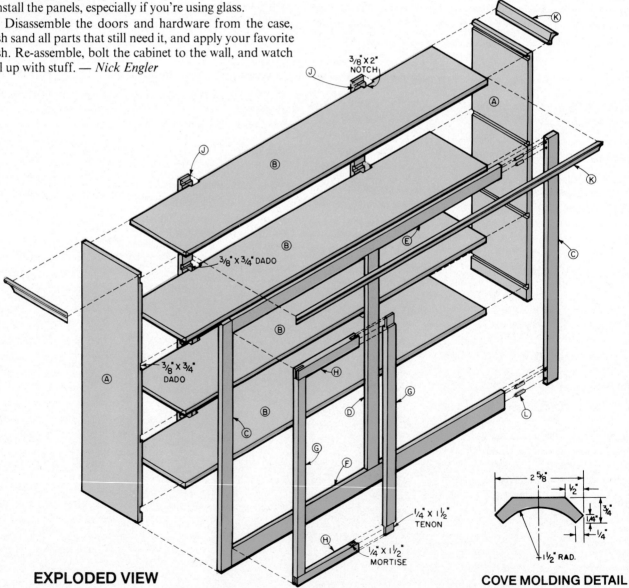

3/8″ X 2″ NOTCH

3/8″ X 3/4″ DADO

3/8″ X 3/4″ DADO

1/4″ X 1/2″ TENON

1/4″ X 1/2″ MORTISE

2 5/8″   1/2″   3/4″   1/4″   1/4″

1 1/2″ RAD.

EXPLODED VIEW

COVE MOLDING DETAIL

Country Rocker

This old-timey rocking chair has many graceful curves — but there's not a single piece of bent wood in it!

ountry wood shops were usually sparsely equipped with only the simplest tools. Consequently, country furniture is usually much simpler than pieces made in the larger cities where woodworkers had access to better equipment. Rarely do you find country furniture with bent or curved wood — this required steam bending machines that the country woodworker just didn't have the money to buy.

But every now and then you run across a country piece in which the craftsman cleverly imitated his big-city counterparts without using expensive equipment. The rocker you see here is a country interpretation of a classic Windsor design. At first glance, you think that many of the parts are gracefully bent. But on closer inspection, you find there's not a single curved piece in the chair! The seat isn't even scooped, though it looks it.

The woodworker who built this chair probably used nothing more complicated than a coping saw and a drawknife to create the curves. You can duplicate this same effect in your home workshop with a bandsaw and a router.

Shaping the Parts

Choose an attractive wood that's not too hard to work, since this project takes a lot of hand-fitting. The rocker you see here was made from butternut. Walnut, mahogany, and chestnut would also be suitable. However, we suggest you avoid cherry, maple, oak and other extremely hard woods. Otherwise, you'll just wear your fingers down to the bone.

Cut all parts to size. Cut the parts with tenons on the ends — legs, stretchers, arms, arm supports, and spindles — 1"-2" longer than indicated in the Bill of Materials. This will give you room to properly size the tenons during assembly.

The seat is glued up from *at least* 3 sections, each section 1-3/4" x 6" x 19". The headrest is made in 2 sections,

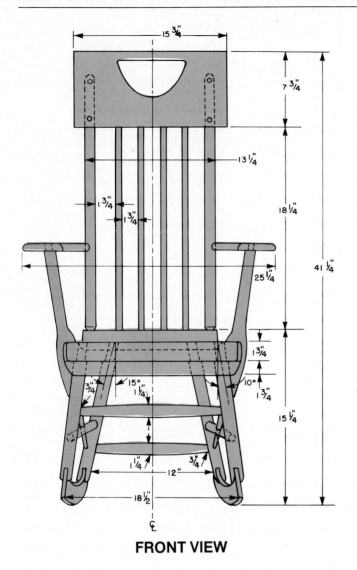

FRONT VIEW

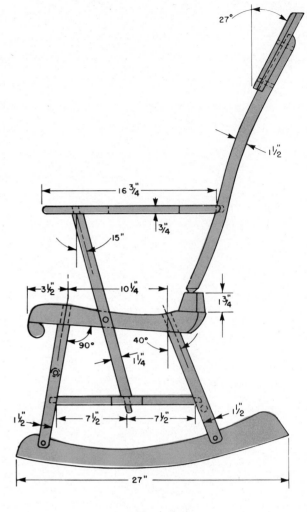

SIDE VIEW

each section 1-3/4″ x 4″ x 16″. The reason for this is that the seat is 'scooped' and the headrest is 'bent' by sawing it on a bandsaw. Most bandsaws have a throat capacity of 6″, so you have to make these parts in sections, cut the sections, then glue them up.

Making the headrest requires a bit of compound cutting on the bandsaw. First saw part of the shape (top or bottom) of the hand-hold in the stock. Tape the waste back to the block to make it square, then cut the long curve. (See Figure 1.) When you glue the two sections together, they will form a single curved piece with a hole for a hand-hold.

(See Figure 2.)

The back brace also requires some fancy bandsaw work. You cut this part with the worktable tilted, but you have to change angles in the middle of the operation. Cut the *back* curve at 7°, and the *front* curve at 20°. (See the Back Brace Profile illustration.)

While you're at the bandsaw, cut the seat sections, arms, arm supports, side stretchers, rockers, and back posts. Don't cut any joinery (such as the notches in the arm supports) or drill any holes just yet; this needs to be done during the actual assembly of the project.

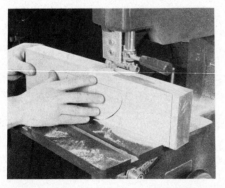

Figure 1. Shape the headrest sections with a 'compound cut' on the bandsaw. Cut the top or bottom of the hand-hold from the stock, tape the waste back on, and cut the curve.

Figure 2. When you glue up the headrest sections, the hand-hold will become a closed moon-shaped hole in the headrest.

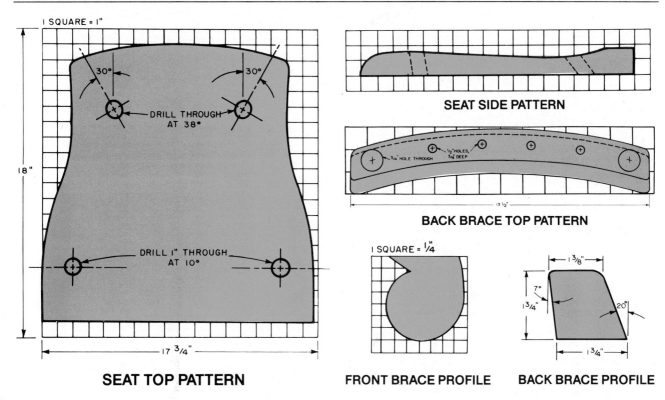

SEAT TOP PATTERN

SEAT SIDE PATTERN

BACK BRACE TOP PATTERN

FRONT BRACE PROFILE　　**BACK BRACE PROFILE**

Round over the edges of all the parts with a router or shaper. (See Figure 3.) Some parts are more rounded than others. The arms, arm supports, side stretchers, and backrest are completely rounded, while all you want to do is 'knock off the corners' of the legs, back posts, and spindles. Some edges are left square until after assembly — the back brace, seat, and rockers.

Several parts are shaped without using either a bandsaw or a router/shaper. Turn the front and back stretchers on a lathe. Cut a V-shaped groove in the back side of the front brace on your table saw. (See Figure 4.) Then round over the front and bottom with a hand plane. (See Figure 5.)

Dry Assembling the Parts

During assembly, cut the joinery *as you go*. Several parts — the rockers, legs, arm supports, and back posts — are joined at odd angles. If your miter gauge or table trunnion is 1°-2° off when you cut or drill a joint, that will throw the rest of the joinery off. So it's best to hand fit each joint.

Begin assembly by joining the legs to the seat. Drill the holes for the legs in the seat at the proper angles — the front legs are joined at 10°; the back legs at 38°. The holes must be drilled on the plane shown in the Seat Pattern illustration.

After drilling the leg holes, carefully carve the tenons on the upper ends of the legs with a chisel or a drawknife. These tenons should be 1/2″-3/4″ longer than actually

Figure 3. Round over the edges of the rocker parts with a router (mounted to a table) or a shaper. But don't round *all* the edges just yet. For some edges, such as the tops of the rockers, you must wait until after assembly.

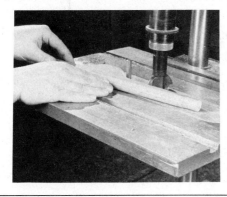

Figure 4. To shape the front brace, first saw a V-shaped groove in the back face on your table saw. Use a hollow-ground planer blade if you have one.

Figure 5. Finish shaping the front brace by rounding over the front and bottom faces with a hand plane.

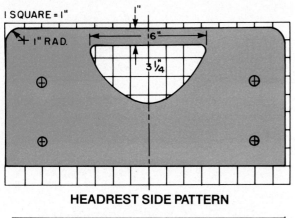

I SQUARE = 1"
1" RAD.
1"
6"
3 1/4

HEADREST SIDE PATTERN

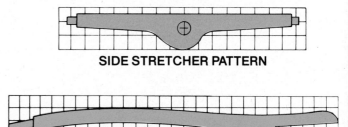

SIDE STRETCHER PATTERN

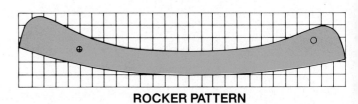

BACK POST PATTERN

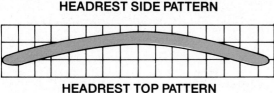

HEADREST TOP PATTERN

ROCKER PATTERN

needed, so that they protrude up above the top surface of the seat when inserted in the holes. Using your bandsaw, cut slot mortises 1/8" wide and 1-3/4" deep in the tenons. This will allow you to lock the legs in the seat by driving wedges into the mortises. (See Figure 6.)

While you're at the bandsaw, cut slot mortises in the bottom ends of the front legs for the rockers. Install the legs in the seat, slide the rocker into the front mortises and turn the front legs until the rockers line up with the back legs. Mark the back legs for the other two slot mortises. (These mortises will be cut at a slight angle.) Then cut the back mortises, and assemble the rocker to the legs. *Don't* drill the holes for the locking pins just yet.

Carefully mark the positions and angles of the stretcher holes. Disassemble the rockers, legs, and seat.

Figure 6. Cut a slot mortise in the leg tenons with a bandsaw. 'Nibble' away the stock at the bottom of the mortise with the blade.

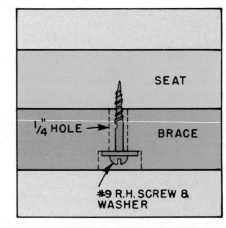

Figure 7. You can use a long 'dowel cutter' or 'plug cutter' to make the tenons on the stretchers, spindles, and several other parts, if you're careful. Make sure the stock is clamped *firmly* to the drill press table and feed the cutter very slowly.

(You'll be doing a lot of this during this phase — disassembling and reassembling.) Drill the holes, then cut the tenons on the ends of the stretcher to match. Also drill the angled holes in the side stretchers for the arm supports. Then reassemble all the parts you've joined so far to make sure everything fits.

> **Tip** ◆ If you have a large (3/4") dowel cutter or plug cutter, you can use this tool to cut the tenons on the stretchers. Just make sure the stock is clamped *firmly* to the drill press table before you begin. (See Figure 7.)

Drill the back brace for the posts and spindles, then attach both the back and front braces to the seat — but *don't* glue these parts down, even when you get to the final assembly. If the braces are glued, the seat won't be able to expand or contract with changes in humidity, and it will eventually split out. Instead, attach these parts with wood screws, countersunk from underneath the seat so they don't show. Drill the pilot holes slightly larger than the screw shanks so the seat can 'breathe with the weather'. (See Figure 8.)

Cut the tenons on the bottom ends of the posts and insert the post in the back brace. Carefully measure and mark the headrest notches at the tops of the posts, then cut these

SEAT

1/4" HOLE

BRACE

#9 R.H. SCREW & WASHER

Figure 8. Attach the front and back braces with round-head wood screws. Drill the pilot holes oversize so the seat can expand and contract with the weather.

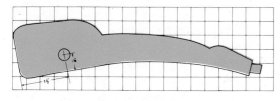

ARM PATTERN

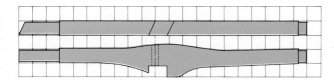

ARM SUPPORT PATTERNS

on a bandsaw. These notches are sawn with a slight side-to-side angle to accommodate the curve of the headrest. Also drill the bottom of the headrest for the spindles. Reinstall the posts and clamp the headrest in place.

Measure for the spindles, cut them off, then cut tenons in both ends. You can use a 1/2″ dowel cutter to make these tenons, if you have one. Remove the headrest, install the spindles, then put the headrest back in place.

Cut the tenons in both ends of the arm supports. The bottom tenons are purposely cut long, so that they protrude from the bottom of the side stretchers approximately 1-3/4″. The top tenons get a slot mortise, so that they can be wedged (just like the legs.) Measure and mark for the angled notch in the sides of the arm supports and cut the notches. Install the arm supports in the side stretchers but *don't* peg them to the seat yet.

Cut the tenons in the back ends of the arms. Then mark the back posts for arm holes, and mark the arms for arm support holes. Disassemble the back posts, headrest, and spindles. Drill all the remaining holes, then reassemble everything to check for fit.

Final Assembly and Finishing

Disassemble the rocker and finish sand any parts that need it. Then reassemble the seat, legs, rockers, stretchers and *arm supports* with glue. When you assemble the rockers, drill through the bottom of the legs and insert locking pins, as shown in the Exploded View. But, once again, *don't* peg the arm support to the seat yet. After the entire seat assembly is glued up, but before the glue sets, drive wedges into the slot mortises on the top ends of the legs. Then clamp the seat assembly with band clamps and wait for the glue to dry.

When the glue dries, sand off the tops of the legs flush with the seat. Attach the front and back braces with screws (but no glue), then glue the back posts, spindles, headrest, and arms in place. Clamp the headrest to the posts, then drill it for dowels, as shown in the Exploded View. When the assembly is glued up, but before the glue dries, drive wedges in the mortises in the arm supports. Finally, peg the arm supports to the seat.

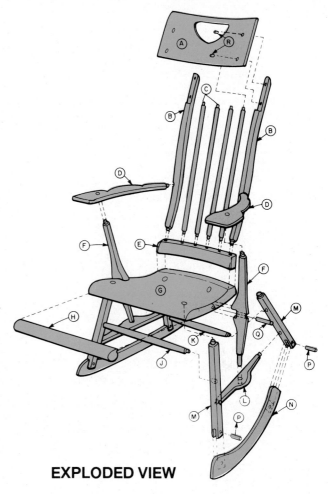

EXPLODED VIEW

Let the glue dry, then sand the tops of the arm support flush with the arms. Remove all glue beads with a chisel, then round any edges that still need it — the sides of the seat, bottom edge of the headrest, top edge of the rockers, for instance. Go over the entire rocker with fine sandpaper, then apply the finish of your choice. — *Nick Engler*

BILL OF MATERIALS — Country Rocker

(Finished Dimensions in Inches)

A.	Headrest	1-3/4 x 7-3/4 x 15-3/4
B.	Back Posts (2)	1-3/4 x 2 x 27-1/2
C.	Spindles (4)	3/4 x 3/4 x 19-3/4
D.	Arms (2)	3/4 x 4-1/2 x 17-1/2
E.	Back Brace	1-3/4 x 3 x 13-1/2
F.	Arm Supports (2)	1-1/4 x 2-3/8 x 21-1/2
G.	Seat	1-3/4 x 17-3/4 x 18
H.	Front Brace	1-3/4 x 1-3/4 x 17-3/4
J.	Front Stretcher	1-1/4 dia. x 15-3/4
K.	Back Stretcher	1-1/4 dia. x 13
L.	Side Stretchers (2)	3/4 x 2-1/2 x 16-1/2
M.	Legs (4)	1-1/2 x 1-1/2 x 14
N.	Rockers (2)	3/4 x 4-3/4 x 27
P.	Dowels (4)	1/2 dia. x 1-1/2
Q.	Dowels (2)	1/2 dia. x 2-1/2
R.	Dowels (4)	1/2 dia. x 1-1/4

The Metropolitan Museum of Art, Rogers Fund, 1925

Tip-and-Turn Table

This classic occasional table adds class to any occasion.

This walnut table, now on display at the Metropolitan Museum of Art in New York City, is an excellent example of tripod Chippendale tables. This particular piece was manufactured in Philadelphia during the height of the furniture boom from 1750 to 1780.

These 'occasional tables' were quite popular — and quite ingeniously designed. The top is hinged on the underside to tilt vertically, so that the table could be stored against a wall until needed. And sometimes the table was used in the vertical position as a fire screen, to block or reflect the heat from a hearth.

With the top in the horizontal position, it was used as a tea table, a wine table, or a 'lazy susan'. Underneath the top there is a 'bird cage' fitted to a slotted tenon. A peg fits

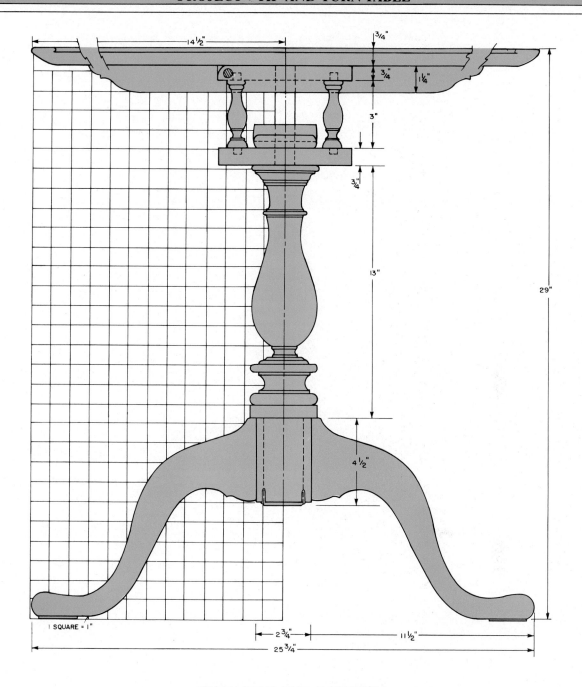

SIDE VIEW AND PATTERN

in the tenon. When the peg is removed, the top and cage re-volve on the pedestal — making it easier for folks to serve themselves from the table.

Considerations

Before you start, give some thought to the stock you'll use. This particular table was made from walnut, as we men-tioned, but you could also use mahogany or cherry — both of those woods were used extensively in the Chippendale

period. Just be certain to use a *hardwood* — wooden hinges and cages made from softwood soon wear out.

Also consider the design of the top. Traditionally, the tops of occasional tables were made from a solid piece of stock, slightly recessed on a lathe to create a lip around the edge. Sometimes the lips were carved to make them look 'pinched', like the edge of a piecrust — hence the name "piecrust tables". We included one possible design for a pie-crust table top with our plans here, as shown in the Piecrust

Pattern illustration. (If you like the piecrust effect, this can be easily duplicated on a Sears Craftsman "Edgecrafter" attachment for your router and router table.) You may also wish to leave the top smooth and slightly round or shape the edge.

Construction

Start by turning the large pedestal and the four small posts of the bird cage. Note that the round tenon (on which the cage revolves) is part of the pedestal. When you're finished turning the pedestal (but while it's still mounted on the lathe) carefully carve the small indentations at the bottom of this part. These indentions make the finished pedestal look scalloped at the base.

Traditionally, the legs of tripod tables are joined to the pedestal by 'French dovetails'. Long dovetails in the legs slide into dovetail slots in the pedestal, as shown in the Exploded View. If you're a traditionalist, cut the dovetail slots and dovetails at this point. Divide the bottom of the pedestal into thirds with a protractor, so you'll know where to mount each leg. Mount the pedestal firmly in a 'cradle' to keep it from rolling, then rout the slots on an overarm router or a router mounted to a router table. (You can also use a Sears Craftsman 'Routercrafter', if you have one.) Cut the dovetails in the leg stock using a table saw or router table. (See Figure 1.) These dovetails should be made *before* you cut the leg from the stock.

If you're not a traditionalist, you may want to dowel the legs to the pedestal, then peg the dowels with small screws to keep the joints from coming apart. (See Figure 2.) This 'pegged dowel' joint holds up well, and is much easier than making French dovetails.

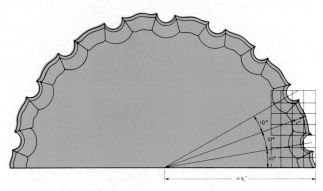

PIECRUST PATTERN

Cut the table top, legs, collar, and top cleats out on a bandsaw. Shape the table top to suit your taste by cutting a lip, piecrust, or simply rounding over the edge. Round the legs with chisels or a drawknife. (See Figure 3.) Remove just a little more stock from the 'ankle' of the leg than you do from other portions, to make the foot look slightly bulbous. Also, round over the 'hinged' edge of the top of the bird cage, as shown in the Side View. If this edge isn't rounded, you won't be able to tip the table up into a vertical position.

Route a 3/8″ deep, 1/2″ wide groove in the collar, straight through the diameter. Make a matching mortise in the round tenon on top of the pedestal by drilling a series of 1/2″ holes, then squaring up the edges with a chisel. And while you're at your drill press, also drill the necessary holes in the collar, bird cage top and bottom, and top cleats. Be careful when you drill the holes for the hinge pins in the cleats and cage top — they must be positioned accurately so that the top will rest firmly on the cage when in the horizontal position.

Assembly

Once all the pieces have been properly cut, shaped, and sanded smooth, spread glue in the dovetail slots in the pedestal and on the dovetails on the legs. Tap the legs into place, then stand the assembly upright on a smooth, flat surface. Use a large carpenter's square to check that the pedestal is perfectly vertical. Also glue the collar to the bottom of the bird cage, then glue cage top, bottom, and posts together to form a small box with open sides.

When the glue has cured, place the table top upside down on your workbench. Place the bird cage bottom up, centered in the top, and mark it for position. Attach the top

Figure 1. Cut the dovetails in the leg stock **before** you cut the shape of the legs.

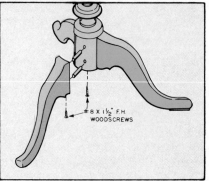

Figure 2. If you don't have the time or the equipment to make French dovetails, you can dowel the legs to the pedestal. 'Peg' the bottom dowels with small screws to keep the joint from pulling apart.

Figure 3. Round the legs with a a drawknife, removing a little more stock from the 'ankle' of the leg than you do from other portions. This will make the foot look slightly bulbous.

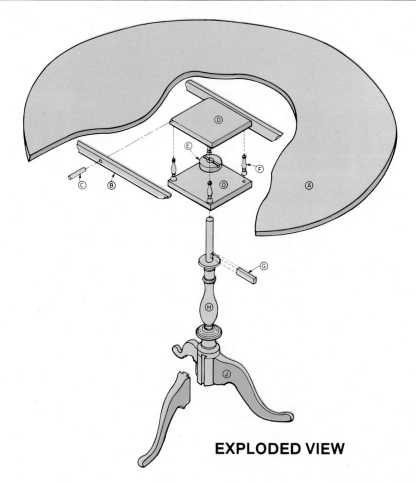

EXPLODED VIEW

cleats to the top with glue and screws, one cleat on either side of the cage. Leave 1/32"-1/16" between the cleats and the cage so the two pieces won't bind. Wax the hinge pins with paraffin (to keep the wood from wearing away quickly), then insert them through the top cleats into the cage top. 'Peg' the pins in place by nailing small brads through the cage top into the pins. Check that the hinge action is smooth and that the cage top doesn't bind against the table top.

Tip ◆ As designed, the table top does not lock in either the horizontal or vertical position. This might prove dangerous — if you set something heavy on the edge of the table at just the right spot, the top will tip up suddenly, dashing whatever you had on the table to the floor. To avoid this, we suggest you attach a simple 'turn button' to the underside of the table, as shown in Figure 4. This turn button hooks over the top edge of the bird cage, opposite the hinge, and locks the table in the horizontal position.

Turn the table top assembly right side up and slip the bird cage over the round tenon on the top of the pedestal. Insert the peg so that it goes through the tenons and rests in the slot in the collar — you may have to do a little hand work to get these parts to fit just right. When everything is fitted and the table tips, turns, and locks in place, stain and finish the piece to suit. — *Monte Burch*

Figure 4. A 'turn button', screwed to the underside of the table top, hooks over the top edge of the bird cage and locks the table in a horizontal position. To tip the table up, rotate the turn button so the flange disengages the cage.

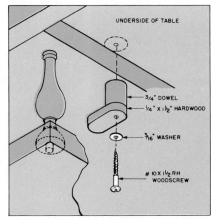

UNDERSIDE OF TABLE

3/4" DOWEL
1/4" X 1 1/2" HARDWOOD
3/16" WASHER
10 X 1 1/2 RH WOODSCREW

BILL OF MATERIALS — Tip-and-Turn Table

(Finished Dimensions in Inches)

A.	Table Top	28 dia. x 3/4
B.	Top Cleats (2)	3/4 x 1-1/4 x 20
C.	Hinge Pins (2)	3/8 dia. x 1-1/2
D.	Bird Cage Top/Bottom (2)	3/4 x 7 x 7
E.	Locking Collar	3 dia. x 3/4
F.	Bird Cage Posts (4)	1 dia. x 4-3/8
G.	Locking Peg	1/2 x 1 x 3
H.	Pedestal	3-1/2 dia. x 22
J.	Legs (3)	1-1/2 x 10-3/8 x 12

Double Planter

Two plants in the space of one!

What better way is there to dress up a sunny window than with a hanging plant? Unless, of course, you can hang *two* plants. This quick project will enable you to suspend a couple of plants where you thought you only had room for one!

Cut one 8″ disc and two 7″ discs from 3/4″ thick hardwood stock. (If you have to glue up stock for the discs, be sure to use a *waterproof* glue, such as resorcinol.) Round the edges of all three discs, then cut holes in two of them to form rings. (See Figure 1.) In the bottom of each ring or disc, drill three 3/4″ holes, 120° apart, halfway through the stock. Change to a 5/16″ bit and complete the holes. (See the Section A diagram.)

Cut a length of 1/4″ diameter rope 76″-78″ long and thread it up through the rings and hanger, then down again. As you go, tie knots to suspend the wooden pieces. But *don't* pull the knots tight just yet. Cut a second length of rope 40″-42″ long, thread it through the rings and hanger, then wrap it around the first rope. (See Figure 2.) Hang up the planter to check that the rings are level. If they're out of kilter, loosen the appropriate knots and 'roll' them up or down the ropes. When you've got all the rings where you want them, pull the knots tight.

As shown, this hanging planter will hold standard 4″ and 5″ clay pots. But you can change the size of the rings to hold almost any pot. Just remember that the outside diameter of the ring should be 3″ more than the diameter of the pot it will hold. — *Nick Engler*

Figure 1. Round the edges of the wooden discs, then make a piercing cut with a scroll saw or jigsaw to form a ring.

BILL OF MATERIALS — Double Planter	
(Finished Dimensions in Inches)	
A. Top and Bottom Discs (2)	7 dia. x 3/4
B. Middle Disc	8 dia. x 3/4
Hardware	
2″ Welded Ring	
1/4″ Manila Rope (10′)	

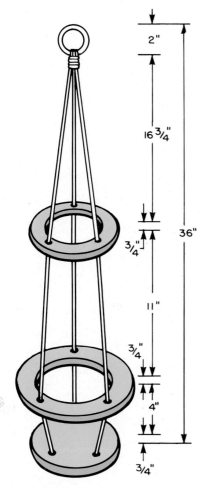

ISOMETRIC VIEW

2"

16 ³/₄"

36"

³/₄"

11"

³/₄"

4"

³/₄"

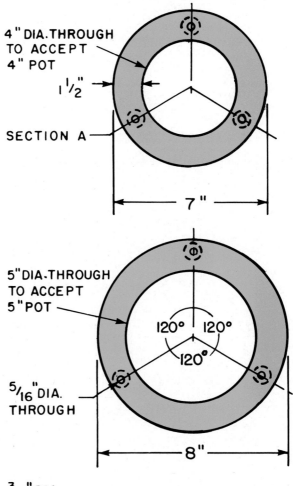

4" DIA. THROUGH
TO ACCEPT
4" POT

1¹/₂"

SECTION A

7"

5" DIA. THROUGH
TO ACCEPT
5" POT

120° 120°

120°

⁵/₁₆" DIA.
THROUGH

8"

³/₄" DIA.
COUNTERSUNK ³/₈"

7"

RING & DISC LAYOUTS

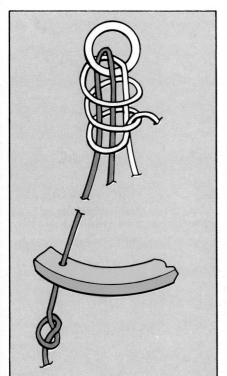

Figure 2. While the rings look to be suspended with three separate ropes, they actually hang on two. Thread them through the rings and hanger as shown.

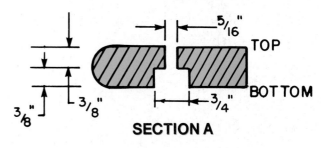

⁵/₁₆"

TOP

³/₈" ³/₈"

³/₄"

BOTTOM

SECTION A

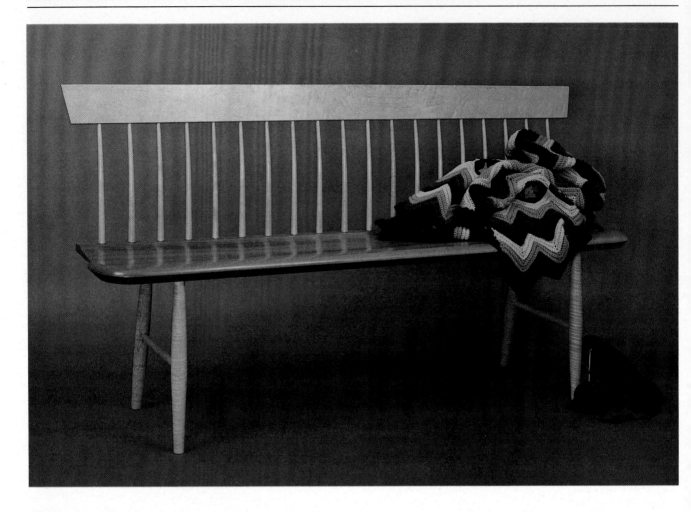

Shaker Settee

Simplicity, grace, and painstaking attention to details make this bench a classic among classics.

There is no better way to gain an appreciation for Shaker furniture than to build a replica of a Shaker piece. The graceful simplicity is immediately attractive; but as you work your way through a Shaker project you begin to notice little details, elegant touches that enhance the design and reinforce the integrity of the whole. By the time you're finished, you think, "The woodworker who designed this piece really knew his wood!"

The bench you see here is a reproduction of a piece that was made in the Enfield, New Hampshire Shaker community about half past the nineteenth century. I first ran across a picture of it in John Kassay's book on Shaker artifacts. Right away it struck a chord deep within me. When you first look at it, it looks like an old Windsor settee from the eighteenth century. The next time you look, it appears to be ultra-modern. There's just one explanation: The design is *timeless*.

Selecting Stock

A special project like this requires special care, starting with the selection of wood. Traditionally, the seats of these settees were made from Eastern white pine and all the other parts were made from rock maple. These days, it's difficult to find a white pine plank thick enough, long enough, and clear enough to make a good bench. And I just didn't want to glue up a plank from smaller pieces — I somehow felt that would have been a violation of the designer's original intent. So I looked for a good substitute and eventually found a good piece of poplar — all heartwood, so there was no variation in the color.

While I was casting about for the seat, I began to pick out the maple to make the other parts, a board here and a board there. I'm partial to figured maple, so I was pretty picky. But I eventually got what I wanted. The legs are curly maple, as you can see, and the backrest has a little curl and many bird's-eyes. The stock is striking, but not so striking that it 'pulls' your eye and detracts from the overall design.

The spindles are not figured at all, and for a good reason. Straight grain is much easier to bend than figured wood — curly maple often cracks when you put it in a press. Straight grain is also stronger, and these spindles have to take quite a bit of what engineers call 'lateral thrust' when you lean back against the backrest.

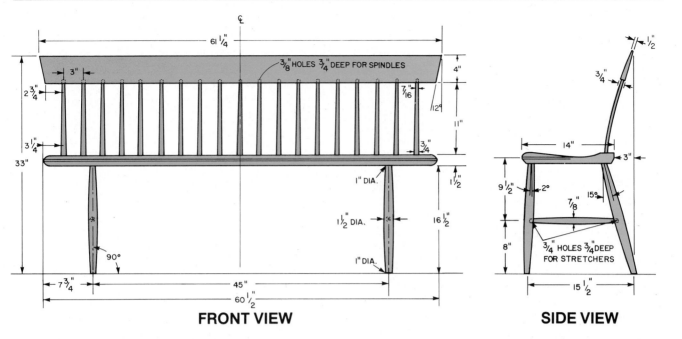

FRONT VIEW   **SIDE VIEW**

Cutting the Seat, Backrest, and Legs

Once I had collected the stock, it was time to start cutting it up. I can't tell you how the Shakers worked their wood — the Shaker brother who built the original bench probably didn't have the advantage of power tools — but I'll tell you how I duplicated the same effects.

(An interesting aside here: I say that Shaker brother didn't have power tools, but I'm not completely sure. The Shakers invented the grand-daddy of all power tools — the circular saw — in the 1830's. The credit goes to a woman, Sister Tabitha Babbit, who got the idea from her spinning wheel.)

The first thing I tackled was the seat. It would have taken forever to scoop it out by hand, so I cut a couple of giant coves on my radial arm saw. (See Figure 1.) Don't hurry this operation, don't feed the wood too fast, and make sure you have plenty of support on the outfeed end. Take small bites, just 1/16″ at a pass, until the cove reaches the proper depth.

After scooping out most of the stock, cut the chamfers in the front and back edges on a jointer. (See Figure 2.) Here's one of those little details I was talking about. The front chamfer is made at 45°, but the back chamfer is only 20°. The reason? The Shaker brother understood that if he made the back chamfer too steep, he would remove too much stock and weaken those spots where the spindles and back legs join the seat. But if he left the back square, the profile of the seat would look awkward. So he made a compromise, one that preserves the integrity of both the joinery *and* the design.

Tip ◆ I cut the coves first, and chamfers second. But if I had it to do over again, I'd cut the *chamfers* first. As you can see, once the seat is scooped out, there's not a lot left on the topside to keep it flat against the jointer fence.

The cove cut and joining saves a lot of time, but the seat still requires a lot of hand work. Cut the contours in

Figure 1. Use a radial arm saw to rough out the seat. Angle the blade at 45° and make multiple cove cuts.

Figure 2. Chamfer the front and back edge of the seat on the jointer. When chamfering, always tilt the fence in towards the knives — it's safer and more accurate.

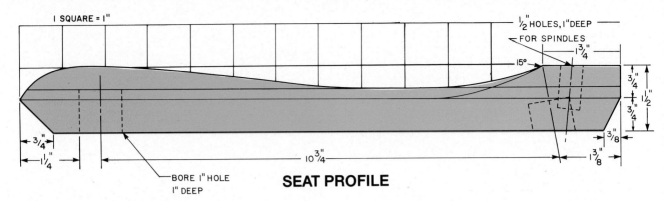

SEAT PROFILE

either end with a coping saw, then carefully rasp, scrape, and sand the rest of the stock away until you achieve the same profile as shown in the Seat Profile illustration. While you're working, it will help to clamp a long straight board to the seat, so that the front edge of the board is 1-3/4″ from the back edge of the seat. (See Figure 3.) This board helps preserve a 'hard' line between the flat and curved areas of the seat. Otherwise, you'd round over this line while scraping and sanding, and part of the design would be lost.

Resaw the backrest on a bandsaw. You don't have to tilt the table very much to make the taper — I tilted mine just a hair past 2°. (See Figure 4.) Then join the surfaces smooth.

> **Tip ◆** If you're using figured stock like I did, set your jointer to remove just a whisper — 1/32″ or less at each pass. This will help keep the grain from tearing out.

Turn the legs and stretchers on a lathe. And here's another detail to watch for: Be sure to score the center of the legs, as shown in the drawings. The score doesn't have to be much, just a light line. This is not just a decoration, it makes a handy centerline when you drill the legs for the dowel-ends of the stretchers.

Bending the Spindles

While you're set up for lathe work, also turn the spindles. These parts are quite delicate, so you may need to use a

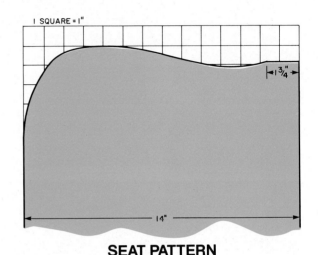

SEAT PATTERN

steadyrest to keep them from whipping on the lathe.

Once turned, the spindles are steamed and then bent slightly in a press. Many woodworkers shy away from bending wood, but it's really quite easy. The only step that's even slightly difficult is making the press. The rest of it is a snap.

The thing you've got to remember is that steamed wood, once released from a press, springs back slightly. On the average, it loses about 20% of its curve. So I cut the curve in the press so that it was slightly exaggerated. (See

Figure 3. Finish shaping the seat by rasping, scraping, and sanding away the remaining stock. Clamp a board to the back edge to preserve a hard line between the curved and flat areas of the seat.

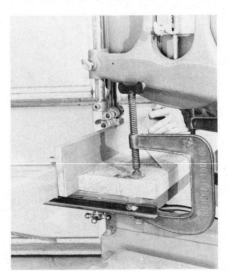

Figure 4. Cut the taper in the backrest by resawing the stock on a bandsaw. You don't have to angle the table much, just 2°.

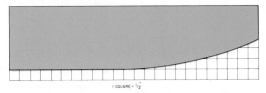

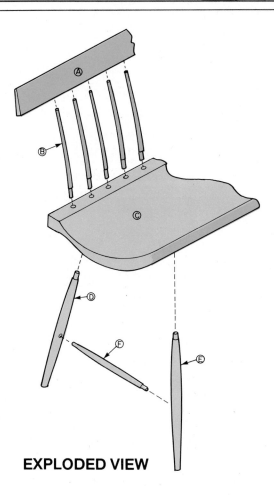

EXPLODED VIEW

lay them in the bottom part of the press. Put the top part on and tighten the clamps. (See Figure 6.) You have to do this fairly quickly; steamed wood begins to harden almost immediately after you remove the heat.

Let the spindles sit in the press for *at least* a week. As you can see, I could only bend four spindles at a time, so it took me five weeks just to complete this step. (Here's yet another detail: Notice that there are 19 spindles on this settee. Why 19? All Shaker chairs and benches had an *odd number* of spindles. This made it easier for the woodworker to center the middle spindle so the finished piece was perfectly symmetrical.) When you remove the spindles from the press, scrape and sand them smooth.

Assembling and Finishing the Settee

Once you've cut and shaped all the parts, finish sand them. I'm pretty careful about this chore. Proper sanding can enhance a finished project more than all the fancy joinery in the world. I try never to touch the wood with coarse sandpaper (50# and 80#). Instead, I scrape the wood smooth, then start with 100# or 120# and go all the way up to 250#. Try it; you'll see it makes a real difference in the way the finished bench looks.

Once the bench is sanded, assemble the pieces with carpenter's (yellow) glue. Apply plenty of glue to each joint and wipe off the excess with a damp rag. This will raise the grain slightly where you wipe, but you can sand it down smooth again after the glue dries. Wiping the glue away is a lot safer than removing glue beads with a chisel and possibly gouging the surface.

Finish the bench however you want. If you'd like a suggestion, I applied three coats of Deft, rubbing each coat out with 0000 steel wool. This always gives me a good, durable finish that's a pleasure to look at and pleasant to touch.

That's it. If you get the impression this settee takes a long time to build, you're right. If you begin a project like this worried about how long it's going to take, you might as well never start. The design almost demands a peaceful, unhurried approach, so that you take the time to discover all the intriguing details I mentioned. And if they were alive today, there's probably a few Shakers who would tell you the same thing. — *Bob Pinter*

the Press Pattern illustration.) Also, steamed wood is very soft. If there are any hard edges on the inside surface of the press, these edges will emboss the wood, making it look 'dented'. And these dents, I found from experience, are all but impossible to remove. So after ruining my first batch of spindles, I carefully carved and sanded round grooves on the inside of the press.

When it comes time to do the bending, you don't have to actually steam the spindles. I boiled them in a big roaster pan. (See Figure 5.) Let them cook for 45-50 minutes, then

Figure 5. To get the spindles soft enough to bend, boil them for 45-50 minutes. Then lay them in the bottom part of the press.

Figure 6. Once the spindles are in place, *quickly* clamp the top on the press. You only have a few minutes to perform this operation before the wood hardens again.

BILL OF MATERIALS — Shaker Settee		
(Finished Dimensions in Inches)		
A.	Backrest	3/4 x 4 x 61-1/4
B.	Spindles (19)	11/16 dia. x 13-1/4
C.	Seat	1-1/2 x 14 x 60-1/2
D.	Back Legs (2)	1-1/2 dia. x 18
E.	Front Legs (2)	1-1/2 dia. x 17-1/2
F.	Stretchers (2)	7/8" dia. x 13

Colonial Cradle

It's portable, it's safe, and it can be quickly filled with wonderful memories.

For an infant, bouncing over nineteenth-century roads in a horse-drawn wagon could be just as dangerous as zipping along twentieth-century highways. Today, we have car seats to minimize the risk. Back then, the 'Pennsylvania Dutch' cabinetmaker who designed this cradle added six small knobs — three on each side — so the mother could tie her child in while traveling. As an added safety feature, he made the cradle quite narrow so the baby couldn't be bumped from side to side.

Choosing Dimensions and Materials

Twentieth-century infants who have used this cradle have demonstrated that it may be a bit too narrow. The baby outgrows it rapidly. To help extend the usefulness of this piece, we've provided *two* sets of dimensions on the End View diagram. If you build it according to the dimensions on the right, the baby will have more room to grow. If you stick to the dimensions on the left, you can make an authentic reproduction of this classic cradle as it now appears in the Philadelphia Museum of Art.

After you've decided on the dimensions, choose your materials. The original cradle is made from pine and walnut, but any straight-grained, knot-free lumber can be used. (Don't use plywood; it splinters too easily.) We recommend a close-grained hardwood such as maple or cherry, as these materials make strong corner posts and rockers.

As originally designed, the headboard, footboard, and sides were 1-1/4″ thick — '5/4' stock was quite common a hundred years ago. You can still find thick planks at some lumber yards that cater to craftsmen, or you can have them custom sawn and planed. However, it may be far easier (and the cradle will be a lot lighter) if you simply adjust the dimensions slightly to make these pieces out of 3/4″ thick stock. Make the mortises and tenons 3/8″ wide instead of 1/2″, and make the bottom frame assembly 1/2″ longer and 1/2″ wider than shown. (See the Side Detail and Bottom Detail diagrams.)

Cutting the Patterns and the Joints

Cut all parts to size. To form the tenons on the headboard, footboard, sides, and sun shields, cut a 3/8″ x 7/8″ rabbet along an edge, turn the board over, and cut another rabbet along the same edge. (If you're working with 3/4″ thick stock, cut 3/16″ x 7/8″ rabbets.) Notch the top and bottom

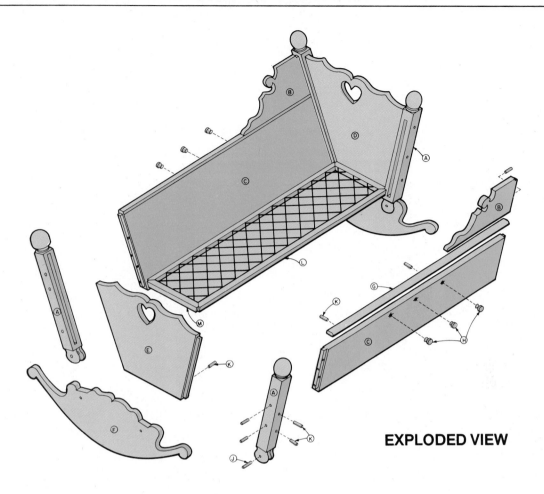

EXPLODED VIEW

of the tenons where needed with a bandsaw (see Figure 1), then chamfer the 'inside' edge of each tenon at 45°, as shown in the Corner Post Cross Section diagram. Use a sander, surform, or *very* sharp block plane to make the chamfer.

Enlarge *half* of the End View drawing (either the right or the left, depending on which dimensions you're working with), then 'flop' the enlargement to make complete patterns for the headboard, footboard, and rockers. Also enlarge the Side View to make a pattern for the sun shields. You may modify the patterns to suit your own tastes, but *don't* omit the holes in the headboard and footboard. These heart-shaped cutouts serve as handholds, making it easier to carry the cradle from room to room. Cut the patterns with a jigsaw or sabre saw.

To make the corner posts, first turn the ends of the posts on a lathe, *then* cut the mortises. (*Do not* cut the mortises first, or the posts will be unbalanced when you turn them.) If you don't have a mortiser to make the mortises, no matter. You have several simple options: You can rout 1/2" x 7/8" (or 3/8" x 7/8") stopped grooves in the posts, then square the ends of the grooves with a chisel. (See Figure 2.) Or you can round the ends of the tenons with a

Figure 2. There are two ways to fit a tenon to a routed mortise: (A) You can square the rounded ends of the mortise with a chisel to match the tenon.

Figure 1. After cutting two rabbets to form a tenon, complete the tenon by notching the top and bottom on a bandsaw.

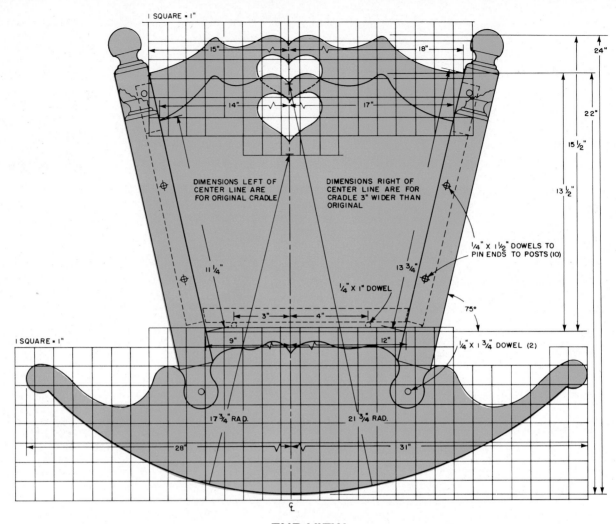

I SQUARE = I"

15"   18"

14"   17"

24"

22"

15½"

13½"

DIMENSIONS LEFT OF
CENTER LINE ARE
FOR ORIGINAL CRADLE

DIMENSIONS RIGHT OF
CENTER LINE ARE FOR
CRADLE 3" WIDER THAN
ORIGINAL

¼" X 1½" DOWELS TO
PIN ENDS TO POSTS (10)

11¼"   13¾"

¼" X 1" DOWEL

75°

I SQUARE = I"

9"   12"

¼" X 1¾" DOWEL (2)

17¾" RAD.   21¾" RAD.

28"   31"

3"

END VIEW

rasp to fit the routed grooves. (See Figure 3.) Either method will produce strong joints.

To complete the joinery, cut a 3/4″ slot in the bottom ends of the post with a bandsaw. Do not drill the posts for dowels just yet; wait for final assembly.

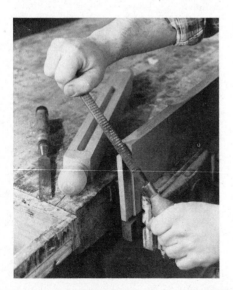

Figure 3. Or (B) you can round the bottom and top of the tenon to match the mortise.

Assembly and Finish

'Dry assemble' the cradle to make sure that all parts fit properly. Don't worry if you have to do some work with chisels and rasps to fit the tenons to the mortises; this is normal.

Once you've gotten everything to fit properly, disassemble the cradle and finish sand all the parts. Then reassemble it, gluing each part as you go. Clamp the entire assembly with band clamps.

When the glue has set, carefully drill the corner posts for dowels. (See the Side View, End View, and Corner Post Cross Section diagrams.) Except for the dowels that hold the rockers to the posts, you don't want the dowels to go all the way through the posts. To prevent drilling too far, put a depth stop on your bit. Spread a little glue in the complete dowel holes, tap the dowels in place, and sand them flush with the surface of the posts.

Sand down the cradle once again, rounding any hard corners. In particular, round the side trim and the edges of the sun shields. Finish the cradle with a non-toxic finish such as mineral oil or 'salad bowl' finish. If the baby isn't due for a little while, you can also use Danish oil — this penetrating finish becomes non-toxic after it sets up for thirty days.

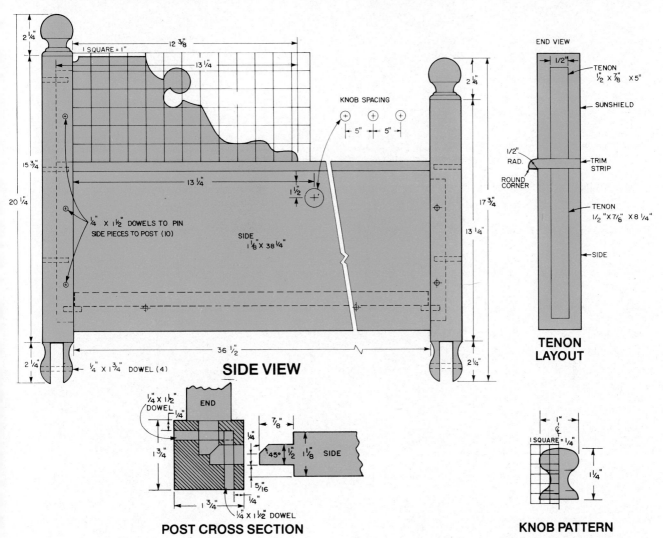

SIDE VIEW

TENON LAYOUT

POST CROSS SECTION

KNOB PATTERN

Weaving the Bottom

Wait until the rest of the cradle is complete to make a bottom for it, so that you can fit the bottom in place. The original cradle used a woven rope bottom (see Figure 4), but you can use something more modern, if you wish. Both furniture webbing and spring mattress supports are easy to install. However, don't make a plywood or plank bottom. Whatever bottom you decide on, it should allow the mattress to 'breathe' underneath.

If you choose to make the woven rope bottom, make a frame from 3/4" x 3/4" hardwood stock. Drill 3/8" holes through the frame parts where shown in the Bottom Frame diagram, and cut 3/8" x 3/8" grooves in the outside edges. (These grooves make it possible to weave the rope in and out of the holes without having the rope project beyond the edges of the frame.) Use cotton traverse curtain cord for the 'rope', and follow the pattern shown.

To assemble the frame in the cradle, drill 1/4" holes, 1/2" deep in the headboard, footboard, and sides where shown in the End View and Side View. Glue 1" long dowels in these holes and let them stick out as 'support brackets' for the frame. Lay the frame in place, then lay a 2" thick foam rubber mattress on top of the frame. If you wish, sew a washable cotton cover for the mattress. — *Bob Gould*

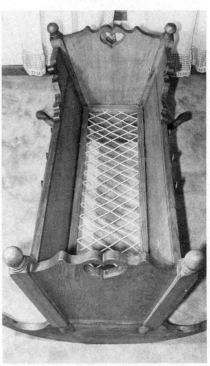

Figure 4. To make an accurate reproduction of the original cradle, install a woven rope bottom to support the mattress.

BILL OF MATERIALS — Colonial Cradle

(Finished Dimensions in Inches)

A.	Corner Posts (4)	1-3/4 x 1-3/4 x 20-1/4 (Head)
		1-3/4 x 1-3/4 x 17-3/4 (Foot)
B.	Sun Shields (2)	1-1/8 x 5-3/4 x 13-1/4
C.	Sides (2)	1-1/8 x 9 x 38-1/4
D.	Headboard	1-1/8 x 15 x 15-1/2
E.	Footboard	1-1/8 x 13-1/2 x 14
F.	Rockers (2)	3/4 x 9 x 28
G.	Side Trim (2)	3/8 x 1-1/2 x 36-1/2

H.	Knobs (6)	1 dia. x 1-1/4
J.	Dowels (4)	1/4 dia. x 1-3/4
K.	Dowels (28)	1/4 dia. x 1-1/2
L.	Frame Sides (2)	3/4 x 3/4 x 36-1/2
M.	Frame Head/Foot (2)	3/4 x 3/4 x 9-1/2

Hardware

1/4" Curtain Cord (50 ft.)

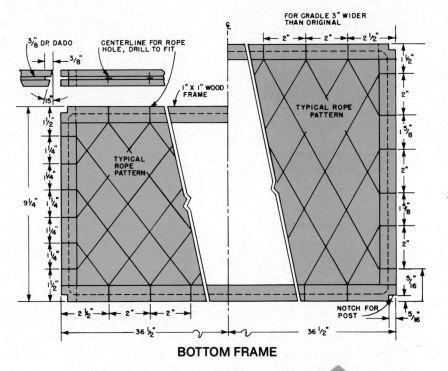

BOTTOM FRAME

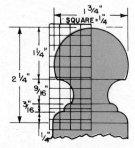

POST TOP PATTERN

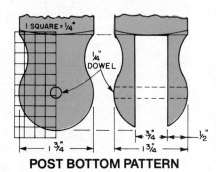

POST BOTTOM PATTERN

TIPS
COLONIAL CRADLE

It's extremely difficult (if not impossible) to accurately judge the depth of the hole you're making with a hand-held drill. Many craftsmen put a mark on the drill bit with a marker, or wrap a rubber band around the bit to let them know when to stop. But marks wear off and rubber bands slip.

◆ Several tool suppliers and hardware stores have recently begun to offer 'depth stops' or 'drill stops' that serve as a positive stop for your hand drill. (See Figure A.) These metal collars come in different sizes and slip onto your drill bits. They can be fastened in place with set screws.

◆ You can also make your own depth stops (also shown in Figure A) from hardwood scraps and two small screws. Fasten two small pieces of wood together with #4 roundhead wood screws. Drill a hole

1/16" smaller than the bit you want to stop through these two pieces where they're joined. Loosen the screws, slip the homemade stop on your drill bit, and tighten the screws again to secure the stop in position.

Figure A. You can purchase metal depth stops (left) at some hardware stores, or you can make your own (right) from hardwood scraps.

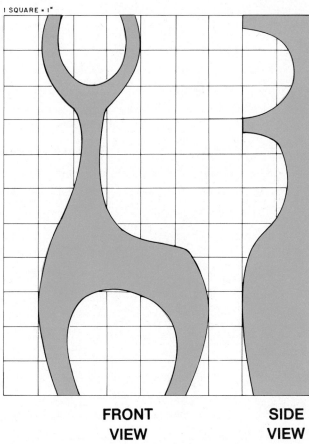

I SQUARE = I"

FRONT VIEW　　　　**SIDE VIEW**

Sculpted Deer

They look carved, they feel carved — but there's no carving involved!

At first glance, these handsome figurines look as if they took hours — maybe days — to make. The reindeer shapes appear to be carefully hand-carved. But the truth is: This project takes minutes! All you need is a bandsaw and a small drum sander.

The deer is roughed out with a *compound cut* on your bandsaw. This is the very same technique you use to make cabriole legs. Just cut the first profile in the stock; tape the waste back on the workpiece; turn the workpiece 90° and cut the second profile. When you remove all the waste, you'll have a shape that curves through three dimensions.

Cut the deer profiles in this order: First, cut the side profile. Tape the waste back on the workpiece, and cut the *interior* curves of the legs and the antlers. Finally, cut the *exterior* curves of the front profile. (See Figure 1.) Sand out the millmarks with a 1" (or smaller) drum sander.

As shown in the patterns, the deer is cut from a 2" x 5" x 11" block. However, you can make different enlargements of the same pattern to make deers of varying sizes. (The smaller deer in the picture is 9-1/2" high.) You can also make the deer face either right or left by flopping the front pattern. — *Nick Engler*

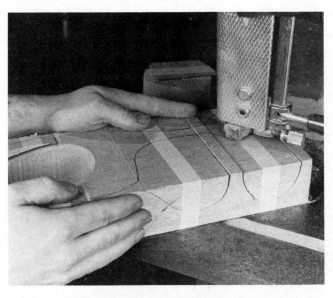

Figure 1. Cut the side profile of the deer first. Then tape the waste back on the workpiece, and cut the front profile.

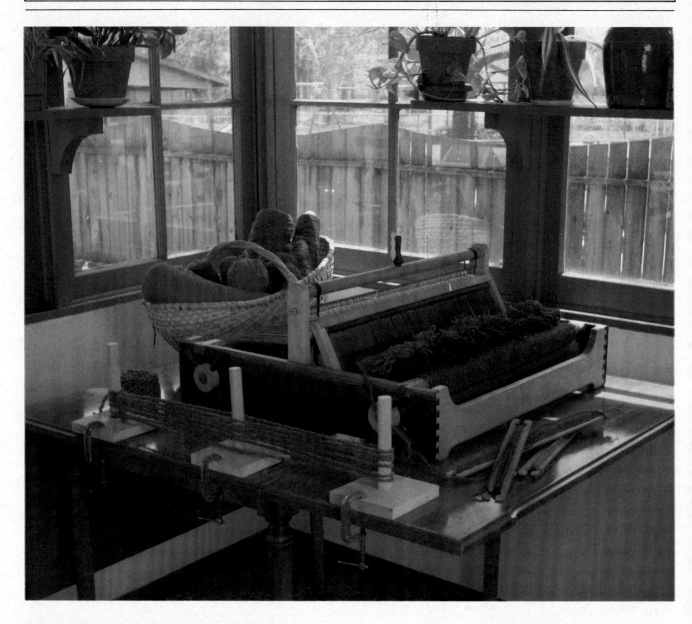

Tabletop Loom

Does someone you know want to learn how to weave? This simple, attractive loom — designed and tested by a weaving instructor — will help them get started right.

I've always thought that looms are beautiful, intriguing objects. The way the polished wood parts slide together silently and effortlessly, the way the shuttles dance back and forth trailing yarn, the way the rainbow colors intertwine in ever-changing patterns as the weaver works — all this is a sight to behold.

So when my wife announced that she was interested in the craft, I jumped at the chance to build a loom for her. But I didn't start out with a big floor model. There was no sense in putting in the time and expense until Donna learned the basics of weaving and found out if she wanted to go for the big time. A weaver in town suggested that we begin with a simple tabletop loom, so that's what I built.

But First, Some Terminology

The first step in making a loom — even a simple loom — is learning how a loom works. And to understand how a loom works, you have to know the parts of a loom and what each one of them does.

The weaver stretches yarn over two **beams,** the back beam and the front or 'breast' beam. Just below each beam is a **roller** or 'warp beam', as it's sometimes called. The yarn (or 'warp') winds around these rollers and is held taut.

The warp yarn runs through two or more **harnesses,** mounted between the beams. These harnesses move up and down, several inches in either direction. There are several

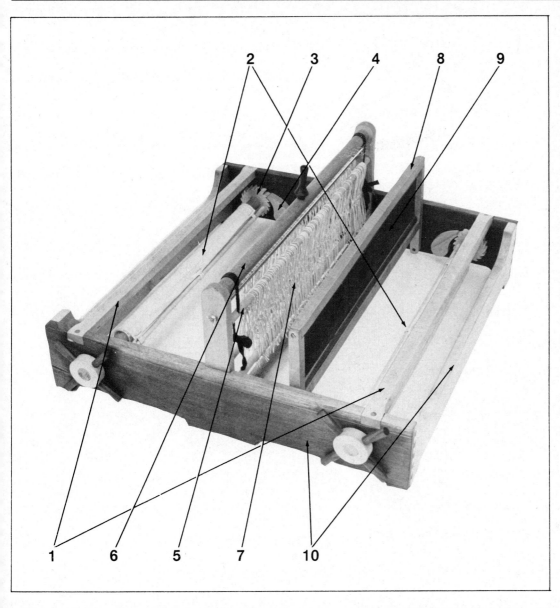

Figure 1. Briefly, here are the important parts of a counterbalance loom: The 'warp' yarn is stretched over two *beams* (1) and tied to the *rollers* (2) located underneath the beams. A *rachet* (3) and *pawl* (4) at the end of each roller keeps the yarn taut. There are two or more *harnesses* (5) in the middle of the loom, supported by *counterbalance bars* (6). Each strand of warp yarn is threaded through one of the many *heddles* (7) that make up the harnesses. As the 'weft' yarn is woven with the warp yarn, the weft is compacted by a *beater bar* (8). This beater bar holds a comb-like *reed* (9) that can be changed according to the weaver's needs. All the parts of the loom are mounted in the *frame* (10).

different mechanisms that can be employed to move harnesses, but the one I decided to use in this loom is called a **counterbalance.** The proper name for this type of loom is a 'two-harness counterbalance loom'.

The harnesses are made up of **heddles.** Each strand of yarn runs through an eye in a heddle. As a harness moves, the heddles pull the yarn along with it. Since the harnesses in this loom are counterbalanced, one harness goes up when the other goes down. Half the strands are pulled up, the other half down. The distance between the strands when they are pulled apart is the 'shed'. A large shed makes it easy to run a **shuttle** between the strands, trailing yarn perpendicular to the yarn already mounted on the loom. (Weavers call this the 'weft'.)

Once a weft is laid down, it is compacted against the weft strands that have gone before it by a **beater bar.** Mounted in this beater bar is a **reed,** a metal comb which actually does the compacting. Reeds come in several sizes or 'dents'. (The dent is a number that indicates the wires per inch in a reed.) The weaver must be able to change reeds

and adjust the dent according to the yarn he or she uses, so the beater bar must come apart easily.

As the weft is intertwined with the warp and the weaving appears, the weaver rolls up the finished weaving on the front roller and lets out unwoven yarn from the back roller. Each roller is then locked in place by a **rachet** and **pawl.** The rachet is located at the end of the roller, and the pawl is mounted just beside it.

All the parts — beams, rollers, harnesses, beater bar, pawls — are mounted in the **frame** of the loom. Refer to Figure 1 as you build this loom to remind yourself what each part is called and where they go.

Cutting and Shaping the Parts

Traditionally, looms are built from *very* hard woods, such as maple or cherry. There's two reasons for this. First of all, these woods can be sanded and polished until they're glass-smooth. This helps the yarn glide across the beams. Second, the wooden parts that move would soon wear out if they were made from soft woods.

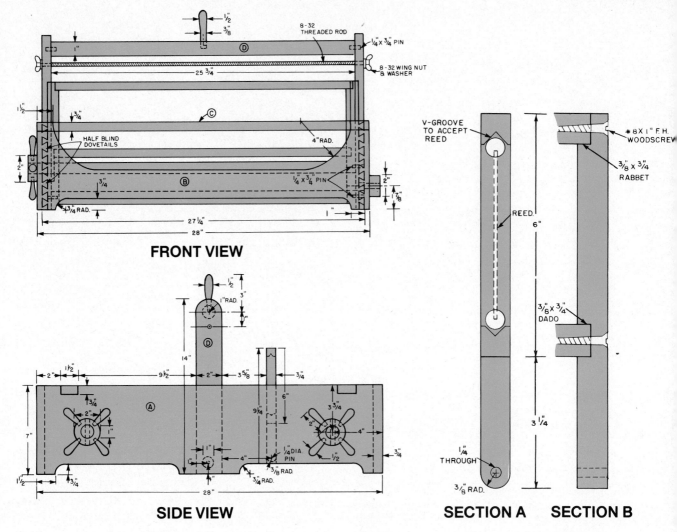

FRONT VIEW

SIDE VIEW

SECTION A **SECTION B**

I elected to make all the moving parts and any parts that come in contact with the yarn from rock maple. The dowels in this project — which I bought at the local hardware store — are beech, another extremely hard wood. The frame sides are walnut. Walnut is somewhat soft; but the sides don't move, they don't contact the yarn, and the darker wood sets off the dovetails.

Most of the parts in this loom that need shaping are shaped with a bandsaw or coping saw. After you cut all the parts to size, then saw the cut-outs on the frame parts. Also round the top ends of the harness supports. Remove all millmarks from the sawn parts with a drum sander.

Lay out the rachet by scribing a 3″ diameter circle, then a 2-1/2″ circle inside that. Divide the circles in half, then quarters, eighths, and finally sixteenths. With a straightedge, draw a line from the point that one of the radial lines intersects the 3″ circle down to the point that the radial beside it intersects the 2-1/2″ circle. This will make a single tooth on the rachet. (See Figure 2.) Continue until you have drawn all sixteen teeth. Then cut the teeth on your bandsaw — cut the radial lines down to the 2-1/2″ circle, then go back and cut the sloping lines. (See Figure 3.) After you've made the rachets, bandsaw matching pawls. The ends of the pawls should fit snugly against the teeth of the rachets. (See the Rachet and Pawl Detail illustration.)

Figure 2. To lay out the rachet, draw two concentric circles and divide them into sixteenths. Then trace diagonal lines from one circle to the next until you have laid out what looks like a gear.

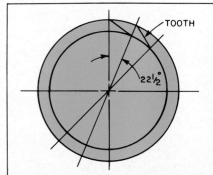

Figure 3. Cut the rachet on a bandsaw. Cut in on the radial lines, stopping at the smaller circle. Then cut the diagonal lines to make the teeth.

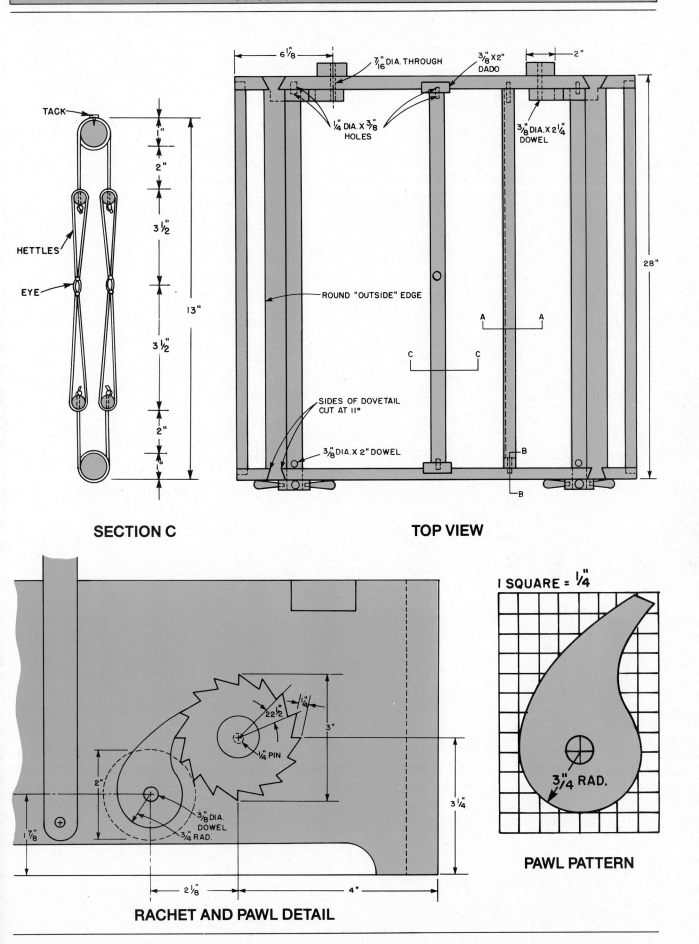

SECTION C

TOP VIEW

6⅛"

7/16" DIA. THROUGH

3/8" X 2" DADO

2"

¼" DIA. X ⅜" HOLES

3/8" DIA. X 2¼" DOWEL

TACK

1"

2"

3½"

13"

3½"

2"

1"

HETTLES

EYE

28"

ROUND "OUTSIDE" EDGE

A   A

C   C

SIDES OF DOVETAIL CUT AT 11°

3/8" DIA. X 2" DOWEL

B

B

RACHET AND PAWL DETAIL

22½°

¼"

3"

¼ PIN

3¼"

2"

3/8" DIA. DOWEL

¾" RAD.

1⅞"

2⅛"

4"

PAWL PATTERN

I SQUARE = ¼"

¾" RAD.

119

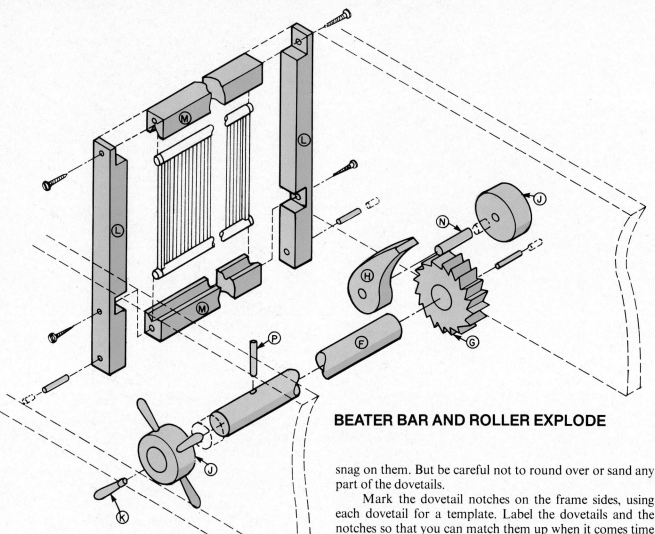

BEATER BAR AND ROLLER EXPLODE

snag on them. But be careful not to round over or sand any part of the dovetails.

Mark the dovetail notches on the frame sides, using each dovetail for a template. Label the dovetails and the notches so that you can match them up when it comes time for assembly. Saw the sides of the notches with a back saw or 'dovetail' saw, then clean out the bottom of the notch with a chisel.

You can make the knobs that turn the rollers and pawls with a 2-1/4″ holesaw, if you have one. (See Figure 5.) Or you can saw them out on your bandsaw. Remove the millmarks with a belt sander or disc sander.

Cut the dovetails in the ends of the beams on the band-saw. Then use a router or shaper to round the front corners of the breast beam and the back corners of the back beam. (See Figure 4.) Carefully sand out any millmarks. These beams must be round and smooth so that the yarn won't

Figure 4. Use a router (or shaper) and a quarter-round bit to round over the back corners of the back beam and the front corners of the breast beam.

Figure 5. You can make the 2″ diameter knobs with a 2-1/4″ holesaw. Remove the millmarks with a belt sander or disc sander.

If you want, turn the levers that stick out of the sides of the roller knobs on a lathe. If you don't have a lathe, 1/2″ dowels work just as well. However you decide to make them, remember you'll need *nine* levers — the extra lever sits on top of the upper counterbalance bar.

Joinery and Assembly

Once you've cut and shaped the parts, begin to join them. Dry assemble the loom as you go, carefully hand fitting each part to the next.

Start with the frame. I joined the front and back to the sides with half-blind dovetails. This joint looks difficult to make, but actually it's very easy — providing you have a router and a dovetail template. (See Figure 6.) If you don't have the equipment (or you're not partial to dovetails), there are two other joints that I would recommend — finger joints or locking tongue-and-rabbet joints. All of these joints are strong enough to keep the frame square under the tension and stress of weaving.

After you've joined the frame parts, disassemble them and cut a dado in the frame sides of the harness supports. These supports are inset in the sides to help keep them straight up and down. But *don't* lap the parts. If you cut a matching dado in the supports to make a lap joint, the supports will be slightly weakened.

Also cut rabbets and dadoes in the beater bar stiles to accept the rails. On your table saw, cut V-grooves in the rails to hold the reeds. The positions of the dadoes and the shape of the grooves may need to be adjusted somewhat to accommodate your reeds. Buy the reeds *before* you make the loom, then measure the reeds carefully before you join the parts of the beater bar. You can purchase these reeds from a weaving supply store near you, or via mail. Here are several mail-order suppliers:

Whitaker Reed Company
P.O. Box 172
Worcester, MA 01602

Nasco
901 Janesville Avenue
Fort Atkinson, WI 53538

Leclerc Corporation
Highway 9 North
P.O. Box 491
Plattsburg, NY 12901

Nasco West
1524 Princeton Avenue
Modesto, CA 95352

Drill holes in the frame sides and supports to accommodate the counterbalance bars, rollers, pawls, and beater bars. And while you're at the drill press, drill the pawls, rachets, knobs, beater bar stiles, and the ends of the rollers and counterbalance bars, as shown in the illustrations.

Dry assemble the loom to make sure everything fits. You'll need some help for this step; it gets a bit tricky fitting all the pins and dowels in all the holes all at once.

When you're sure all the parts go together like they're supposed to, disassemble the loom and finish sand *everything*. Make sure all surfaces are glass-smooth, so there's no splinters to snag the yarn. There are just too many corners and nooks in this project to properly sand it after it's glued up.

> **Tip** ◆ To speed up the sanding, use *flutter sheets* to polish the round surfaces and knock off the hard corners. (See Figure 7.) These are available from most tool suppliers.

Reassemble the loom, using a high-grade aliphatic resin glue (yellow glue). First, glue up the sub-assemblies. Glue the levers in the knobs and upper counterbalance bar, and the counterbalance supports to the frame sides. Assemble the beater bar with wood screws. You can glue the lower rail in place if you want, but *don't* glue the upper rail in place. The weaver must be able to remove this rail and change reeds, remember?

When the glue on the sub-assemblies has dried, insert the pins in the counterbalance bars and beater bars, then insert these pins in the proper holes in the supports and sides. Glue the front and back to the sides, then glue the beams in place. Clamp all parts together and check the frame for squareness. If necessary, adjust the clamps so the frame is square.

> **Tip** ◆ Wherever one part rubs against another — such as the pins that turn in the counterbalance supports or the dowels and rollers in the sides — *wax* both the moving parts and the inside of the holes. Wax insures that the loom will operate smoothly and it helps keep the wood from wearing away.

Figure 6. If you use half-blind dovetails to join the frame parts, these can be easily made with a router and a dovetail template.

Figure 7. 'Flutter sheets' are a real time-saver when you want to sand and polish round surfaces or knock the hard corners off stock.

After the glue has dried on the main assembly, insert the pins in the ends of the rollers, then insert the rollers part way through the side. Glue the rachets on the rollers, making sure the outside edge of the rachet is flush with the roller end. Insert the pins in the holes on the other side, then glue the stops and roller knobs in place on the rollers. *Be careful* not to get any glue on the rollers or sides that might interfere with the movement of the rollers.

Let the glue dry completely, then remove any glue beads with a chisel. Sand down any joints that need to be 'trued up'. Then finish with a *penetrating* finish, such as Danish oil or tung oil. Avoid building finishes such as varnish or polyurethane — these will just gum up the works.

Stringing Up the Loom

When the finish is dry, the next step is to string up the harnesses between the counterbalance bars. But to do this, you first need to make approximately 100 heddles.

The heddles are made from string, and each one must be tied exactly the same as the next. To do this you need to build a jig, as shown in the Heddle Jig illustration. To use the jig, drape a length of heavy cotton string over the top dowel in the jig. Tie a square knot below the second dowel, then another below the third — this will make the 'eye' in the heddle. (See Figure 8.) Finish the heddle by tying the string below the bottom dowel.

Drill 1/4″ diameter holes through the harness bars, 1/2″ from each end. String the heddles on the bars to make two harnesses, each with 50 heddles. (Fifty heddles is a minimum number for a harness. Later on, you — or your weaver — may want to add more. So keep the jig.)

Cut a pair of 28″ shoelaces in half, thread the shoe

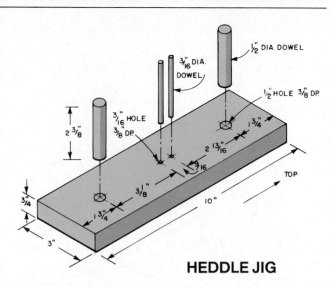

HEDDLE JIG

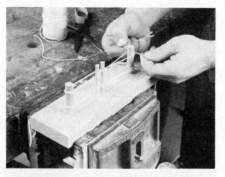

Figure 8. When you tie the heddles, use a 'heddle jig'. This not only saves time; it insures you that all the heddles will be exactly the same.

Figure 9. Center the harnesses between the counterbalance bars and tie them off. But don't tie the knots too tight; you may want to untie them someday to add or subtract heddles.

Figure 10. Sew two cloth aprons with three loops on the end. (Use muslin, light canvas, or cotton.) Insert 3/8″ dowels in the loops and staple the aprons to the rollers.

laces through the harness bars of one harness, and tie a knot in one end. Loop the top shoelaces once around the upper counterbalance bar, then thread the other end through the upper harness bars of the second harness. Make sure the lever (in the counterbalance bar) is straight up and down, and adjust the position of the harnesses until they're centered between the counterbalance bars. Then tie a knot in the other end of the upper laces. Repeat for the bottom laces. (See Figure 9.)

You may have to tie and retie all the knots several times before you get the harnesses properly centered — so don't tie the knots too tight. You don't want to tighten the knots even after you center the harnesses. Leave them loose enough so that your weaver can untie them, if need be, to add or subtract heddles.

Tip ◆ When the harnesses are centered, drive a thumbtack through the upper laces into the counterbalance bar. This will keep the laces from slipping when the weaver needs to move the harnesses up or down.

Insert a threaded rod through the holes in the supports, just under the upper counterbalance bar. Put washers and wing nuts on either side of this bar. This allows the

weaver to adjust the tension on the counterbalance mechanism, so that the harnesses will stay up or down when he or she throws the lever.

Finally sew (or get your weaver to sew) two cloth 'aprons', 24″ wide and 8″-12″ long. These aprons should have three small loops on one end. Insert a 3/8″ diameter dowel through these loops and staple the aprons to the rollers. (See Figure 10.) You see, the warp yarn shouldn't be attached directly to the rollers — the yarn may slip. The weaver ties the yarns to the dowels at the ends of the aprons.

Two Essential Accessories

That finishes off the loom. But as I mentioned before, a weaver needs more than just a loom to begin weaving. There are two important accessories you should make to really finish the project.

First, make three *warping blocks,* as shown in the Warping Block Detail. These are nothing more than dowels inserted into a base. The weaver clamps these blocks to the edge of a table and winds the warp yarn between them — this automatically measures the length of each strand.

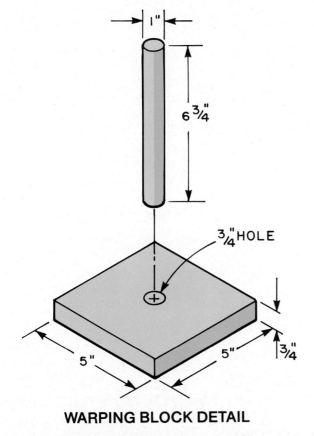

WARPING BLOCK DETAIL

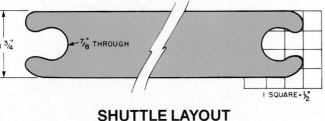

SHUTTLE LAYOUT

Next make several *shuttles,* according to the Shuttle Layout. Drill a hole near the end of a 1/8″ thick board, then cut in from each end on a bandsaw. Your weaver will need 3-4 of these shuttles — one for each color of yarn to be used in the weaving. The weaver may also need shuttles of varying lengths — 12″, 18″ and 23″ are the most common. (The reason for this is that when you wind the yarn on the shuttle, the shuttle-and-yarn combination gets thicker. But you don't want it to get too thick, or you won't be able to 'throw' the shuttle through the shed. So weavers use longer shuttles for heavy yarn.)

Sand and polish the warping blocks and shuttles smooth, then finish them with a penetrating finish. And the project's finished — for you. The rest is up to your weaver.

Further Information

If you'd like to learn more about looms and loom design before you actually build your own, there are many good books you can refer to at your library. I found that one was particularly helpful — "The Weaving, Spinning, and Dyeing Book," by Rachel Brown. If your library doesn't have it, you can order it through a bookstore from the publisher, Alfred A. Knopf in New York. — *Nick Engler*

Special thanks to Deedee Tuss, weaving instructor at the University of Dayton, for her help in designing and testing this loom.

BILL OF MATERIALS — Tabletop Loom	
(Finished Dimensions in Inches)	
Loom	
A. Frame Sides (2)	3/4 x 7 x 28
B. Frame Front/Back (2)	3/4 x 7 x 27-1/4
C. Back/Breast Beams (2)	3/4 x 1-1/2 x 28
D. Counterbalance Supports (2)	3/4 x 2 x 14
E. Counterbalance Bars (2)	1 dia. x 25-3/4
F. Rollers (2)	1 dia. x 28
G. Rachets (2)	3 dia. x 3/4
H. Pawls (2)	3/4 x 1-1/2 x 2-3/4
J. Knobs (4)	2 dia. x 3/4
K. Levers (9)	1/2 dia. x 2
L. Beater Bar Stiles (2)	3/4 x 3/4 x 9-1/4
M. Beater Bar Rails (2)	3/4 x 3/4 x 27-1/4
N. Dowels (2)	3/8 dia. x 2-1/4
P. Stop Dowels (2)	3/8 dia. x 2
Q. Harness Bars (4)	1/2 dia. x 25
R. Apron Bars (2)	3/8 dia. x 24
Accessories	
S. Warping Block Bases (3)	3/4 x 5 x 5
T. Warping Block Dowels (3)	1 dia. x 6-3/4
U. Shuttles (3-6)	1/8 x 1-3/4 x (variable)
Hardware	

1/4″ dia. x 3/4″ Metal Pins (8)
24″ Reed
Heavy Cotton String (200′)
28″ Shoelaces (1 pair)
Thumbtacks (2)
#8 x 1″ Flathead Wood Screws (4)
8-32 Threaded Rod (28-1/4″)
8-32 Wing Nuts and Washers (2)

Twelve-Dot Clock

A simple inlay technique produces an elegant clock that tells time "on the dot."

Over the centuries, mankind has spent enormous amounts of time devising better ways to tell time. Here's our small contribution to this noble endeavor: A wooden clock with an inlaid face.

Make the clock 'frame' on your lathe, as a faceplate turning. Glue the frame stock to an 11-1/2" scrap wood disc. (Tip: Put a piece of newspaper between the stock and the disc to help separate the two pieces later on.) Let the glue cure for *at least* 24 hours, then attach the disc to a faceplate. Turn the back of the frame first, cutting the rabbet that will hold the clock face. (See Figure 1.)

Separate the frame from the disc with a chisel, then glue the *back* of the frame to the disc. Once again, let the glue cure for 24 hours, then turn the front of the frame.

Cut the clock face from 1/4" thick stock. 'Fancy' wood — something with burls and curls — looks best. Draw a 6-1/2" circle on the face, then divide that circle into 12 equal sections. Where each section line intersects the circle, drill a 1/2" hole, 1/8" deep for the hour inlays.

Using a 1/2" plug cutter, cut the inlays from a wood that contrasts with the face. (See Figure 2.) Glue the inlays

Figure 1. Turn the back of the frame first, cutting a rabbet 1/4" wide and 1-5/8" deep.

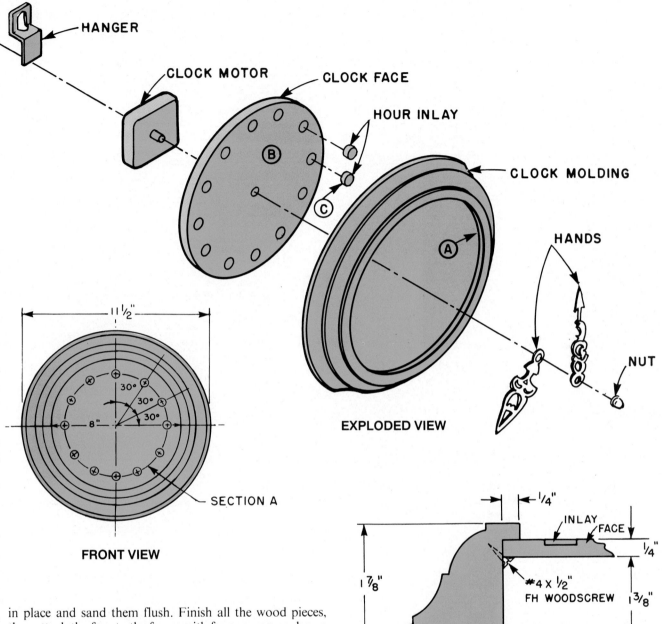

HANGER

CLOCK MOTOR

CLOCK FACE

HOUR INLAY

CLOCK MOLDING

HANDS

NUT

EXPLODED VIEW

FRONT VIEW

**MOLDING
SECTION A**

in place and sand them flush. Finish all the wood pieces, then attach the face to the frame with four screws, as shown in Section A. Finally, assemble the clock motor and hands to the clock. — *Nick Engler*

Figure 2. Cut the hour inlays with a 1/2″ plug cutter, and drill 1/2″ holes in the clock face to accept the inlays. The inlays and the clock face should be made of *contrasting* woods.

BILL OF MATERIALS — Twelve-Dot Clock

(Finished Dimensions in Inches)

A.	Frame	11-1/2 dia. x 1-7/8
B.	Face	8-1/2 dia. x 1/4
C.	Hour Inlays (12)	1/2 dia. x 1/8

Hardware

Clock Motor, Hanger, Hands
(4) #4 x 1/2 F.H. Woodscrews

Curio Cabinet

This glass case lets you view your treasures from all sides.

There's no better way to display your collectables than in a lighted glass 'curio cabinet' with a mirrored back and bottom. The glass protects each piece from dust and children, while the mirrors let you view your collection from all angles.

Glass and mirrors, however, are heavy and fragile. A display case must be designed and built to support the weight of these materials without distorting. The curio cabinet you see here appears delicate — the case has a vast expanse of glass in an unobtrusive wooden frame — but there is hidden reinforcement where it counts. It will provide a safe place for your most delicate treasures for generations.

Building the Base

When building a large, heavy piece of furniture, it's always best to begin at the bottom. But this once, you can save time by making both the base and the top frames, since these pieces are exactly the same. (See the Base Exploded View and Top Exploded View.) Round the side and front edges of these frames, then set the top frame aside — you won't need it for a while yet.

Glue a C-shaped shell together to make the drawer cavity in the base. (The back of this shell can be 3/4″ thick plywood, since it will never be seen.) When the glue is dry, attach two frames — one on top, one on the bottom — to this shell. Make a drawer to fit the cavity, then attach molding to the base side's drawer front, as shown in the Base Exploded View. This molding must separate where the drawer front meets the base side, so that the drawer can open. However, when the drawer is closed the molding should appear to be continuous.

Making the Cabinet

Build the cabinet frames (two sides and a door) from clear, straight hardwood. *This is important!* If any of the rails or stiles have the slightest warp or bend, the cabinet will be distorted and the door will not close properly.

Figure 1. If you cut the rabbets in the frame parts with a table saw, make sure that the waste stock is on the outside of *both* the rip fence and the saw blade.

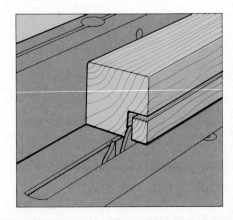

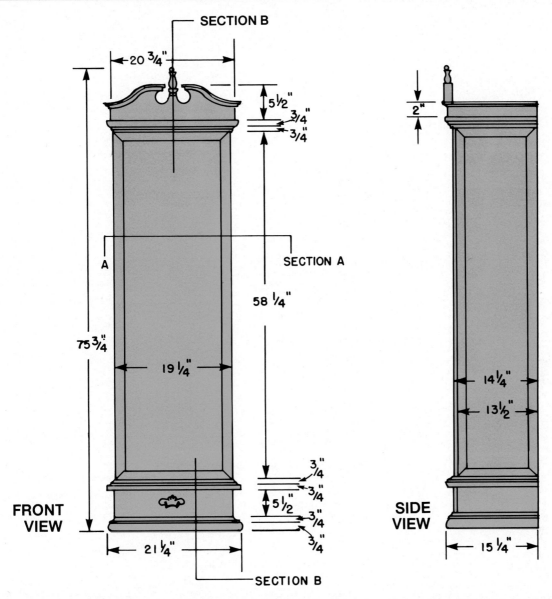

SECTION B

20 3/4"

5 1/2"

3/4"

3/4"

SECTION A

58 1/4"

75 3/4"

19 1/4"

FRONT VIEW

3/4"

3/4"

5 1/2"

3/4"

3/4"

21 1/4"

SECTION B

2"

14 1/4"

13 1/2"

SIDE VIEW

15 1/4"

If you use a table saw to make the rabbets in the rails and stiles, cut with the waste stock to the outside of **both** the rip fence and the saw blade. (See Figure 1.) If you make your second pass with the waste stock between the blade and the fence, the waste will kick back — possibly causing damage or injury. (See Figure 2.) After you've cut the rab-

bets and mitered the ends of the frame parts, reinforce the miter joints with splines. (See the Cabinet Exploded View.)

The door needs extra reinforcement, since it swings free. Before you assemble the door frame, rout shallow grooves in the backsides of the rails and stiles, as shown in Figure 3. After you assemble the door frame, and before

Figure 2. If you make the second pass with the waste between the fence and the blade, it will kick back.

Figure 3. Route shallow grooves in the backside of the door frame parts to accept L-brackets. These brackets will reinforce the mitered joints.

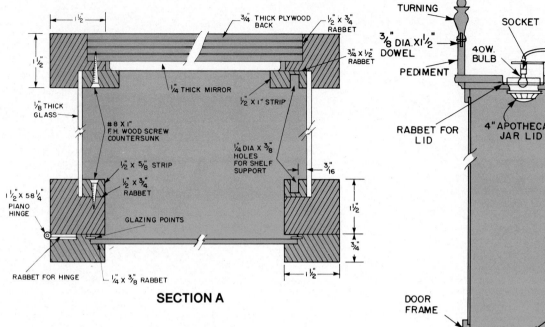

SECTION A

SECTION B

you attach it to the cabinet, inset L-brackets in these grooves at each of the corners. (See Figure 4.) *Be sure* that these L-brackets don't interfere with or partially cover the rabbets for the glass or hinge. (See Section A.)

While the glue is setting up on the frame, construct another C-shaped shell to form the cabinet. The back of this shell can be made from 3/4" thick plywood, since it will eventually be hidden by a mirror. The top and bottom, however, should be made from hardwood. If you want the finished cabinet to be lighted, cut a hole and a rabbet in the top to accept a lens. We used the lid to a 4" apothecary jar (available at most discount stores) for the lens. (See Section B.) It looks real fancy, better than many expensive light fixtures.

Notch the back corners of the side frames with a coping saw, as shown in the detail in the Cabinet Exploded View, so that they will fit properly against the back of the shell. Then assemble the side frames to the shell with glue and screws. You may think that we mismeasured the top and bottom of the shell when you find that both parts are cut 1/8" smaller than the frames all the way around. There's a good reason for this: When you finally add the top and bottom molding, the molding strips will be slightly recessed, making the joinery look neater and completely hiding the rough edges of the cabinet shell.

Position the assembled cabinet shell on the base, equidistant from the front and sides and flush with the back. Screw the cabinet down to the base. (Don't glue it in place, in case you need to disassemble the pieces for repair or moving.) Attach the bottom molding to the shell with glue and brads. Leave the top molding and the door unattached for now.

Topping Off

Remember the top frame we advised you to make back when you were building the base? Well, drag it out and blow off the sawdust. Glue and screw the pediment front and sides to the base, as shown in the Pediment Exploded

View. If you wish, make a small turning and dowel it to the pediment front. Then screw (but don't glue) the completed pediment to the cabinet, centering it just as you centered the cabinet on the base.

To make the curved moldings for the pediment, first trace the curve of the pediment on 3/4" stock. With a compass or a divider, draw a parallel curve 3/4" below the first curve, as shown in Figure 5. Cut this second (parallel) curve with a bandsaw, then shape the curved edge to match the straight molding. (See Figure 6.) After shaping, cut the

Figure 4. Install the L-brackets in the grooves after you assemble the door frame. But be sure the brackets do not cover up the rabbets for the glass or piano hinge.

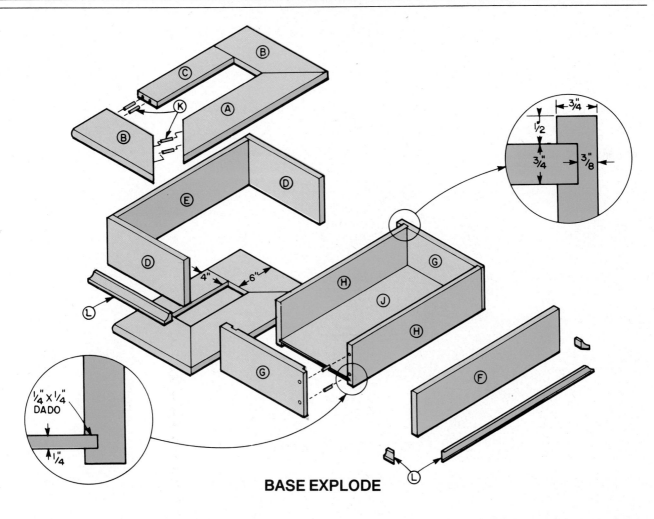

BASE EXPLODE

molding from the stock by sawing the first curve. (See Figure 7.) The result will be a curved molding that fits the pediment perfectly. Attach all the remaining molding to the cabinet top and pediment with glue and brads.

Warning: *Do not* try to cut the molding first, then try to shape it. Not only is this next to impossible; it's very dangerous.

Put the door frame in place to make sure that it fits the cabinet properly. If it's too snug (and it probably will be), plane down the rails until there's a 1/16″ gap top and bot-

tom. If you haven't done so already, rout a rabbet in the back left side of the door frame to accept a piano hinge. (See Section A.) Screw this hinge to the door frame, then screw the door to the cabinet. Make sure it opens and closes properly without having to be forced. Install a magnetic or locking catch to keep the door closed. (A locking catch will keep 'unauthorized persons' from handling your valuables — and leaving fingerprints on the glass shelves.)

Cut and fit the retaining strips to hold the mirror and glass in place. Use 1/8″ or 1/4″ thick scraps of hardwood to

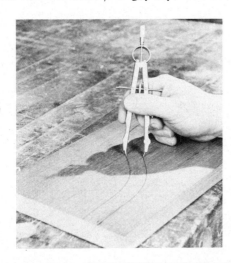

Figure 5. To make the curved molding for the pediment, first trace the pediment curve on 3/4″ thick stock. Using a compass or divider, draw a parallel curve 3/4″ below the first curve.

Figure 6. Cut the second (parallel) curve on a bandsaw, then shape the edge to match the other moldings.

represent the glass or mirrors while fitting these parts, but *do not* install the mirror or glass just yet. After you've fit these parts, drill 1/4″ holes, 3/8″ deep in the vertical strips, as shown in Section A. These holes will hold the shelf supports, and their position will vary depending on what you want to display in the cabinet and how many shelves you need. To increase the usefulness of this display case, you may want to drill holes every 2″-4″ so the shelves can be added, subtracted, and adjusted to many different levels.

Figure 7. After shaping, cut the molding from the stock by sawing the first (pediment) curve.

Figure 8. Metal shelf supports (available in most hardware stores) fit in 1/4″ holes and hold the glass shelves in place.

Installing the Mirrors and Glass

When all parts have been made, take a minute to admire your work, then disassemble the retaining strips, door frame, and hardware from the cabinet. Finish sand all parts and assemblies, including the case, the door frame, and the retaining strips for the mirrors and glass. Then apply a finish, *before* installing the mirrors or glass. We recommend a finish that seals the wood and provides protection against humidity — such as tung oil or tung oil mixed with spar varnish — to minimize distortion of the frames with changes in the weather.

After finishing, install a light as shown in Section B, if you've elected to make a lighted case. Then put the back mirror, bottom mirror, and glass sides in place. You'll need help! This step requires an extra set of arms to hold these parts in place when they're being fastened down. All mirror and glass parts should be cut 1/8″-1/4″ smaller than the frame size to let the wooden frames expand and contract without cracking the glass. Screw (but *don't* glue) the retaining strip in place.

Hang the door frame on its hinge and install the glass door panel with glazing points. Tip: If the glass rattles against the points when you open or close the door, wedge tiny pieces of felt between the glass and the points. Reinstall

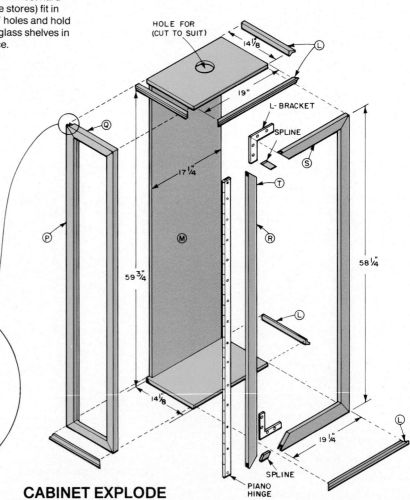

CABINET EXPLODE

the door catch, then clean off all fingerprints from the glass and mirrors.

Fit shelf supports in to the holes in the vertical retaining strips where you want to hang the shelves. (See Figure 8.) Put the glass shelves in place, then clean off any fingerprints. (If you handle the shelves with paper towels or cotton gloves, these will help prevent fingerprints and cut down on the amount of cleaning you have to do afterwards.)

One last tip: If you have small children, you may want to use plastic or safety glass instead of regular window glass. General Glass Industries of 444 East 10th Street, New York, NY 10009, makes a glass-and-plastic safety glazing called "Stormlite." This product (or products like it) are available from many local glass dealers and window repair shops. — *Jay Hedden*

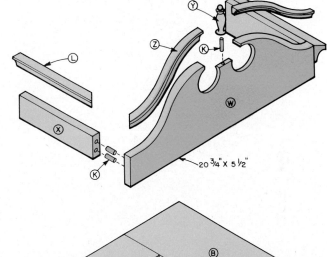

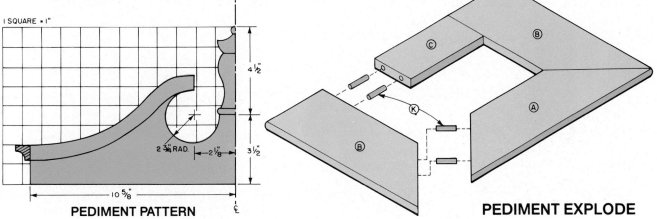

PEDIMENT PATTERN

PEDIMENT EXPLODE

BILL OF MATERIALS — Curio Cabinet

(Finished Dimensions in Inches)

Base

A.	Frame Fronts (2)	3/4 x 6 x 21-1/4
B.	Frame Sides (4)	3/4 x 6 x 15-1/4
C.	Frame Backs (2)	3/4 x 4 x 9-1/4
D.	Base Sides (2)	3/4 x 5-1/2 x 13-1/2
E.	Base Back	3/4 x 5-1/2 x 17-3/4
F.	Drawer False Front	3/4 x 5-1/2 x 19-1/4
G.	Drawer Sides (2)	3/4 x 5-1/4 x 12-3/4
H.	Drawer Back and Front (2)	3/4 x 5-1/4 x 16-7/8
J.	Drawer Bottom	1/4 x 11-1/4 x 16-5/8
K.	Dowels (20)	3/8 dia. x 1-1/2
L.	Cove Molding (total)	3/4 x 3/4 x 50-3/4

Cabinet

L.	Cove Molding (total)	3/4 x 3/4 x 100-1/4
M.	Cabinet Back	3/4 x 17-1/4 x 58-1/4
N.	Cabinet Top and Bottom (2)	3/4 x 14-1/8 x 19
P.	Side Frame Stiles (4)	1-1/2 x 1-1/2 x 58-1/4
Q.	Side Frame Rails (4)	1-1/2 x 1-1/2 x 13-1/2
R.	Door Frame Stiles (2)	3/4 x 1-1/2 x 58-1/4
S.	Door Frame Rails (2)	3/4 x 1-1/2 x 19-1/4
T.	Frame Splines (12)	1/4 x 3/4 x 2-1/8
U.	Retaining Strips (total)	1/2 x 1 x 134
V.	Retaining Strips (total)	1/2 x 5/8 x 154-1/2

Pediment

A.	Frame Front	3/4 x 6 x 21-1/4
B.	Frame Sides (2)	3/4 x 6 x 15-1/4
C.	Frame Back	3/4 x 4 x 9-1/4
K.	Dowels (13)	3/8 dia. x 1-1/2
L.	Cove Molding (total)	3/4 x 3/4 x 31-1/2
W.	Pediment Front	3/4 x 5-1/2 x 20-3/4
X.	Pediment Sides (2)	3/4 x 2 x 14-1/4
Y.	Turning	1-1/2 dia. x 3-1/2
Z.	Curved Cove Moldings (2)	3/4 x 3/4 x 9-3/8

Hardware

#8 x 1 Flathead Wood Screws (24)
#10 x 1-1/4 Flathead Wood Screws (2-3 dozen)
1-1/2 x 58-1/4 Piano Hinge and Screws
Door Catch (Magnetic or Locking)
Drawer Pull
Glazing Points (12)
Shelf Supports (2 dozen)
4″ Apothecary Jar Lid
Light, Socket, Cord, and In-line Switch
1/8 x 3/4 Steel Strap, Mounting Screws and Nut
1/8 x 11-1/4 x 56 Glass Side Panels (2)
1/8 x 17 x 56 Glass Door Panel
1/4 x 16 x 58 Back Mirror
1/4 x 12-1/2 x 16-1/4 Bottom Mirror

Wooden Attaché

As a businessman, your attaché case says a lot about you. Why not say it with the elegance and warmth of wood?

In the book "Dress for Success," author John T. Molley offers this advice about briefcases and attachés: "Attaché cases are always positive symbols of success, regardless of what they carry, and a lot more of them than you think are used only to carry lunch."

So why put your lunch in an expensive looking briefcase? Because it's *impressive* — and impressions are important in business. And what could be more impressive than a handcrafted case made from rich hardwoods?

Wood Selection and Joinery

A briefcase is a simple project to build — it's nothing more than a box with a handle, really. But if you want this box to survive everyday use (and abuse), you must be careful about what woods you use and how you put them together.

Choose woods that take a lot of punishment and don't expand and contract too much with changes in the weather. The stock should be very hard, close-grained, and rich in natural oils to keep out the moisture. Rosewood and teak are the best choices, but they are quite expensive and sometimes hard to find. Maple, cherry, birch, and elm are also acceptable — the case you see here was made from 'spalted' elm and rosewood. Avoid walnut, mahogany, oak — all of these have open grains, and walnut and mahogany are too soft.

If you want your briefcase to have flush panels, use plywood for the sides. Plywood does not 'breathe with the weather' nearly as much as solid wood. If you want raised panels, use solid wood. Cut these panels 1/8″-1/4″ small and set them in grooves, free to react to changes in temperature and humidity without splitting or warping. Join the

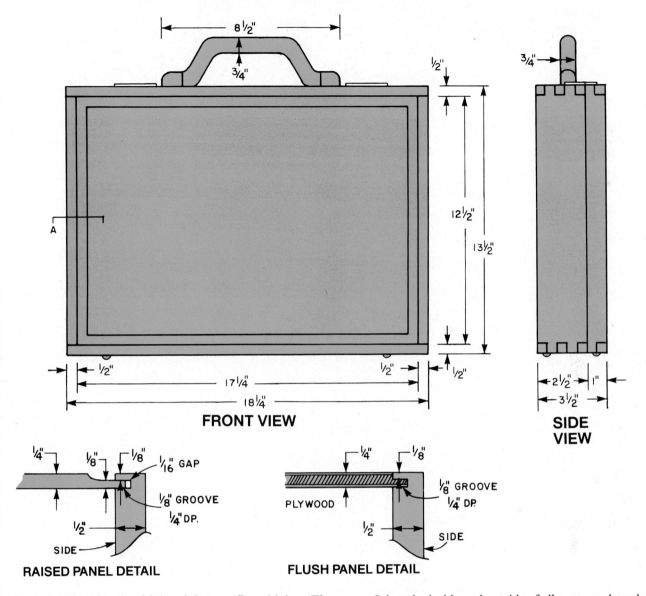

FRONT VIEW

SIDE VIEW

RAISED PANEL DETAIL

FLUSH PANEL DETAIL

front, back, and ends with box joints or 'finger' joints. The interlocking fingers stand up well under the strain of every-day travel and keep the case square.

Making the Case

Glue up 1/4″ thick stock for the sides (if you're making raised panels). Pay attention to the grain direction — the grain should run top to bottom in the case as you hold it by the handle. When the glue is dry, cut the sides, front, back, and ends to size.

Select the inside and outside of all parts, and mark the inside with a large "X". Lay out the finger joints on the *inside* of the front, back, and ends with a *scratch awl*. (See Figure 1.) You can make either 1/4″ or 1/2″ fingers, which-ever you prefer. Once you've laid out the joint, cut the fin-gers with a dado blade — the inside of the board should face you and the outside should face the blade as you begin the cut. (See Figure 2.)

Figure 1. Lay out the finger joints on the *inside* face of the boards with a scratch awl. The awl scores the wood grain to reduce the chances of splinter-ing when you cut.

Figure 2. Cut the fingers on your table saw with a dado blade. The inside face of the board should face away from the blade as you begin the cut.

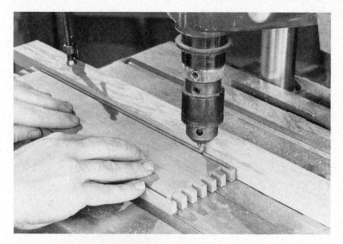

Figure 3. Use your drill press as a router to rout the grooves in the front, back, and ends for the panels. Take your time; this setup cuts much slower than a regular router.

Figure 4. Use a 'core box' router bit to form the raised panels.

Figure 5. Carefully cut the lid from the completed case on your table saw. Use a hollow-ground planer blade for a smooth cut.

Figure 6. Install 'dowel buttons' on the back of the case to serve as feet.

Tip ◆ Using a scratch awl for layout and properly orienting the wood when you cut it is the best way to get good, clean fingers. The scratch awl tears the wood grain between the fingers. If you face the layout lines away from the blade, this will keep the wood from chipping out on the backside of the cut.

Rout a 1/8″ wide, 1/4″ deep stop-groove on the insides of the back, front, and ends, as shown in the Case Partial Explode illustration. (See Figure 3.) These grooves will hold the panels. They should stop 1/4″ from the ends of the fingers — otherwise, you'll see the grooves when you assemble the case.

Cut a 1/8″ deep, 1/4″ wide rabbet in the edges of the panels, so that the panel will fit in the grooves. If you're making raised panels, use a 'core box' bit in your router to widen the rabbets and round the sides of the 'steps'. (See Figure 4.)

Dry assemble the sides, front, back, and ends to be sure that they all fit properly. Disassemble the case and finish sand the inside faces of all parts and (if you've made raised panels) the outside faces of the side panels. Glue up the case — but *don't* glue the panels in place. Just let them sit loose in the grooves. If they're glued in place, they will pull the entire case out of shape.

Let the glue cure, then sand the outside to 'true up' the finger joints. Carefully cut the lid from the box on your table saw. (See Figure 5.) Use a hollow-ground planer blade to get a smooth cut.

Hardware and Handles

Mortise out the back of the lid and the box for a piano hinge, then hinge the lid on the box. Make sure that when the lid is closed, it sits square on the box. Then rout out the front of the box for the latches, as needed. We used a combination lock-and-latch (called a "Prestolock") on the case shown here. It's available from:

The Cleveland Luggage Company
626 Huron Road
Cleveland, OH 44115

When the case is hinged and latched, make 'lips' for the inside of the box, as shown in the Section A. These lips, which fit inside the case like a picture frame, serve several functions: They keep the lid square on the box; they help keep the rain out of the inside; and they hide the backs of the latches where you mortised through the wood. Round the tops of the lips with sandpaper, check that the case opens and closes freely, then glue the lips in place.

With the lips in place, install a lid support on the inside of the box to prop the lid open. Also install 'feet' on the back of the case. (See Figure 6.) These feet are nothing more than commercial 'dowel buttons', available from most hardware stores and tool suppliers. They keep the back of the case from getting scratches when you set it down.

Finally, install a handle between the latches, centered in the front of the case. You can use a commercially-made leather handle (also available from the Cleveland Luggage Company), or make your own wooden handle, as we did.

If you make your own, remember that the handle

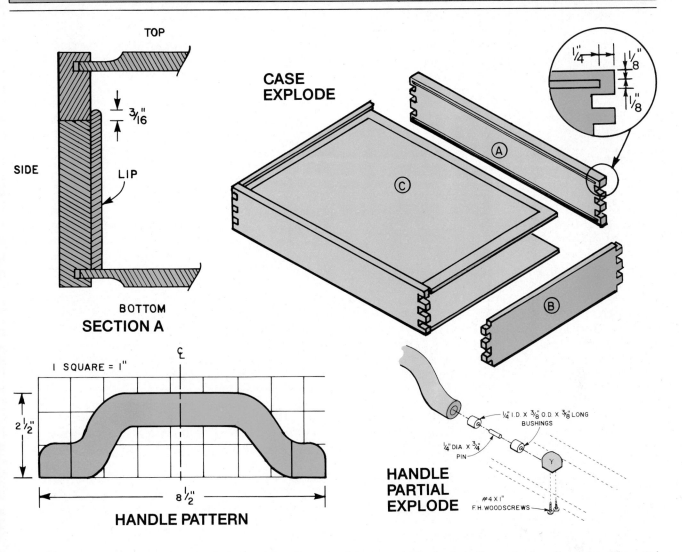

TOP

SIDE

LIP

BOTTOM

SECTION A

CASE
EXPLODE

(A)

(C)

(B)

$\frac{3}{16}''$

$\frac{1}{4}''$ $\frac{1}{8}''$ $\frac{1}{8}''$

I SQUARE = I"

$2\frac{1}{2}''$

$8\frac{1}{2}''$

HANDLE PATTERN

HANDLE PARTIAL EXPLODE

$\frac{1}{4}''$ I.D. X $\frac{3}{8}''$ O.D. X $\frac{3}{8}''$ LONG BUSHINGS

$\frac{1}{4}''$ DIA. X $\frac{3}{4}''$ PIN

(Y)

#4 X I" F.H. WOODSCREWS

takes more abuse than any other part of the brief case. Therefore, it needs to be reinforced in several different ways.

First of all, glue up your own 3/4″ 'plywood' to make the handle, using leftover 1/4″ thick stock from the side panels. The grain direction of the middle layer must run perpendicular to the grain of the top and bottom layer. (See Figure 7.) This will keep the handle from breaking as you carry the case.

Tip ◆ Use a waterproof glue, such as epoxy or resorcinol, to glue up the stock for the handle. This will prevent the sweat from your hands from dissolving the glue and delaminating the stock.

Round the corners of the handle with chisels and rasps, then sand it smooth. Remember to leave the bottom corners — the part of the handle that is attached to the case — square. When the handle is rounded so that it fits your hand comfortably, saw off the ends where shown in the Handle Pattern.

Drill the handle and the handle ends to accept small bronze bushings. (These bushings are available from most companies that supply bearings or fix electric motors.) Glue the bushings in the holes with epoxy, so that the edge of the bushing is flush with the edge of the wood. After the glue

dries, assemble the handle to the handle ends with metal pins, as shown in the Handle Partial Explode illustration. The pins act as a hinge from the handle, while the bushings keep the wood from wearing away.

Temporarily, clamp the handle to the case and check the hinge action. It should flop freely in both directions. If not, you'll need to remove the ends and carve away some more stock from the bottom of the handle.

Figure 7. Glue up your own 'plywood' for the handle. The grain direction of the middle layer should be perpendicular to the grain of the top and bottom layers.

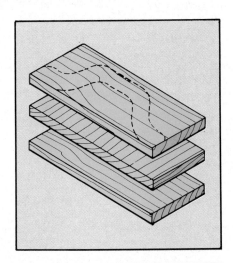

When the handle is rounded so that the hinges work correctly, reassemble the ends and glue the ends to the case. Be careful not to get any glue between the ends and the handle. When the glue is dry, reinforce this joint with several small screws, countersunk from the inside of the case.

Finishing the Case

Remove all hardware from the completed case and finish sand any parts that still need it. Then apply a finish to all wood surfaces, both inside and out.

The finish you use must be waterproof, and it must not spot when raindrops hit it. It must not be too brittle so that it 'breathes' with the wood when the weather changes — or when you go from the outside to the inside and back again. And it should be easy to repair so that you can fix scratches quickly. The best finish we know of that meets all these qualifications is actually a *combination* of finishes — tung oil and spar varnish.

Start by applying a coat of straight tung oil. Rub it on with your bare hands — the heat from your hands will help the finish to penetrate the wood. For the second and third coats, mix one part spar varnish to two parts tung oil. 'Wet' sand between each coat with very fine sandpaper, applying a little tung oil to the paper. After the final coat, rub out the final finish with rottenstone and oil. Then wax the finished case with lemon oil or a paste wax.

Take care of the outside of the case by occasionally wiping it with lemon oil or waxing it. If the case gets scratched, lightly sand the damaged area, then rub in the tung-oil-and-spar-varnish mixture.

Lining the Case

Lining your finished briefcase and making a portfolio requires a few leatherworking tools. But only a few — a punch to make the holes for the stitches, a 'star wheel' to accurately space the stitches, two needles to do the stitching, and a 'setter' and 'anvil' to set the snaps. (See Figure 8.) The total comes to less than $15.

Cut out the leather parts according to the patterns or the measurements in the Bill of Materials. We used two types and tones of leather. The portfolio front, card pocket, pen holder, and strap were cut from a stiffened, light cowhide; all the other parts were cut from a darker, much more flexible pigskin.

All the parts are stitched together using the same technique: First glue the parts together with rubber cement to hold them in place. With the star wheel, trace where you want to put the stitches. (See Figure 9.) The star wheel leaves tiny indentations that mark where each stitch begins and ends. Punch a hole at each indentation — you'll never be able to force the needles through the leather otherwise. (See Figure 10.) Cut a length of waxed string and thread a needle on each end. Push one needle through the first hole and pull the string halfway through. Then push one needle down through the second hole, and the other needle up through the same hole. Repeat for all succeeding holes, making a classic 'over-and-under' stitch. (See Figure 11.)

The leather parts must be stitched together in the proper order. To show this order, we've provided three successive explodes, showing how the portfolio goes together. First, stitch the top trim, card pocket, and pen holder to the portfolio front, as shown in the Portfolio Explode 1 illustration. Also install two 'male' snaps. You'll use the bottom snap when the portfolio is empty, and the top snap when it's full.

Sew the front pocket and gussets to the sides of the portfolio front, as shown in Portfolio Explode 2. These parts are stitched together all at once in three layers. Don't attach the pocket first, and then the gussets — or the other way around. When the portfolio is assembled, sew it to the liner, as shown in Portfolio Explode 3. Attach a 'female' snap to the strap, and sew the strap to the top of the liner.

Figure 10. Use a small punch to make holes in the leather at each mark left by the star wheel.

Figure 11. With two needles and one length of string, sew the leather together with a standard 'over-and-under' stitch.

Figure 8. You only need a few tools to do the leatherworking on this project: (clockwise from the top) A hole punch, a star wheel, a snap setter and anvil, and two needles.

Figure 9. With a star wheel, trace where you want to sew the leather. This will mark the beginning and end of each stitch.

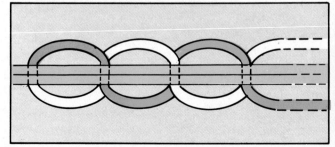

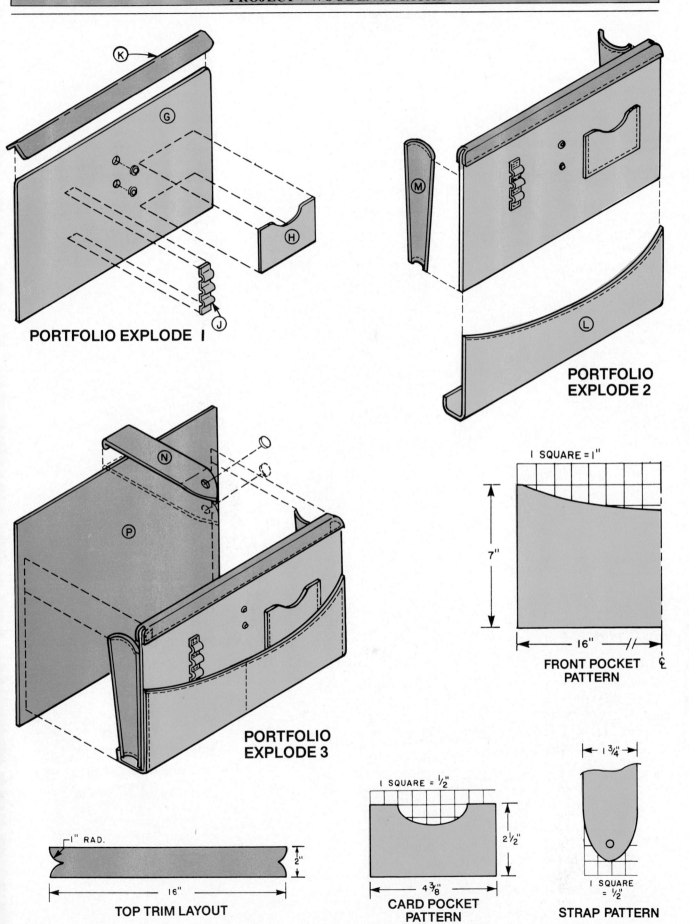

PORTFOLIO EXPLODE 1

PORTFOLIO EXPLODE 2

PORTFOLIO EXPLODE 3

1 SQUARE = 1"

7"

16"

FRONT POCKET PATTERN

1" RAD.

2"

16"

TOP TRIM LAYOUT

1 SQUARE = 1/2"

2 1/2"

4 3/8"

CARD POCKET PATTERN

1 3/4"

1 SQUARE = 1/2"

STRAP PATTERN

Glue the liner with the portfolio in the inside of the lid, using contact cement. Reinforce the strap by driving several small brass brads through the strap into the front of the lid. (See Figure 12.) Finally, glue another liner (this one *without* a portfolio) in the bottom of the case.

And that's it! You'll quickly find that your business acquaintances are doubly impressed with your new attaché — once because of the elegance and warmth of the handcrafted wood, and once again because *you* are the craftsman. — *Nick Engler*

Figure 12. Reinforce the strap by nailing it to the inside of the lid with small brads.

BILL OF MATERIALS — Wooden Attaché

(Finished Dimensions in Inches)

Attaché (Wood)

A.	Front/Back (2)	1/2 x 3-1/2 x 18-1/4
B.	Ends (2)	1/2 x 3-1/2 x 13-1/2
C.	Raised Side Panels (2)	1/4 x 12-7/8 x 17-9/16
	Flush Side Panels (2)	1/4 x 13 x 17-3/4
D.	Handle	3/4 x 2-1/2 x 8-1/2
E.	Front/Back Lips (2)	1/8 x 2-5/8 x 17-1/4
F.	End Lips (2)	1/8 x 2-5/8 x 12-1/2

Portfolio (Leather)

G.	Portfolio Front	3/32 x 10 x 16
H.	Card Pocket	3/32 x 2-1/2 x 4-3/8
J.	Pen Holder	3/32 x 3/4 x 4-1/2
K.	Top Trim	1/16 x 2 x 16
L.	Front Pocket	1/16 x 7 x 16

M.	Gussets (2)	1/16 x 3 x 8
N.	Strap	3/32 x 1-3/4 x 7-1/4
P.	Liners (2)	1/16 x 12-1/4 x 17

Hardware

1/4" I.D. x 3/8" O.D. x 3/8" Bronze Bushings (4)
1/4" dia. x 3/4" Steel Pins (2)
#4 x 1" Flathead Wood Screws (4)
1" x 17-1/4" Piano Hinge and Mounting Screws
Latches/Locks and Mounting Screws (1 pair)
Lid Support and Mounting Screws
Dowel Buttons (4)
'Male' Snaps (2)
'Female' Snap
Waxed String (50')

TIPS
WOODEN ATTACHÉ

Finger joints are a snap to make with a simple jig that attaches to the miter gauge of your table saw. This jig is just a flat piece of wood with a spacer board sticking out of the front face, the same size as the fingers you want to cut. Beside the spacer is a dado that passes over the dado blade. The dimensions of the spacer, dado, and the distance between them changes according to the size of the fingers you want to make, as shown in the illustration. The bolts that mount the jig to the miter gauge are set in slots, so you can change the horizontal position of the spacer.

◆ To use this jig, first adjust the spacer so that it's *exactly* the same distance away from the dado blade as the width of the finger. Put a board against the face of the jig and slide it over till it butts up against the spacer. Cut the first dado (which forms the first finger), then move the board over again so that the spacer sits in the dado you just cut. Cut the next dado and repeat until all fingers are formed. The spacer will insure that all the fingers are accurately spaced.

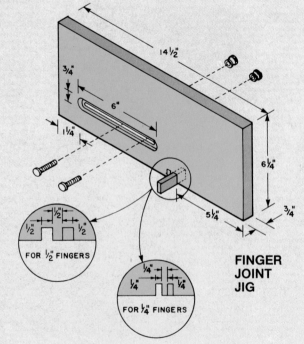

FINGER JOINT JIG

FOR 1/2" FINGERS

FOR 1/4" FINGERS

Bird-in-Tree Puzzle

Here's a traditional child's toy with a little something extra.

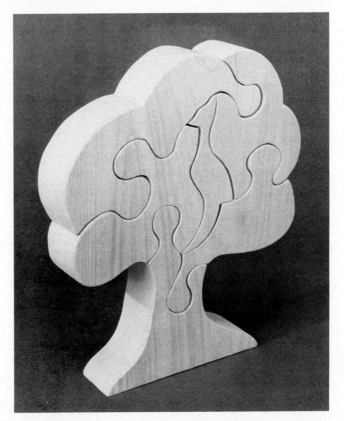

Puzzles are popular with children (and parents) possibly because they are one of the few toys that come apart with no need to break them. This particular puzzle offers a little something extra: When it's assembled, it stands up. And one of the pieces becomes a bird nesting in the branches.

Cut this puzzle from an 11″ x 11-3/4″ block *at least* 1-1/2″ thick. (The puzzle you see here is 2″ thick). If the stock is too thin, the puzzle will tip over or the pieces will fall apart when your child tries to assemble them.

You can use a jigsaw to cut the pieces, but it's slow going, especially in thick, hard stock. To speed things up, we've designed the curves of this project so that they can be easily cut with a 3/16″ or 1/8″ bandsaw blade. After you've cut the pieces apart, remove the millmarks with a small drum sander. Once again, this project is designed so that you can easily sand the small interior curves with a 1/2″ drum sander. These sanders are available from most tool suppliers.

If you want to color the pieces of the puzzle, use food colors, diluted 1 to 1 with water, like a stain. We suggest you paint the bird red, the upper parts of the tree green, and mix green and red food coloring to make a brown for the trunk. Let the colors dry for at least 24 hours, then seal them in with a non-toxic finish such as mineral oil or salad-bowl dressing. — *Nick Engler*

1 SQUARE = 1″

PUZZLE PATTERN

Photo courtesy Sotheby Parke Bernet

Blockfront Dresser

If you missed your bid on the original, here's how to build a replica!

I n January of 1983, this charming little dressing table sold at an auction at Sotheby Parke Bernet in New York City for $687,500, the highest price ever paid for a piece of American Furniture.

Not only is this piece valuable, it's also distinctly American. 'Blockfront' furniture (so called because of the protruding blocks on either side of the case) originated in Boston around 1730. The style quickly became popular in the colonies, and craftsmen in other areas began to turn out blockfront chests, desks, and dressers in great numbers.

This piece is widely considered to be the finest surviving example of blockfront design. It was commissioned by George Gibbs, Jr. and built around 1765 by cabinetmakers of the prestigious Goddard-Townsend school of Newport, Rhode Island. Gibbs was a ship's captain and senior partner in Gibbs & Channing, one of Rhode Island's largest merchant fleets. The dressing table descended through the Gibbs family for five generations before it was finally sold at the auction.

The replica that we've designed is not quite exact. It looks the same on the outside, but we've simplified the joinery somewhat so that it can be made with modern power tools. American craftsmen of the Chippendale period (1750-1780) typically 'overbuilt' their furniture with many locking joints. There were several reasons for this: First of all, metal hardware was hard to come by in the colonies. It

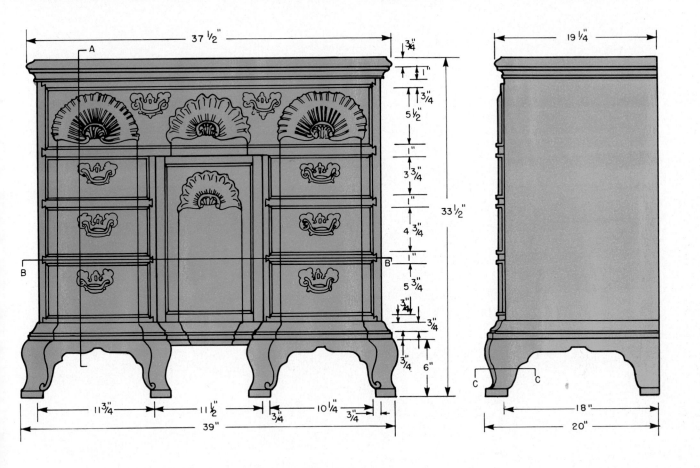

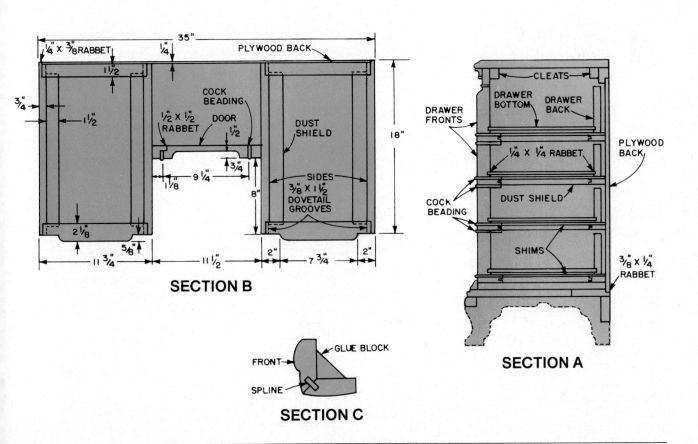

SECTION B

SECTION A

GLUE BLOCK

FRONT

SPLINE

SECTION C

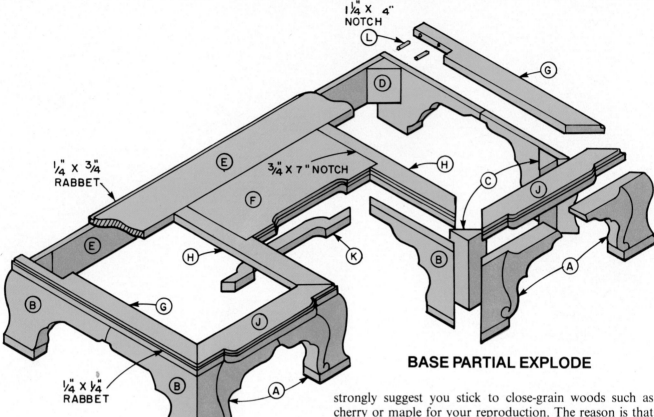

1¼" X 4" NOTCH

¼" X ¾" RABBET

¾" X 7" NOTCH

¼" X ¼" RABBET

BASE PARTIAL EXPLODE

strongly suggest you stick to close-grain woods such as cherry or maple for your reproduction. The reason is that this project requires considerable wood carving — four shells (two raised and two recessed), plus details on four of the six legs. You'll find than when carving, a close-grain wood gives you more control and yields better results than open-grain. Of course, you can also avoid the whole issue by simply substituting ready made pressed wood "carvings" (available from several woodworking suppliers) for the real thing.

Making the Base

Start with the base — actually two half-bases, each a mirror image of the other. Each half-base consists of three shaped feet, two across the front and one on the 'outside' at the back. The feet are joined to a frame, whose front profile follows the distinctive contour of the dresser. The frame also has a small decorative rabbet around the outside.

Tip ◆ It's easiest to make this rabbet with a hand-held router *after* you've finished the base.

was often cheaper to make a dovetail to hold two boards together than it was to fasten them with wood screws. Second, the glues of this period were not as durable as modern glues. The craftsmen knew they had to depend on the joinery to hold the piece together after the glue deteriorated.

If you're a purist and want to build an **exact** replica of the Gibbs dresser — inside and out — we suggest you get a copy of the July/August 1980 issue of "Fine Woodworking" magazine. (There's a blockfront dresser on the cover). It contains several excellent articles on Chippendale joinery and building blockfront dressers. Otherwise, what we have put together here should suffice. If you're careful and patient, nobody but a furniture expert will be able to tell your finished blockfront from the real McCoy.

Dimensions and Materials

While the joinery isn't original, the dimensions are — but you may want to change those, too. People were smaller in the 1700's than they are today, so the kneehole of the dresser is too small for the average person today. If you want this piece to be usable, adjust the dimensions so that person can fit their legs in the kneehole. (The standard measurements for a kneehole in a modern dresser are 18"-20" wide, 22"-24" tall, and 16"-18" deep.) If you wish to make an historical replica for show, stick to the dimensions given.

The preferred wood of the Chippendale period was mahogany, and the original Gibbs dresser was made from this wood. But American craftsmen also used other native hardwoods. If you don't want to use mahogany, we

Figure 1. To shape the parts for the legs, begin by mitering one end of the stock at 45°. *Don't* miter the stock for the back side legs.

142

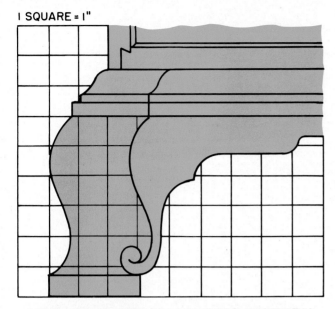

I SQUARE = I"

LEG AND BOTTOM MOLDING PATTERN

The half-bases are joined at the back by two boards that are glued and doweled into notches cut in the frame, and just doweled to the back side feet. Note that the notches are blind, so that the joinery doesn't show on the outside. (See the Base Partial Explode illustration.)

Perhaps the only thing tricky about the base is shaping the feet. Each foot is made from two pieces of thick stock, joined at the corner with a simple miter. Use 1-1/2" thick stock for the side pieces, and 2-1/8" thick stock for the front pieces. (The front pieces must be thicker so they can be

carved and contoured.)

Cut the pieces to length and miter the ends, where needed. (See Figure 1.) Both ends of the front pieces are mitered; but only one end of the side pieces. Using a table saw, cut a 3/4" deep by 3" wide cove in the outside face of each piece, 3/4" from the bottom. (See Figure 2.) If you're using a 10" blade, feed the stock at an angle of 58° to blade. Don't cut the cove all in one pass; take small 'bites', raising the blade just 1/8" at a time.

Tip ◆ To keep your fingers out of harm's way when cutting coves, use a fingerboard to hold the stock against the fence and a push block to feed the stock.

After you've cut the coves, clamp the pieces in a vise and round the top portions with a plane or rasp. (See Figure 3.) Trace the shape of the feet on the inside face of each piece, and cut it out with a bandsaw or coping saw. (See Figure 4.) Finally, carve the contour and details into the two front pieces.

Making the Cabinet Case

Like the base, the cabinet case is actually two half-cases. Each half-case is a simple box. The sides of this box can be glued up from solid stock, or made from cabinet-grade ply-wood with veneer tape applied to the front edge. The dust shields make the structure rigid and also serve as slides for the drawers. The front and back rails of the dust shields are dovetailed and fit into stopped slots in the sides. (See the Case Partial Explode.) There are several methods for cutting these slots, but perhaps the easiest is to use a router with a dovetail bit. (See Figure 5.) The dovetails on the ends

Figure 2. Cut a cove in the front of the stock on your table saw or radial arm saw. Take small 'bites', running the stock over the blade at 58°. Use a push block and finger-board to help control the cut.

Figure 3. Round over the top front edge of the leg stock with hand planes and rasps.

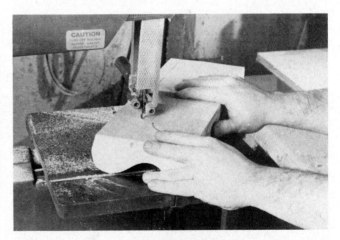

Figure 4. Finishing shaping the legs by cutting the contours with a bandsaw.

Figure 5. Rout the dovetail slots in the sides with a hand-held router. Since these slots are short — just 1-1/2" long — you can use a wood-en clamp as a fence to guide the router.

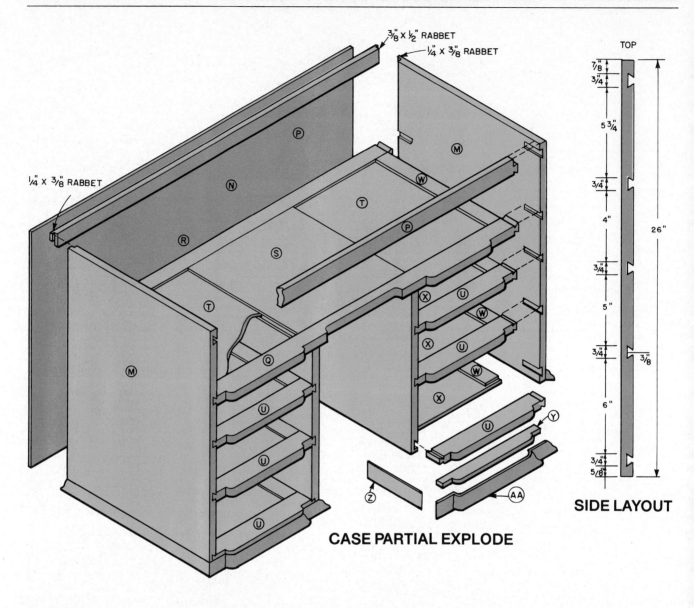

$\frac{3}{8}" \times \frac{1}{2}"$ RABBET

$\frac{1}{4}" \times \frac{3}{8}"$ RABBET

$\frac{1}{4} \times \frac{3}{8}"$ RABBET

CASE PARTIAL EXPLODE

TOP

$\frac{7}{8}"$

$\frac{3}{4}"$

$5\frac{3}{4}"$

$\frac{3}{4}"$

$4"$

$\frac{3}{4}"$

$5"$

$\frac{3}{4}"$

$6"$

$\frac{3}{4}"$

$\frac{5}{8}"$

$26"$

$\frac{3}{8}"$

SIDE LAYOUT

of the rails can be cut with a dovetail saw or a bandsaw. (See Figure 6.)

The front, back, and side rails are grooved on the inside to accept 1/4″ thick panels. These panels are not glued in place, but are allowed to 'float' in the grooves so that they can expand and contract with changes in humidity without stressing the case. The side rails have tenons cut at

Figure 6. Cut the dovetails in the front rails on your bandsaw. Traditionally, the sides of a dovetail are angled at 11°.

both ends that fit into the grooves in the front and back rails, and these tenons are glued in place.

Assembling the dust shields to the sides is a process that requires five arms and a lot of patience. (You can substitute a few wood clamps if you only have two arms.) Slip the front rails into the stopped slots in the sides, then put the side rails in place and clamp them to the sides. Slide the panel into the grooves, and finally fit the back rails to the assembly.

Because this is a rather complex assembly, it's a good idea to 'dry assemble' the sides and dust shields before final gluing. This goes for all assemblies, really. Any errors in the assembly can be corrected before committing expensive wood.

Attaching the Case to the Base

When the case is complete, set it on the base and fit the ogee molding that will hide the joint between the two assemblies. The side pieces of this molding are straight and should pose little problem. But the two front pieces and the piece at the back of the kneehole must follow the contour of the base

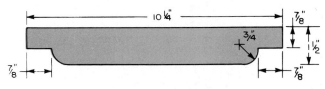

COCK BEADING PROFILE

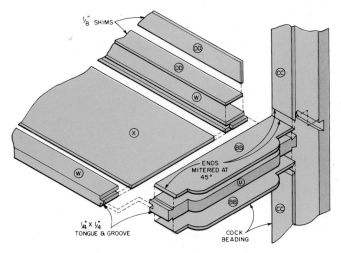

BEADING AND SHIM DETAIL

Details: Cock Beading and Cockle Shells

When you've secured the case to the base, attach 1/8″ thick strips of wood to the top, bottom, and sides of each drawer opening, mitering the adjoining ends. These strips must follow the contour of the case, protrude 1/8″, and should be slightly rounded at the front to create a "cock beading" around the drawer openings. (See the Beading and Shim Detail, and the Cock Beading Profile.) It is interesting that while cock beading on most antique furniture is attached to the drawer fronts, on this one piece it is secured around the openings.

Directly behind the cock beading, glue 1/8″ thick shims to the dust shields and sides, as shown in the illustration. These shims serve as guides for the drawers. Because the drawers will be scraping back and forth across them constantly, make the shims out of an extremely hard wood such as rock maple. Later, when you're finishing the dresser, rub the shims with hot paraffin wax to help the drawers slide smoothly.

At this time, before you make the drawers, carve the four cockle shells that make this dresser so distinctive. There aren't any hard and fast rules as to how to make these ornaments. The old joke applies: Get a piece of wood and chip away everything that doesn't look like a shell. However, we can give you a few tips to help you along.

When making the raised shells, first cut the silhouette of the shell out of 3/4″ thick stock with a jigsaw or scroll saw. Attach the stock to a scrap block, and secure the scrap

and case. To make these pieces, first cut the **outside** contour of the molding in one edge of a board 4″-6″ wide. Shape this contoured edge, using a shaper or router and an ogee bit. (See Figure 7.) When the edge is shaped, cut the **inside** contour, severing the molding from the board. (See Figure 8.) To finish shaping the two front pieces, carve a 90° angle at the bends to make it look as if each piece were made from three mitered pieces. (See Figure 9.)

Once you have fitted the molding, carefully mark its position on the base. Lift the case off the base, and attach the molding to the base frame with glue and 3d finishing nails driven down at an angle from the inside so they don't show. (It's easiest to first glue and clamp the molding in place, then drive the nails after the glue has set up.) With the molding in place, assemble the case to the base by driving wood screws up through the base frame into the case sides.

Figure 7. To make the ogee molding that fits around each blockfront, first cut the *outside* profile on a bandsaw, then shape it with a shaper or router.

Figure 8. After you cut the ogee, cut the molding free of the stock. *Don't* try to cut the molding first, then shape — that can be dangerous.

Figure 9. Carve phony 'miters' in the blockfront ogee molding by hand.

block to your workbench with a bench screw. (See Figure 10.) This bench screw will allow you to turn the piece 360° while you're carving it. (If you don't have a bench screw, you can also use a 1/2″ carriage bolt and wing nut.)

Start carving by tracing the rays with a parting tool, making a series of grooves in the surface. (See Figure 11.) Then round the shell down — round over the edges with a skew chisel until the grooves begin to disappear, then recut the grooves with the parting tool. (See Figure 12 and 13.) Continue in this manner until you've completely rounded the shell. Then round over the convex rays with a skew chisel and hollow out the concave rays with a gouge. (See Figure 14.) Finish shaping the rays with rifflers and fine sandpaper, carefully smoothing the surface. (See Figure 15.)

To carve the recessed shells in the upper drawer and kneehole door, first make sure that the stock is thick enough. The upper drawer front and cabinet door should be at least 1-1/4″ thick. (On the original dresser, the drawer front was carved in one piece from 2-1/4″ thick stock to accommodate *both* the raised and recessed shells). As you carve, work almost exclusively with a gouge; hollowing out each ray. When you've finished, these shells should be about 3/4″ deep at the deepest, just as the raised shells are 3/4″ thick at the thickest.

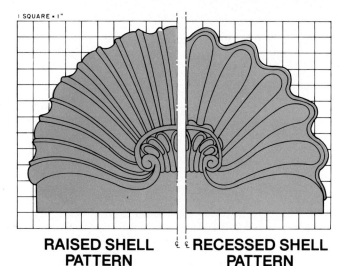

I SQUARE = I″

RAISED SHELL PATTERN **RECESSED SHELL PATTERN**

Figure 12. When you have traced the rays, round over the edge with a skew chisel.

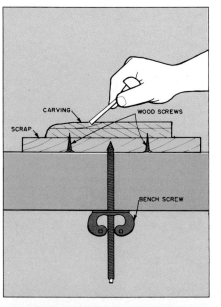

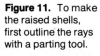

Figure 10. Use a 'bench screw' when carving the raised shells. This simple tool allows you to turn the work 360° as you carve, so you don't have to dance around the workbench.

Figure 11. To make the raised shells, first outline the rays with a parting tool.

Figure 13. Re-trace the rays in the rounded edges with a parting tool again. Continue rounding and tracing, rounding and tracing until the shell assumes the contour you're after.

Figure 14. Shape the convex rays with a skew and the concave rays with a gouge.

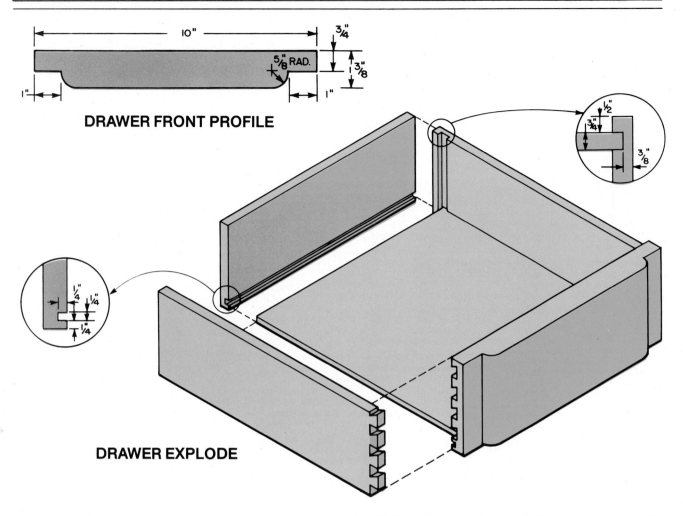

DRAWER FRONT PROFILE

DRAWER EXPLODE

Drawers and A Door

Make the seven drawers, sizing them to fit the completed case. Measure the drawer openings carefully, then build each drawer 1/16″-1/8″ narrower and shorter than the opening you want to fit it into. This will insure that the drawers slide in and out easily.

The fronts of the six small drawers have raised fronts, rounded on each side to follow the contour of the case. (See the Drawer Front Profile illustration.) In the original dresser, half-blind dovetails are used to join the drawer sides to the front, and the front, back, and sides are grooved

Figure 15. Finish up the shells with 'rif-flers'. The file-like tool will quickly smooth over the carving so you won't see the chisel marks.

to hold the bottom panel in place. However, unless you're building an historical replica, you can use whatever drawer construction suits your tastes.

The drawer hardware is Chippendale styling, with brass bails pivoting in pins fitted through a flat brass escutcheon. You can buy these from several hardware suppliers. Here are two suggestions:

Horton Brasses
Nooks Hill Road
P.O. Box 95F
Cromwell, CT 06416

Wolchonok & Son
155 E. 52nd Street
New York, NY 10022

If you want to get really detailed, drill and file a key-hole in each escutcheon, then mortise the front of each drawer under the hardware and install locks. Of course keeping track of all those keys may get to be a bit of a bother.

When you have assembled all seven drawers and fitted them to the openings, glue the raised shell carvings to the front of the large top drawer directly in line with the raised surfaces of the smaller drawers. Also, 'clean up' the recessed shell in the middle of the large drawer with carving tools so that it follows the contour of the rail just below it.

Remove the drawers temporarily, marking them so you know which one fits in what opening. Cut and attach the rails and stiles around the kneehole, as shown in the Kneehole Explode, then glue cock beading on these parts. Fit the door to the opening, mortise for the hinges and lock, and install the door.

It's a puzzle what such a small shallow cabinet in the kneehole of this dresser would be used for, and we are not really sure of its interior dimensions. It's not a secret compartment, since the hinge pins and keyhole are in plain sight. If you wish, you could make it a secret compartment by using "invisible" hinges and a "Tutch-Latch" so the door would appear to be just a shaped panel.

Finishing Up: The Back and Top

As shown in Sections A and B, the outer sides and back brace of the case are rabbeted 1/4″ x 1/4″ and the inner sides and dust shields are shorter by 1/4″ to allow for a plywood back. (If you want to be historically accurate, use 1/4″ thick spruce or fir boards instead of plywood.) Cut and fit the back panel, and attach it to the case with brads.

The last part to be fitted to the dresser is the top. Attach cove-and-bead molding to the sides and front brace, flush with the top edge, in the same manner that you attached ogee molding to the base. Glue cleat strips to the inside of the braces and sides, as shown in the Top Explode illustration. Drill 3-5 holes in each cleat strip, then drive roundhead wood screws up through the strips into the underside of the top. These holes should be somewhat oversized to let the top expand and contract without stressing the case. (For example, if you use #10 screws, drill a pilot for a #14 screw. Use small flat washers to keep the heads of the screws from going through the oversized holes.)

The finish is up to you. If you want to duplicate the original, build up a reddish, glossy finish streaked with black to give the impression of 200 years of proud history.
— *Nick Engler/Jay Hedden*

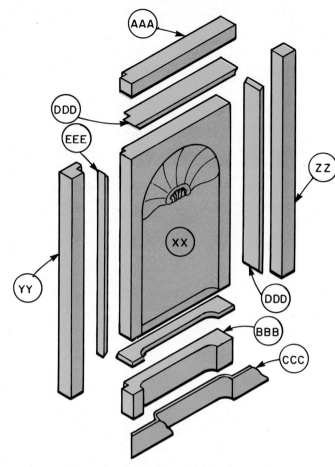

KNEEHOLE CABINET EXPLODE

TIPS
BLOCKFRONT DRESSER

The most time-consuming and tedious step in replicating the Gibbs Dresser is carving the four cockle shells. However, you can cut down considerably on time and frustration by sharpening your chisels properly. Here are some sharpening tips relayed to us by Dick Belcher, professional carver and past president of the National Wood Carver's Association:

When making shells, you have to carve at many different angles to the wood grain. To get your parting tools and gouges to cut both cross-grain and with the grain with equal ease, regrind the profile so the sides slightly lead the bottom or 'nose' of the chisel, as shown. (The traditional method is to grind the profile flat, or with the nose

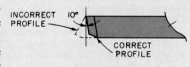

leading the sides. But this may tear the stock when you cut cross-grain.)

If you intend to hit your chisels with a mallet, grind the bevels so that they are no longer than 1/4″. If you wish to carve using only hand or palm pressure, the bevels should be longer. The shorter bevels keep your knuckles up off the wood; longer bevels allow you to lay the chisels flatter and pare away a thin slice.

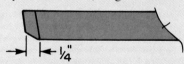

Put a tiny bevel on the edge opposite your main bevel. This will help the chisel stay sharp longer. If you bevel one side and hone the other flat, the edge may 'peen' back, creating a burr and dulling the tool.

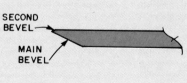

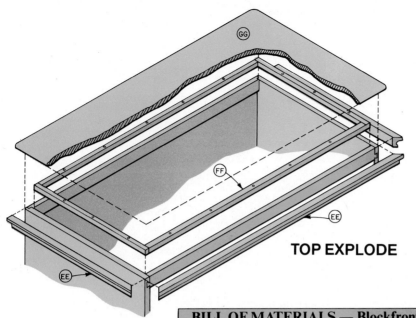

TOP EXPLODE

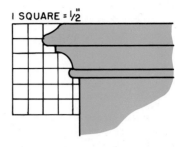

I SQUARE = 1/2"

TOP MOLDING PATTERN

BILL OF MATERIALS — Blockfront Dresser

(Finished Dimensions in Inches)

Base

A.	Front Legs (4)	2-1/8 x 6 x 7-7/8
B.	Side Legs (6)	1-1/2 x 6 x 10
C.	Front Glue Blocks (4)	1-1/4 x 1-1/4 x 6
D.	Back Glue Blocks (2)	1-1/4 x 1-1/4 x 4
E.	Bottom Braces (2)	3/4 x 4 x 36
F.	Cabinet Floor	3/4 x 7 x 11
G.	Outside Base Frame (2)	3/4 x 2 x 19-1/4
H.	Inside Base Frame (2)	3/4 x 2 x 15-1/4
J.	Front Base Frame (2)	3/4 x 2 x 14-1/4
K.	Quarter Round Molding	3/4 x 1-1/2 x 11
L.	Dowels (8)	3/8 dia. x 1-1/2

Case

M.	Sides (2)	3/4 x 18 x 26
N.	Back Panel	1/4 x 25-1/8 x 34-1/4
P.	Top Braces (2)	3/4 x 1-5/8 x 34-1/4
Q.	Top Front Rail	3/4 x 2-1/8 x 34-1/4
R.	Top Back Rail	3/4 x 1-1/2 x 34-1/4
S.	Cabinet Ceiling	3/4 x 13 x 15-1/4
T.	Top Dust Shields (2)	1/4 x 9-1/4 x 15-1/4
U.	Front Rails (6)	3/4 x 2-1/8 x 11
V.	Back Rails (6)	3/4 x 1-1/2 x 11
W.	Side Rails (14)	3/4 x 1-1/2 x 15-1/4
X.	Dust Shields (6)	1/4 x 7-3/4 x 15-1/4
Y.	Front Spacers (2)	5/8 x 2-1/8 x 10-1/4
Z.	Ogee Molding (total)	3/4 x 3/4 x 56-1/2
AA.	Front Ogee Molding (2)	3/4 x 1-3/8 x 13-1/4
BB.	Front Cock Beading (total)	1/8 x 2-1/4 x 190
CC.	Side Cock Beading (total)	1/8 x 1-5/8 x 71-1/2
DD.	Shims (total)	1/8 x 1-1/2 x 227-1/2

Top

EE.	Cove-and-Bead Molding (total)	3/4 x 1 x 74
FF.	Cleat Strip (total)	3/4 x 3/4 x 97
GG.	Top	3/4 x 19-1/4 x 37-1/2

Top Drawer

HH.	Top Drawer Front	1-1/4 x 5-1/2 x 33-1/4
JJ.	Top Drawer Sides (2)	3/4 x 5 x 16-7/8
KK.	Top Drawer Back	3/4 x 5 x 33-1/2
LL.	Top Drawer Bottom	1/4 x 15-3/4 x 33-1/4

Top Middle Drawers (2)

MM.	Top Middle Drawer Fronts (2)	1-1/4 x 3-3/4 x 10
NN.	Top Middle Drawer Sides (4)	3/4 x 3-1/4 x 16-7/8
PP.	Top Middle Drawer Backs (2)	3/4 x 3-1/4 x 9-1/4
QQ.	Drawer Bottoms (2)	1/4 x 9 x 15-3/4

Bottom Middle Drawers (2)

QQ.	Drawer Bottoms (2)	1/4 x 9 x 15-3/4
RR.	Bottom Middle Dr. Fronts (2)	1-1/4 x 4-3/4 x 10
SS.	Bottom Middle Dr. Sides (4)	3/4 x 4-1/4 x 16-7/8
TT.	Bottom Middle Dr. Backs (2)	3/4 x 4-1/4 x 9-1/4

Bottom Drawers (2)

QQ.	Drawer Bottoms (2)	1/4 x 9 x 15-3/4
UU.	Bottom Drawer Fronts (2)	1-1/4 x 5-3/4 x 10
VV.	Bottom Drawer Sides (4)	3/4 x 5-1/4 x 16-7/8
WW.	Bottom Drawer Backs (2)	3/4 x 5-1/4 x 9-1/4

Kneehole Cabinet

XX.	Cabinet Door	1-1/4 x 9-1/4 x 14-7/8
YY.	Left Cabinet Stile	1-1/4 x 1-1/2 x 17-7/8
ZZ.	Right Cabinet Stile	1 x 1-1/4 x 17-7/8
AAA.	Upper Cabinet Rail	1 x 1-1/4 x 9-1/2
BBB.	Lower Cabinet Rail	1-1/4 x 1-1/2 x 9-1/2
CCC.	Cabinet Ogee Molding	3/4 x 1-3/8 x 9-1/2
DDD.	Cabinet Beading (total)	1/8 x 1-3/8 x 34-1/8
EEE.	Left Cabinet Beading	1/8 x 7/8 x 15-1/8

Hardware

#10 x 1-1/4 Roundhead Wood Screws (16)
3/16" Flat Washers (16)
1-1/2" x 1-1/2" Brass Hinges and Mounting Screws (1 pair)
Brass Cabinet Lock and Keyhole Plate
Brass Drawer Pulls (8)

TECHNIQUES

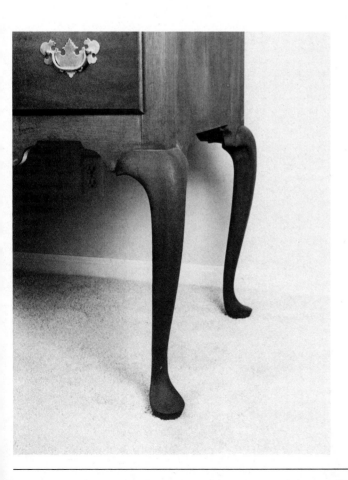

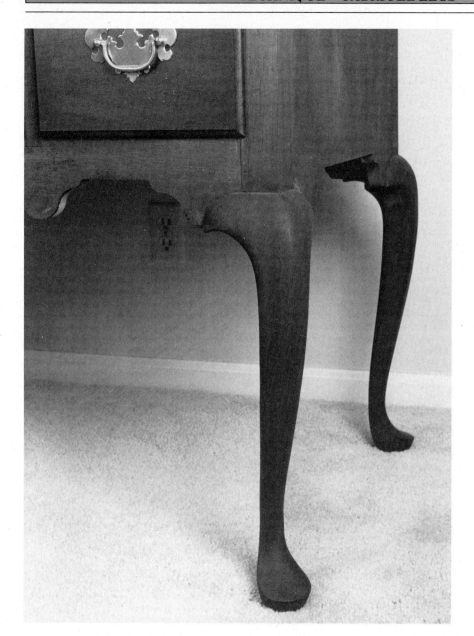

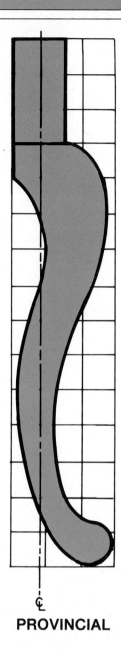

PROVINCIAL

Cabriole Legs

Some say the French invented it, some say the Chinese — but no matter where it originated, the cabriole has a universal appeal.

Cabriole legs (sometimes called "Queen Anne" legs) are perhaps the most graceful of all legs used in furniture. They are popularly considered to have originated with the French, but some historians claim the cabriole was first made by Chinese cabinetmakers who patterned it after the natural shapes of animal legs. (The word 'cabriole' means "to caper" in French, since the shape resembles the foreleg of a capering horse.)

Cabriole legs come in a variety of styles, both modern and traditional. Shown here are just a few: Provincial, 'Reverse' Cabriole, Dutch Foot, and a cabriole that is designed to be partially turned on a lathe. Despite the complex appearance of these legs, they are all relatively easy to make. You can copy the patterns here, copy existing furniture by enlarging drawings of photographs, or design your own.

Cabriole Design

If you design your own, here are several tips to help you along:

Leg Joinery — Before you finalize the cabriole design, plan how you will join the leg to the main assembly. There are many different methods you can use. Some require that you cut a post on top of the leg, some require a post with

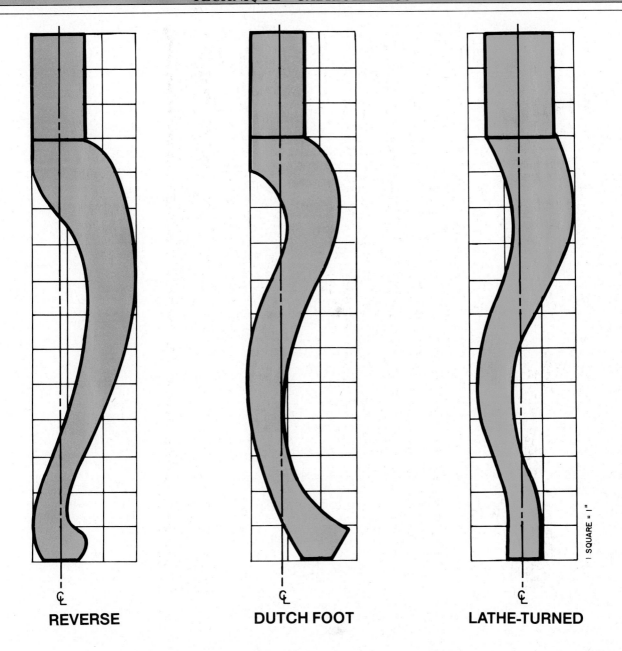

REVERSE   **DUTCH FOOT**   **LATHE-TURNED**

I SQUARE = I"

'shoulders', some require no post at all. Figure 1 shows four possible leg joints. The weakest of these joints is the leg with no post, joined to an apron or frame with a dowel. This should only be used for short legs with little weight to support. Table legs have a short post and are often joined to aprons with a mortise-and-tenon joint. Or you may want to use a hanger bolt and a corner block. (The bolt-and-block method is used in 'knock-down' furniture to make the legs easily detachable.) Cabinet legs have longer posts and shoulders so they can be joined to the case and made an integral part of the framing.

Width of the Cabriole — The curve of the finished three-dimensional leg will appear to be more pronounced than the curve of your two-dimensional pattern. You don't have to start with a wide block to cut a graceful curve. For legs less than 15″ long, use blocks about 2-1/2″ square. For longer legs, the blocks should be 3″-3-1/2″ square. Some designs may require more width at the 'knee'; to get this

width, you can glue smaller blocks on two adjacent faces of the main block. However, an exaggerated knee may create other problems, as described below.

Weak Spots — Neither the knee or the ankle of the cabriole should be too far off the center line of the leg. Exaggerated curves will cut the 'long' grain of the block into shorter lengths and create weak spots. Also, don't make the ankle or other parts of the leg too slender in relation to the rest of the leg. The cabriole may snap at a slender spot if you happen to drag it across the floor or put any sideways pressure on it. (Note: Cabriole legs will always be somewhat more fragile than straight legs, no matter how well you design them. If you examine furniture with cabriole legs in museums, you will generally find one or more repairs at the ankle and other weak points.)

Sawing and Shaping a Cabriole Leg

Once you've settled on a design, make a template. If you

plan to make several legs, glue the paper pattern to posterboard or even 1/8″ thick hardboard, and cut the outline. This reinforced pattern can be used many times without appreciable wear.

Place the template on one face of a leg block and trace around it. Turn the block 90° and do the same on an adjacent face. (See Figure 2.) After you have traced the pattern twice, cut one of these profiles using a bandsaw or jigsaw. *Keep the waste stock;* don't throw it away! Instead, tape the waste back to the block to make it square again. Then turn the block 90° and cut the second profile. (See Figure 3.) When you unwrap the tape and remove the waste, you'll have a rough cabriole leg 'in the square', ready for shaping. (See Figure 4.)

Clamp the post in a vise, or fasten the leg to your workbench between two bench dogs. Use a wood rasp, wood chisel, file, surform or whatever tool you find most convenient to round the leg close to its final shape. (See Figure 5.) Finally, remove all millmarks and scratches with drum sanders, flap sanders or other abrasive devices. Cabri-

ole legs take a lot of hard work, but the results are pleasant and satisfying.

Turning Cabriole Legs

You may have heard that cabriole legs can be turned on a wood lathe. This is not quite true. *Part* of the leg can be turned on the lathe — the top and bottom — but only if the leg is designed for this operation.

In designing the leg, be sure that the post and the foot are in line with each other. Cut out the rough leg as you would an ordinary cabriole, then clamp the leg between the centers of a lathe. **Warning:** Make absolutely certain that the spurs of the drive center and the cup of the cup center are engaged *at least* 1/8″ in the top and bottom of the leg.

At first, use the lathe like a rotating vise. Rasp, chisel, file, and sand the curved portion of the cabriole to its final shape. (See Figure 6.) When you have removed all the surplus stock from the curved, turn the lathe on at its *slowest* speed. (See Figure 7.) Do not go above 600 rpm! Check that the leg is not too far out of balance and that the lathe does

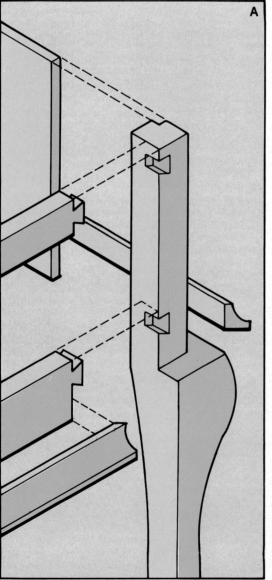

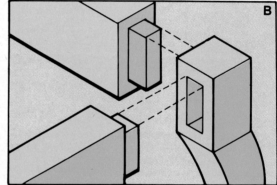

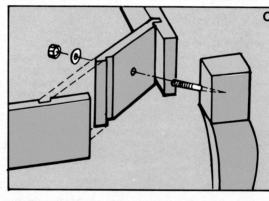

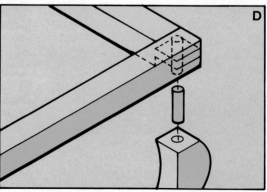

Figure 1. Shown here are just four of the many possible ways to join cabriole legs to a piece of furniture. Cabinet legs (A) often have 'shoulders' and long posts that become part of the cabinet case. You can join table legs to a frame permanently with a mortise-and-tenon joint (B). Or, if you want to make the legs removable, use hanger bolts and corner blocks (C). The simplest method to attach a cabriole is to dowel it to the underside of the table or cabinet (D). But this is also the weakest method. Dowels should only be used in small pieces where the legs will bear very little weight.

not vibrate too much: Stand clear while the leg spins a minute or two, then shut off the machine and make sure the centers are still solidly embedded in the wood.

Start the lathe again. Using lathe tools, shape the top and bottom of the leg. Be careful to keep your hands clear of the spinning off-center (curved) portion of the cabriole. Work from the ends toward the center, moving slowly and cautiously. As you approach the curved part of the leg, your tools will 'hang up' a bit. This is a signal for you to stop; don't try to turn it any farther toward the center. After you have rounded the top and bottom, stop the lathe and sand the rough areas between the curved and turned portions of the leg.

Variations

There are many more variations on cabriole legs than the few shown here. For instance, you can make a 'semi-cabriole' by only cutting the front portion of the profile, leaving the back square. You can carve the foot to make a claw-and-ball leg, as was common in eighteenth century

Chippendale furniture. Some modern variations leave a wide, nearly flat area on the knee. This flat area can be carved, or pressed-wood carvings can be glued to it.

Let your imagination go while designing your own leg. As long as you mind the joinery and the weak spots, a cabriole is one of those few projects in woodworking where almost any variation you can dream up will look great. — *Jay Hedden*

Figure 2. To make a cabriole legs, first trace the pattern on two adjacent sides on your stock, as shown.

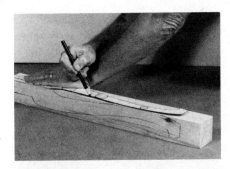

Figure 3. Cut the first profile with a bandsaw or jigsaw, and tape the scrap back onto the board to make it square again. Turn the board 90° and cut the second profile.

Figure 4. When you unwrap the tape and remove all the scraps, you'll have a cabriole in the rough.

Figure 5. To shape the rough cabriole, clamp the post in a vise and attach the leg with files, rasps, chisels, and sandpaper until you get what you want.

Figure 6. To 'turn' a cabriole, first design a leg with the post and foot in line. Cut out a rough and mount it on your lathe, making sure the centers are engaged *at least* 1/8″. Using the lathe like a rotating vice, shape the center portion of the leg with files, rasps, and chisels.

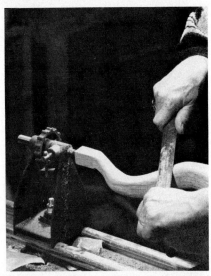

Figure 7. When you have shaped the center part, turn on the lathe at its *lowest* speed. **Do not exceed 600 RPM!** Make sure the spinning leg does not vibrate too much, then turn the foot and post as you would a spindle turning.

Router Joinery

Who says you can't teach an old router some new tricks?

The portable power router is an invaluable workshop tool. And it grows ever more valuable as you learn the many, many router techniques. It's not the sort of tool you take out of its box, switch it on, and use casually. You *must* practice with it to master its use. And you should be prepared to waste some good wood before you begin to get good results.

The router has two primary roles in your workshop. The best-known function is 'edging' or putting a decorative shape on the edges of boards. A lesser-known (but more important) role is *joinery*. A router is an indispensable tool for cutting furniture joints. It's this second role that we'll be discussing in this chapter.

Router Anatomy

But first, let's talk about the router itself: It's mostly a high speed (11,000-23,000 rpm) motor. That motor sits in a frame, and a flat base on the frame allows you to move the router across the surface of a workpiece. But the motor is so fast and creates such a high degree of 'torque', that the frame must be guided if you want to rout a straight line.

There are several ways to guide a router. Most router manufacturers offer 'guide fence' accessories that attach to the router base to help control the path of the cutter or 'bit'. A guide fence bears against the edge of the workpiece and the cutter does its job at a short distance from that edge. (See Figure 1.) If you need to rout a larger distance from the edge than a guide fence will allow, you can use a separate, true board as a fence. Clamp this board to the workpiece and hold the base of the router against it as you cut. (See Figure 2.)

Another way to guide a router is with a 'piloted bit'; i.e., a cutter with a descending pilot or a roller bearing that contacts the edge of the board without cutting it. Simply move the router along the edge of a workpiece, and the pilot will guide the router while the bit cuts the edge. Piloted bits are used primarily for decorative edging; the only such bit that's useful in joinery is the piloted rabbet bit.

Guiding the router is, of course, the whole secret to using this power tool to produce accurate joints. As I mentioned before, you need to practice before you can do this proficiently. But you also need to make a few simple jigs and fixtures.

Cutting Dadoes

You can cut dadoes on a radial arm saw, table saw, with a circular saw, and with a router. Of all these options, the router — when properly guided — will produce the cleanest dadoes in the shortest time.

> **Tip ◆** When cutting dadoes — or any joint — with a router, you'll get the best results if you take small bites. Make several passes, cutting 1/8"-1/4" deeper or wider with each pass. Don't try to 'hog it' and make a big cut in one pass — you'll just screw up the joint.

The most common dadoing procedure is cutting furniture stiles (uprights) for shelves or drawer frames. A router with a 3/4" straight bit, guided by a fixed straightedge, can accomplish this in seconds. For the straightedge, you can use a straight, true board or an extruded metal bar. But I suggest you take fifteen minutes out to make a T-square, custom designed for your router and 3/4" bit.

My T-square, shown in Figure 3, is 12" x 18", made of oak. The right end of the 'T' or crossbar is equal to the distance between the edge of the router base and the 3/4" bit. This greatly speeds the routing setup. All you have to do is place the right end of the T-square against a mark where you want to make a dado, then clamp the T-square down to the workpiece at both ends. (See Figure 4.) To cut the dado, just guide the router along the long arm of the square. If you need to make longer dadoes, make a T-square with a longer arm.

> **Tip ◆** When you build your T-square, take care to join and square the two pieces to produce a true 90° angle. Use yellow glue and four screws to keep this jig true. You might also want to build additional T-squares for 1/2" and 1/4" bits.

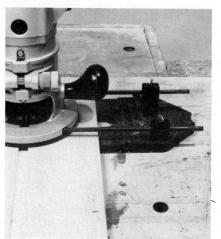

Figure 1. Guide fence accessories are available for most routers. These fences allow you to use the workpiece itself as a straightedge to control the cut.

Figure 2. If you need to make a cut in the middle of the work, too far away from the edge for the guide fence to be of any use, clamp a straight, true board to the workpiece to serve as a fence.

Cutting Stopped Dadoes

Many times, a project plan will call for a 'stopped dado' — a dado that stops short of the board's edge. To make this, you can simply stop the cutter at the desired point and lift the router out of the groove. However, this may mar the dado at the stopped end. There are two acceptable solutions:

The first is to clamp a small block to the workpiece to serve as a 'stop' for your router. (See Figure 5.) When the router base comes up against this block, back up the router in the dado and turn off the motor. Let the bit come to a complete stop, then lift the router off the workpiece.

The second solution is to invest in a 'plunge router'. This tool is similar to an ordinary router in all respects except that the motor can be raised and lowered in the frame *while the motor is running* by simply pressing down on or releasing the handles. You can position the router at any given point, lower the bit into the work with precision, then lift it out again with that same precision when you want to stop the cut.

Cutting Rabbets

You can cut rabbets with all the tools I mentioned before — radial arm saw, table saw, circular saw — but once again, a router is the most convenient and will give you the best results.

There are two easy methods you can use to make a rabbet with a router: Use a straight bit and a guide fence accessory to control how far the bit bites into the edge of the workpiece. Or use a piloted rabbet bit. (See Figure 6.) The disadvantage of using a piloted bit is that you can't adjust the width of the rabbet as you can with a guide fence.

Cutting Mortises

A mortise is nothing more than a dado stopped at both ends. Make these joints with the same equipment you used to make stopped dadoes — either clamp stop blocks to your workpiece, or use a plunge router. However, there are a few things you should know about to help you perform this particular chore quicker and easier.

If you're using an ordinary router and a fence, first drill two holes in the workpiece to mark the beginning and end of the mortise. These holes should be the same width and depth as the mortise you want to cut. Place the router over the work, settling the bit in one hole. With the router in place, adjust the position of your fence and clamp it down. Then just switch on the router and make the cut. (See Figure 7.) Later on, square the rounded ends of the

Figure 3. A simple homemade T-square, reinforced with wood screws, makes router joinery setups a snap.

Figure 4. To position the T-square, first measure where you want the dado and mark the workpiece. Then line up the right side of the T-square with the mark.

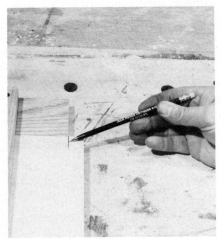

Figure 5. To make a stopped dado or groove, clamp a small block to your workpiece in the path of the router to serve as a 'stop'.

Figure 6. A piloted rabbet bit will cut a rabbet of a fixed width in the edge of a board with no need to use a guide fence.

Figure 7. To mark the beginning and end of a mortise, first drill two stopped holes in the workpiece. Then rout up to these holes — but don't go beyond them.

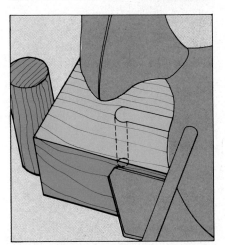

mortise with a chisel — or round the corners of the tenon to fit the routed dado.

You may also want to use a commercially available mortising jig. There are a lot of advantages to these jigs, one of them being that the jig automatically centers the mortise in the workpiece. However, using these jigs is somewhat hairy, even with a plunge router. You must attach a guide template to the router base (this template bears against the jig), then lower the spinning bit into the work. If you forget the template or are off your mark, the bit will engage the jig and chew it up — ruining, possibly, both the jig and the bit.

Making Grooves

Grooves are long dadoes that run in the same direction as the wood grain. And like the dado, you can cut grooves with a router and a guide fence. But if you're making a groove in the edge of a board, you may find it simpler to pass the work across the router, rather than pass the router over the work.

To do this, mount the router upside down under your workbench or on a commercially available router table. (See Figure 8.) There are even 'router plates', available from

Figure 8. To turn your router into a shaper, mount it to a 'router table'. Tables and table inserts are commercially available from many manufacturers.

Figure 9. A 'slotting cutter' is the best bit for cutting grooves in the edges of board. This bit allows you to cut the edge with the board laying on its wide face, so you have more control.

Figure 10. A dovetail template and dovetail bit make quick work of dovetail joints. The template allows you to cut both mating boards at the same time.

Figure 11. With a dovetail bit mounted in your router, and your router mounted to a router table, you can make long 'french' dovetails.

several tool suppliers to help you make your own router table. With the router fixed in this position, it becomes a 'shaper'.

Clamp a hardwood fence to the worktable to guide the stock. Mount a straight bit or a 'slotting cutter' (shown in Figure 9) in the router, then pass the stock across the business end of the tool. If you need to rout a particularly deep or wide groove, the same tip applies here that we mentioned earlier: *Don't take too big of a bite in one pass.* Make several passes, removing 1/8"-1/4" of stock with each pass.

Dovetail and Finger Joints

Two of the most handsome joints in woodworking are the dovetail joint and the finger joint. They are also two of the hardest to cut. But a router and a 'dovetail template' make these operations a breeze.

The dovetail jig automatically aligns the boards so that you can cut both the dovetails and the dovetail slots at the same time. (See Figure 10.) As with the mortising jig, you'll need to attach a guide template to the router base. If you want to make a dovetail joint, mount a dovetail bit in the router chuck. If you want to make a finger joint, use a straight bit.

You can also use a router and a dovetail bit to make 'french dovetails'. French dovetails are long dovetails that slide into dovetail slots. Cut the slots in the same manner that you'd cut a dado or a groove, but use a dovetail bit instead of a straight bit. Then cut the long dovetails in the stock with the router mounted to a router table. (See Figure 11.)

Portability and Permanence

The real advantage to router joinery is that you can cut any size stock, because the tool can be both portable *and* permanent. You can take the tool to the work to cut joinery in large plywood panels that you can't otherwise cut on your radial arm saw or table saw. Or you can fix the router in place, upside down, and bring the stock to the tool.

Just remember: Always guide the router, take small bits, and practice first on scrap wood. You'll end up with clean, professional looking furniture joints every time. — *Burt Murphy*

Scraping By

Cut your sanding chores in half with these simple tools.

Ask any craftsman: What's your least favorite step in the woodworking process? The answer: Sanding. Ask again: What step is the most important to the final look and feel of a project? Same answer: Sanding.

For example, take a good look at the Shaker Settee on the cover of this book. The design is elegantly simple; the joinery is professionally executed; but what really makes this piece a sight to behold is the *finish*. Imagine my surprise when Bob Pinter (the craftsman who built the settee) told me there's nothing special about the finish. He just brushed on a few coats of varnish, then carefully rubbed them down.

What's special, he explained, was the way he prepared the wood before he finished it. "I never start sanding with anything coarser than 100# sandpaper," says Bob. "Fact is,

I usually start with 120# or 150#, then work my way up to 250# or finer. If you start sanding with coarse paper, you just never get the scratches out of the wood. That ruins the final finish."

So what does he use for 'rough sanding,' to remove millmarks and other imperfections? Well, he doesn't rough sand. "I start with *scrapers* — scraping gets the wood smooth in a hurry," Bob claims. "Then I can jump right to finish sanding."

Cabinet scrapers were used for smoothing wood long before the invention of sandpaper and other modern abrasives. And for fine woodworking, there's really nothing that can replace them. When you sand, all you're doing is trading one set of scratches for a finer set. Scraping shears off a thin layer of wood, leaving a fresh, smooth surface. Scrapers are also less expensive to use than sandpaper, and — best yet — quicker. Once you learn the knack of scraping, you can cut your sanding chores in half.

Choosing and Using Scrapers

A cabinet scraper is nothing more than a flat sheet of steel, usually less than 1/16″ thick. They come in several different shapes — the most common shape is rectangular, but you

Figure 1. Cabinet scrapers come in several different shapes, with both curved and straight edges, to fit a variety of wood surfaces.

Figure 2. If you need to scrape a curved surface, turn the scraper and angle it so that it fits the wood.

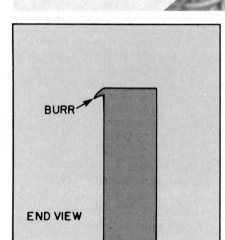

Figure 3. Curved scrapers can be used for one-handed scraping, leaving your other hand free to hold the stock.

BURR

END VIEW

Figure 4. Unlike most cutting tools, a scraper does not have a sharp edge, as shown in the enlarged end view. A small burr on the edge of the scraper shears the wood.

can also find shapers with concave and convex ends or shaped like a french curve to fit a variety of wood surfaces. (See Figure 1.)

To use a scraper, hold it in both hands. Cup your fingers around the sides and press your thumbs against the middle of the backside, as shown in the opening photograph to this chapter. Flex the scraper so that it is slightly 'sprung'; this keeps the corners up off the wood so they don't scratch it. Hold the scraper at a slight angle to the wood (tilting forward), then press down and away from you. If you've done this correctly, the scraper will remove a few tiny curls of wood as it passes over the surface.

When you use a curved scraper, the procedure is similar — except that you don't have to flex the metal to keep the corners off the wood. This means that you can scrape with one hand and hold the stock with the other, if you need to. (See Figures 2 and 3.) Don't be discouraged if you produce sawdust rather than curls right at first. As I mentioned before, scraping takes a knack. As you become more experienced, your hand will just naturally find the right angle and the right pressure for scraping. The wood will be-

gin to peel away more and more quickly.

Sharpening Scrapers

If you're making a lot of sawdust, this can also be the sign of a dull scraper. Scrapers go dull fairly often, so you have to watch for this — and know how to sharpen them.

Unlike most of the cutting tools in your shop, scrapers don't have a sharp edge. A tiny burr on the edge of the metal cuts the wood like a plane, shearing off a microscopic amount of wood with each pass. (See Figure 4.) When this burr wears away, the scraper no longer cuts.

To put a new burr on your scraper, clamp it in a wood vise with a dull edge facing up. Using a fine flat file, file off any traces of the old burr. Hold the file as square to the scraper as you can, you want the new edge to be flat. (See Figure 5.)

When you've removed the old burr, run a *burnisher* across the edge, slightly off-square (80° to 85°). Press down hard and push forward slowly and evenly. (See Figure 6.) The burnisher will 'roll' the new edge over in a long burr. If you want, tip the burnisher in the other direction and put a

Figure 5. To sharpen a scraper, first remove the old burr with a fine flat file. Hold the file square to the scraper.

Figure 6. Finish sharpening by making a burr with a burnisher. Hold the burnisher just off-square, tilted at 80°-85°.

Figure 7. Molding scrapers will smooth intricately contoured surfaces. They usually come in sets, with 4-8 blades in a set.

Figure 8. A scraper holder flexes the scraper and holds it at the proper angle to the wood, while all you do is push it across the surface. It saves your aching fingers.

burr on the other side of the scraper. Craftsmen generally put four burrs on their scraper — two on the top, two on the bottom. When one burr wears out, they just turn the scraper and use another.

Sharpening a curved scraper takes more time, but the procedure is the same. Use a round file to remove the old burrs on the concave surfaces, a flat file on the convex surfaces. Run the burnisher along the edges with as long a stroke as possible; you want the burr to be fairly even all around the scraper.

Other Scraping Tools

As you become more proficient at scraping, you'll begin to rely on scrapers more and more. And you may want to invest in other scraping tools to help cut your sanding chores even further. There are two that I would recommend:

Molding scrapers are made especially to scrape intricately shaped or contoured surfaces smooth. Anyone who has tried to preserve a hard corner while sanding a molding edge will immediately appreciate the value of these tools. (They're also great for removing glue beads in tight cor-

ners.) Molding scrapers usually come with a handle and several interchangeable blades, ground to fit a variety of contours. (See Figure 7.) Sample brand names: Shaper-Scraper, Contoured Scraper.

If you do a lot of scraping, you'll find your fingers tire quickly. It takes a lot of muscle to keep the scraper blade flexed and held at the proper angle to the work. A *scraper holder* is a real finger saver. This tool looks and handles like a spokeshave. A backup plate and simple clamp hold the blade at the optimum angle, while a thumbscrew in the back of the plate keeps the blade flexed. (See Figure 8.) Kunz is the only company I know that makes a scraper holder, but there may be others.

If you're interested in purchasing a set of scrapers, or any of the other tools I mentioned, you'll find they're available from most mail-order tool suppliers. You'll also find they're pretty cheap. A scraper can pay for itself in just one or two woodworking projects, when you consider what you'd normally spend for sandpaper. — *Nick Engler*

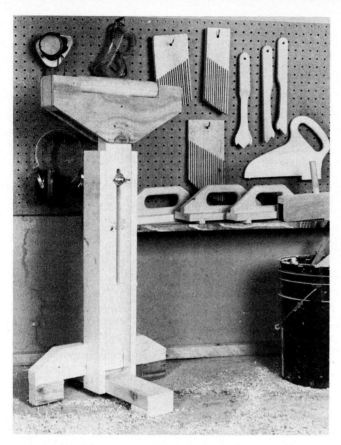

Safety Tools

These simple devices provide an 'extra hand' whenever you need one — and help keep your own hands out of danger.

Safety is always the first consideration when working with power tools. And while a careful operator is the very best safety device, he can get help from the homemade tools shown here — a support stand, fingerboards, push sticks, shoes, and blocks. Each of them will help hold the wood, give you better control over your work, and keep your hands and fingers away from whirling blades, bits, and cutters.

Danger Zones

All power tools (or, for that matter, any tool with moving parts) have danger zones — areas where you cannot put your fingers, hands, or other parts of your body without risk. For example, the danger zone on a table saw extends 2″-3″ out from the saw blade in all directions. Keep your hands outside this area while the blade is running and you'll be relatively safe. But once inside the danger zone, the slightest miscalculation could cause serious injury.

Safety tools reach inside the danger zones for you when you need to maneuver stock close to a blade. They also keep you from losing your balance and possibly falling into the machinery. Better yet, they increase your control and accuracy so that you get better results. They are absolutely indispensable tools for anyone who works with power tools, and after you've used them for a while you'll wonder how you ever did without them.

All of the safety devices shown here can be made in an evening's time with some scrap wood. However, be careful that you don't use *scrappy* wood. The stock you use should be straight-grained and free of knots, checks, and splits. A push stick that might break while you're using it would be more dangerous than using no push stick at all. Also, with the exception of the support stand, use **only** wood and glue. Now and again, you might graze a blade with one or more of these devices. When you do, you don't want the blade to hit a nail or screw.

Push Sticks

Perhaps the most common safety device is the **push stick** we just mentioned. They can be used for any number of operations when you need to push a piece of wood or hold it in place, but they are most useful for finishing a cut — pushing the end of a board past a blade. (See Figure 1.)

Push sticks come in a variety of shapes and styles, but they all have several things in common: A handle (to grip the stick), a heel (to hold the wood), and a shaft (to hold the handle and the heel apart). You can cut the push stick shown here from a single piece of 3/4″ thick stock, about 12″ long, using a bandsaw or jigsaw. Round the handle slightly with a rasp and sandpaper to make it more comfortable to grip and to reduce the risk of splinters.

Make at least two push sticks — there will be times when you'll need one for each hand. You might also want to make several types of push sticks, for different operations. One useful variation is the **reversible push stick.** This looks like a salad fork and has two heels. Make the stick out of hardwood and cut the heels and shaft 1/4″ thick. This will allow you to push stock past a saw blade when there is less than 3/4″ between the blade and the rip fence. (See Figure 2.) Depending on where you position the fence, turn the stick so that the handle bulges out away from the blade. This will keep your hand as far away from the danger zone as possible.

Figure 1. Use push sticks to help finish a rip cut, pushing the end of the board safely past the blade.

Push Shoes and Push Blocks

Jointers can be scary tools, especially when you surface the face of a board 1″ thick or less. **Push shoes** and **push blocks** remove some of the danger from this chore. They are also useful for sawing, molding, and shaping. Both devices are shaped like a concrete trowel. The only difference is that the push shoe has a heel to grip the edge of the board.

Make at least one shoe and one block. Use the block to hold down the wood on the outfeed side of the jointer, and the shoe to feed the wood into the knives. (See Figure 3.) You may also want to make shoes and blocks of several widths for different widths of stock.

A **saw-handle push shoe** solves the problem of how to safely surface short, narrow boards on a jointer. (See Figure 4.) As the name implies, this device looks like a saw handle, but does the same job as a push shoe. You can cut one from a single piece of 3/4″ thick stock, using a jigsaw or coping saw.

A **fence shoe** is used mostly for ripping operations in which you need to slice a narrow strip from thin stock. (See Figure 5.) This shoe straddles the rip fence and rides along it as you push the wood past the blade. The handle is usually just a dowel sticking out from the top (though some fancier fence shoes have handles like hand planes), and two heels — one on each side of the fence. The double heels allow you to use the shoe with the rip fence clamped to either the right or left of the blade.

Figure 2. A reversible push stick will easily reach into places that your fingers can't. Notice that the stick is turned so that the handle bulges *away* from the blade.

Figure 3. Use a push block to keep a board flat on the outfeed table of your joiner, and a push shoe to feed the board over the knives.

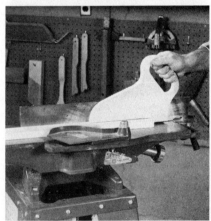

Figure 4. A saw-handle push shoe is used to saw or join narrow boards.

Figure 5. A fence shoe pushes a thin board past a rip blade to safely complete the cut.

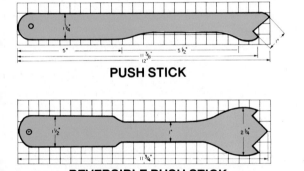

PUSH STICK

REVERSIBLE PUSH STICK

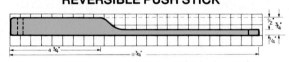

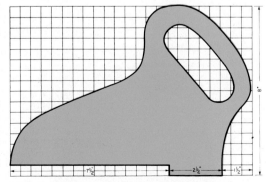

SAW-HANDLE PUSH SHOE

Fingerboards

Fingerboards (also called featherboards) are clamped to the worktable or fence of a power tool as 'hold-ins' or 'hold-downs', depending on how they are placed. (See Figure 6.) The figures of these boards flex in one direction as the wood is fed past them. If the wood tries to kick back, the fingers prevent it.

There are times when you'll need both a hold-down and a hold-in, so it's a good idea to make at least two fingerboards. You may also want to make fingerboards of different widths and thicknesses of different operations. Cut the angled end of the fingerboard either straight or at a slight curve. (A curved fingerboard makes it easier to adjust the pressure on the work, but it doesn't prevent kickbacks as well as a straight board.) If straight, cut at 30°. Make the fingers with a table saw, radial arm saw, or bandsaw.

When using fingerboards, clamp them to the power tool so that the fingers are angled in the same direction that you will feed the work. The fingers should press against the stock just **before** the stock reaches the blade or cutter. (See Figures 7 and 8.) Don't position the fingerboards beside, over or after the blade; this will bind the blade as it cuts. There are a few exceptions to this rule: You may want a fingerboard to hold the stock after it clears the knives during some jointing and molding operations. However, be sure the position of the fingerboards doesn't bind the knives or otherwise interfere with their operation.

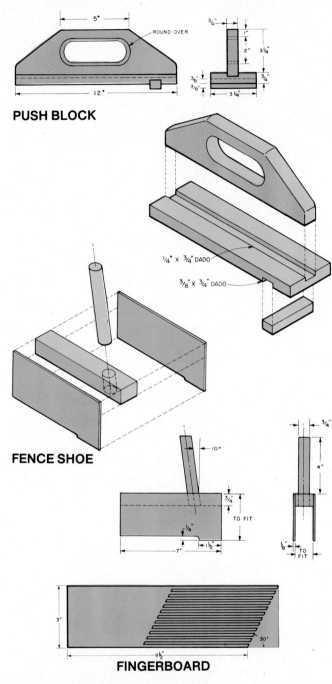

PUSH BLOCK

FENCE SHOE

FINGERBOARD

Figure 6. Fingerboards can be clamped to your worktable or to an extension fence to hold the stock against the rip fence or down on the table.

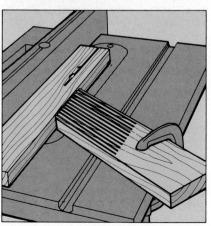

Figure 7. Fingerboards should be angled in the same direction as the feed, and the fingers should put pressure on the stock *before* it gets to the blade.

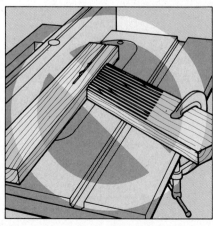

Figure 8. If the fingers press against the stock while it's being cut, the blade will bind.

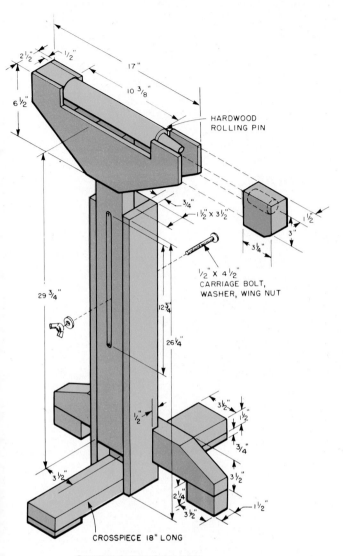

2½" **½"**

17"

6½"

10 ⅜"

HARDWOOD
ROLLING PIN

¾"

1½" × 3½"

½"

3"

3¾"

½" × 4½"
CARRIAGE BOLT,
WASHER, WING NUT

29 ¾"

12¾"

26¼"

3½"

½"

3½"

¾"

3½"

½"

2¼"

3½"

1½"

3½"

CROSSPIECE 18" LONG

SUPPORT STAND

Support Stands

Unlike the other safety tools described here, a **support stand** will not reach into a danger zone to push small pieces of wood past a blade. Instead, this device helps you keep control and balance when working with long, large boards so that you don't fall into the machinery.

A support stand is simply a roller on a post that can be adjusted to the same height as your worktable. The roller can be a hardwood rolling pin that you can pick up in any dime store; the post can be two 2x4's that slide together. Once the post has been set to the proper height, the roller will catch the work as you feed it past the blade and off the table. (See Figure 9.) This saves you the inconvenience of having to find a helper when you want to rip long stock.

Cut the pieces of the stand from clear lumber and sand the faces that will slide together. You can turn the roller on a lathe, but it may be better to use a cheap rolling pin — most of these have nylon bushings and metal axles that will wear a long time. Drill holes in the roller support blocks to fit the handles. Cut the groove in the sliding post with a router. Finally, nail and glue all these pieces together as shown.

To adjust the support stand, first position the stand 1"-5" out from the power tool. Lay a long, straight board across the roller and the worktable. Then raise or lower the stand until the board rests flush on the worktable. (See Figure 10.) If you need to put the stand so far away from the table that the stock 'droops' before the roller catches it, adjust the height a fraction of an inch below the table. Either that, or use two support stands.

Use these safety tools by themselves or in combination, as the occasion requires. (Figure 9 shows how a push stick, a fingerboard, and a support stand can combine to make a resawing operation a little easier and a lot safer.) You can leave these tools unfinished if you like — most woodworkers do — but a few craftsman like to paint them a glowing red or yellow. The bright colors make the safety tools stand out in your shop and help remind you what they're there for. — *Jay Hedden/Nick Engler*

Figure 9. A support stand can be used on either the infeed or outfeed side of the worktable to support long boards while they're being cut.

Figure 10. To properly adjust the height of a support stand, lay a long, straight board across the stand and the worktable. Then raise or lower the roller so that the board lays flat on the table.

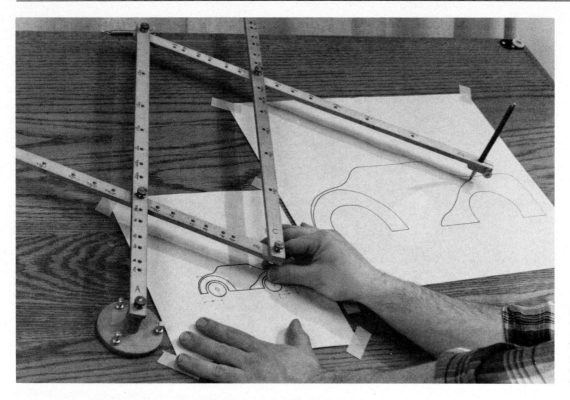

Figure 1. To enlarge drawings with a pantograph, simply trace the original with the stylus. The pantograph will draw an enlarged copy with the pencil.

Enlarging Patterns

These simple techniques help you make mountains out of molehills.

Because of space limitations, magazines and books often present woodworking patterns on a grid of squares, with instructions to "enlarge the drawing to make a full-size pattern." Simpler said than done, right?

Not quite — enlarging patterns can be a simple matter if you know a few tricks. There are two techniques for making full-scale drawings that are no more difficult than connecting the dots on a child's game or tracing a line with your finger. And you don't need any 'artistic ability' — just some patience.

Using a Pantograph

Perhaps the simplest method for enlarging drawings is by using a *pantograph*. This tool consists of four bars put together to form a parallelogram with pivots at each corner. There is also a *fulcrum* to fix the pantograph to the drawing surface, a *stylus* to trace the pattern, and a *pencil* to make the enlargement. There are several inexpensive ($25-$50) pantographs available through art supply stores and some mail-order tool companies. Or you can make your own following the diagrams shown here.

To use a pantograph, first fasten the fulcrum to the lower left hand side of your drawing surface with stick pins or screws. (If you don't have a drafting table, use a piece of plywood for a drawing surface.) Adjust the position of the

pivots to make the enlargement you require — most pantographs will enlarge a drawing between 1-1/4 and 10 times. For example, if the drawing is labeled "1/4 scale", adjust the pantograph to enlarge 4 times. Remember that all four pivots *must* be positioned for the same enlargement.

If the scale of the drawing isn't labeled (many of them aren't in this book), you can find it by performing this simple calculation: First find the size that each square represents. There should be a call-out on the grid telling you that "1 square = 2 inches" or some other measurement. Next, measure the actual size of the squares. Let's say that in this case, the squares are 1/2″ to a side. Now divide the represented size by the actual size. Two divided by 1/2 equals 4. Adjust the pantograph to enlarge the drawing 4 times. Here's the equation written out:

$$\frac{\text{Represented Size}}{\text{Actual Size}} = \text{Enlargement Required}$$

Once you've adjusted the tool for the proper enlargement, tape the pattern you want to enlarge under the stylus. Tape a blank sheet of paper under the pencil. Roughly trace the circumference of the drawing with the stylus to make sure that the pencil will stay on the paper. You may have to shift the paper, the drawing, the fulcrum, or a combination of all three.

With everything properly adjusted and positioned, carefully trace the drawing with the stylus. (See Figure 1.) The pencil will automatically make an enlarged copy on the paper. If there are gaps in the lines of the copy, adjust the height of the pencil so the lead rests firmly on the paper.

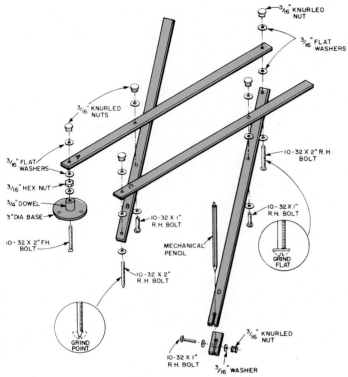

PANTOGRAPH EXPLODE

If you need to make an enlargement outside the normal range of the pantograph, make it in two steps. For example, you can enlarge a drawing 9 times by enlarging the original 3 times, then enlarging the copy 3 times again — 3 times 3 equals 9. To enlarge a drawing 20 times, enlarge the original 4 times, then enlarging the copy 5 times — 4 times 5 equals 20.

The Squares Method

Enlarging by squares requires more imagination than using a pantograph, but less equipment. Begin by finding the size that each square in the drawing represents. Let's presume that once again, 1 square = 2 inches. Draw a grid of 2″ squares on a piece of paper large enough to accommodate the full-size pattern — make the same number of squares horizontally and vertically as there are in the original drawing.

Next, number the horizontal and vertical lines on both the drawing and the grid you have just made. Carefully examine the drawing and note where each pattern line intersects a grid line. Make a pencil dot at the corresponding point on your full-size grid. Repeat for every point of intersection. After you've marked all the dots, use a straightedge, french curves, or 'flexible curve' to join these dots. (See Figure 2.) If the resulting full-size pattern doesn't look quite right, adjust the lines to make it look better.

Here's a tip that may make this chore go a little faster: If the pattern is symmetrical; that is, both halves are exactly the same, then only enlarge *half* the drawing. After you

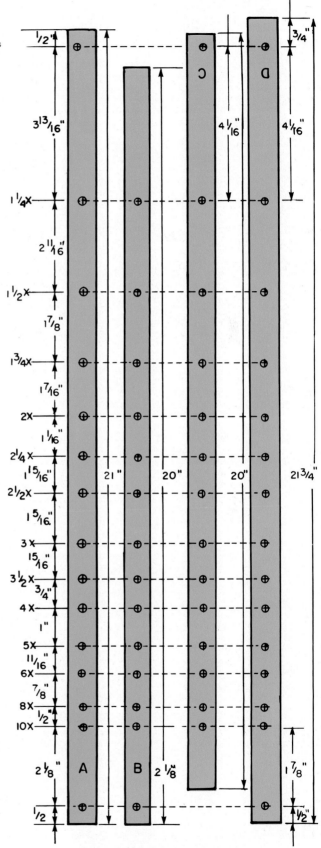

PANTOGRAPH LAYOUT

make the enlargement, fold the paper along the center line and cut out the pattern — you automatically create the full shape.

Enlarging Patterns from Photos

Now and again, woodworkers find a photograph of a piece of furniture that they would like to make. You can enlarge these photos to make full size patterns by using a pantograph or the squares method. If you use the squares method and you don't want to harm the original photograph, you can draw a grid over the picture (but not on it) by using ordinary plastic kitchen wrap and a fine-tipped marker. (See Figure 3.)

As an example, assume that a caption under the photograph of a small chest says that it's 30″ high, 25″ wide, and 14″ deep. In the photo, the chest is 5″ high. If you use a pantograph, you'll need to enlarge the picture 6 times — 30 divided by 5 equals 6.

If you use the squares method, decide what full-scale measurement each square should represent. In this example, let's make a grid where 1 square = 3 inches. First draw a rectangle around the chest. The sides of this rectangle should just touch the top, bottom, and sides of the chest. Since the chest is 30″ high, this rectangle will have to be divided into 10 equal sections, top to bottom — 30 divided by 3 equals 10.

To do this simply, use a metric ruler. Place this ruler with the "0" mark on the top line, and angle it back and forth till the bottom line intersects a measurement that is easily divisible by 10. In this case, 20 centimeters works nicely. Make a mark every 2 centimeters — 20 divided by 10 equals 2. (See Figure 4.) Then draw horizontal lines through these marks, parallel to the top and bottom of the rectangle. (The same technique works whether you want to divide a rectangle into 9, 14, or 25 sections. Just find a measurement on the ruler that is easily divisible by 9, 14, or 25.)

To draw the vertical lines of the grid, measure the distance between the horizontal lines. In our example, you'll

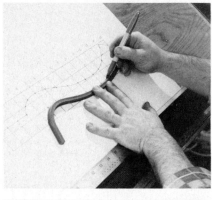

Figure 2. After marking the full-size grid where the pattern lines should intersect, connect the points of intersection. A 'flexible curve', available at most art supply stores, will help you draw the curved parts of the pattern.

Figure 3. To protect a photograph while you enlarge it, tape a sheet of plastic kitchen wrap over it. Then draw a grid on the plastic with a marker.

find that the horizontal lines are exactly 1/2″ apart. Put marks on the top and bottom lines, 1/2″ apart, then draw vertical lines through these marks parallel to the sides of the rectangle.

Whether you use a pantograph or the squares method to enlarge drawings and photographs, keep this in mind: Your enlargement will be just a little different than the original, as will be the enlargements made by every other craftsman who attempts the same project. That assures you that your finished project will be (in its own way) an original. In an age of mass production and conformity, that's not a drawback; it's a definite plus. — *Jay Hedden/Nick Engler*

Figure 4. To divide the distance between two parallel lines into 10 equal parts, position a metric ruler so that one line intersects the "0" mark. Angle the ruler back and forth until the other line intersects a measurement that is easily divisible by 10 — in this case, 20 cm. Make a mark every 2 cm., then draw lines through the marks parallel to the first two lines.

Turning Tips

There are no hard and fast rules in lathe turning. But here are a few good tips to help you develop your own techniques.

Of all the tools in your shop, the wood lathe may be the most unique, the most personal — and the most fun!

Many pros consider turning to be the most creative form of woodworking. There are no strict rules — just wade in with a chisel and find what works for you. When you turn 'free form', you don't even have to worry about dimensions, just let the design evolve on the lathe. If you make a mistake, simply incorporate it into the project as if you had planned it. You can even start *and* finish a project on one machine without taking the time for a half-dozen different setups.

But if there aren't any rules, where do you start? Well, actually there are a *few* rules. And beyond that, there are a whole lot of professional tips that we can offer to help you find your own way.

Turning Basics

Let's begin with a quick review of the basics: There are *three* fundamental turning techniques — scraping, shearing, and cutting. (See Figure 1.)

Scraping is, by far, the easiest. Adjust your tool rest so that the top edge of the rest is 1/8″-1/4″ above the center of the work. Hold the chisel horizontal to the floor and feed it into the stock so that the chisel is *almost* (but not quite) perpendicular to the surface of the stock. The chisel will scrape away sawdust and splinters from the wood, leaving a rough surface.

Shearing is much faster than scraping, but it can be much trickier — especially with a skew chisel. To shear, raise the tool rest so that it's just 1/8″-1/4″ below the top edge of the work. Hold the chisel horizontal and feed it into the wood so that the *heel* cuts into the wood. (See Figure 2.) Be careful not to let the points or corners of the chisel touch the wood — this will gouge big chunks out of the surface. Try shearing on scrap stock first until you get the hang of it. When you're shearing correctly, the wood will peel away from the work in long curls.

Somewhere in between scraping and shearing is **cutting**. To cut, you can adjust the tool rest to any height from the center of the stock up to the top. Hold and feed the chisel so that it touches the work at an angle too steep to scrape, and not steep enough to shear. The wood will peel away in small curls.

As you can tell, there are no clear divisions between these three turning techniques. Scraping becomes cutting as you change the angle of the chisel. Raise the tool rest, and cutting passes into shearing. You'll probably use all three in the course of a single project — most experienced turners do.

Basic Lathe Tools and Tool Care

There are five essential wood chisels that you'll need to accomplish a turning project — gouge, skew, round nose, spear point, and parting tool. (See Figure 3.)

The **gouge** rounds the stock and makes concave curves (called 'coves'). It can be used to scrape, cut, or shear.

The **skew** makes the convex curves ('beads') and the flat parts of the turning ('flats'). It's usually used only to cut and shear; skews do a poor job of scraping.

Figure 2. There's two tricks you must learn in order to shear: Cut with the 'heel' of the chisel, and don't let the point dig into the wood.

Figure 3. There are five basic turning tools. From left to right, these are the *gouge*, the *skew*, the *round nose*, the *spear point*, and the *parting tool*.

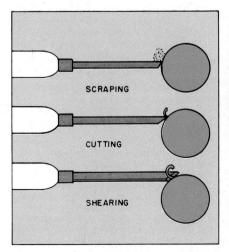

Figure 1. There are three fundamental turning techniques — scraping, cutting and shearing. The difference between them is *how* you remove the wood from the work. *Scraping*, as the name implies, scrapes the wood away as sawdust and splinters. *Shearing* shears the wood off in long curls, like a hand plane. *Cutting* is somewhere in between scraping and shearing.

SCRAPING

CUTTING

SHEARING

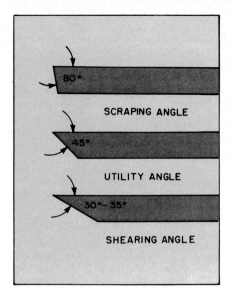

Figure 4. Grind your scraping tools at 80° and your shearing tools at 30°-35°. Chisels that are used for a variety of operations — scraping, shearing, and cutting — should be beveled at 45°.

SCRAPING ANGLE

UTILITY ANGLE

SHEARING ANGLE

Figure 5. To keep your tool rest flat and smooth, file off the hard corners on the shanks of your chisels.

Figure 6. To find the center of square or rectangular stock, draw two diagonal lines from corner to corner. Where the lines intersect marks the center.

The **round nose** also makes coves. It's especially useful when you're cutting into end grain. The round nose is used to scrape *only*.

The **spear point** defines the sharp lines between beads, and will help you get down into deep crevices in the turning. It's used mostly to scrape and cut; it's difficult to shear with a skew because the point wants to bite into the wood.

The **parting tool** will size a turning when dimensions are important, and it parts the waste stock from the finished project. It's a scraping and cutting tool only.

Those descriptions are just suggestions; they aren't meant to be taken as the Bible. As you gain experience as a turner, you'll begin to prefer certain tools for certain operations. Some woodworkers make flats with a gouge and use the skew like a spear point. Experiment with your tools, and if something works for you, stick with it.

How you use a particular tool is a whole lot less important than how you sharpen them. Turning tools must be razor sharp, and they must be sharpened at the proper angle if you're going to get good results.

So what's the proper angle? Well, that depends a lot on how you use each tool and what cutting technique you use. Scraping tools should be ground and sharpened at 80°. Most pros prefer an angle of 30°-35° for shearing — the longer bevel gives you a better approach and more control over the tool. As you might guess, cutting tools should be ground somewhere in between — 45° is about right.

Most turning chisels are ground at 45° at the factory. This is considered a 'utility' angle. Even though it's best for cutting, it can be used for scraping and shearing. However, you'll quickly find that your lathe work will go faster and you'll get better results if you regrind some of your chisels.

We suggest you try this: Grind your round nose to 80°, since this works best as a scraping tool. Put a 30° bevel on the skew for easy shearing. Notice that the skew is beveled on *both* sides, so that you can use it with the heel facing in either direction. If you have the money, buy an extra gouge and grind one at 30° and leave the other at 45°. Also leave the spear point and parting tool at 45°. (See Figure 4.) This setup gives a turner a good selection of chisels *and* bevels for a variety of operations and techniques.

One more tip on chisels: When you regrind your tools, knock the hard corners off the shanks with a file. (See Figure 5.) This keeps the shank of the chisels from biting into the tool rest when you turn. The tool rest stays flat, and the chisels glide back and forth across it easily.

Mounting Stock on the Lathe

So much for basics. The only way you'll learn more about turning is to actually try it. So select a piece of wood and mount it on your lathe.

To mount stock, you first have to find the center. If the stock is square, simply draw two diagonal lines from corner to corner. Where the lines cross is the center of the stock. (See Figure 6.) Do this for both ends.

For round stock, use a 'center finder' (available from most tool suppliers) to mark two lines on the ends of the work. (See Figure 7.) Once again, where the lines cross marks the center of the stock. If the stock is irregularly shaped, lay a small carpenter's square on the end of the wood so that the 'point' of the square is flush with one edge — any edge. Mark two lines at right angles to each other where the square lays on the wood. Then remove the square and draw a third line between the points where the first two lines run off the edge of the wood. Divide this third line in half, and you'll have the center of the stock — or pretty close to it. (See Figure 8.)

Once you've found the centers, unscrew your drive center from the lathe, place the point at the center of one end, and drive it into the wood with a mallet. (See Figure 9.)

Figure 7. Use a 'center finder' to find the center of round stock. These are available from most tool suppliers, or you can make your own.

Figure 8. To find the center of irregularly shaped stock, use a carpenter's square and mark a right triangle on the end. Divide the hypotenuse (longest side) of this triangle in two, and that will show you the center — or close to it.

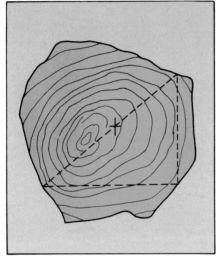

Figure 9. Seat the drive center and cup center in the stock with a mallet. The centers should engage the stock *at least* 1/16″ to be safe.

The spurs of the drive center must bite *at least* 1/16″ into the wood. Do the same with the cup center on the other end of the stock. If the wood is very hard, you may want to drill small holes for the points — this will keep the stock from splitting when you pound on the centers.

Mount the drive center and cup center back on your lathe. Wax the cup center with paste wax to keep it from heating up and burning the wood as it turns. *Don't* use oil; this may stain the wood. If you plan on doing a lot of turning, invest in a 'live' cup center. The cup in a live center revolves on a ball bearing. This eliminates the danger of burning altogether.

Put the stock between the centers. Advance either the drive center or the cup center (depending on the design of your lathe) until the centers hold the stock good and tight. Remember, the spurs and cup must bite into the wood at least 1/16″ in order for the stock to be properly mounted. This keeps the work from jumping out of the lathe (and possibly hitting you) when you try to turn it.

Adjust the tool rest so that it's no further than 1/8″-1/4″ away from the work. This narrows the dangerous 'pinch point' between the work and the tool rest. It also reduces the chance that the lathe may grab the chisel out of your hands if you accidently gouge the wood. You can tell a turner who keeps his tool rest too far from the stock by the number of cuts in the ceiling above his lathe.

Revolve the stock one or two revolutions by hand to make sure it clears the rest. Then turn on the lathe for a minute or two to make sure the stock turns smoothly and it

doesn't vibrate too much. Don't be alarmed if there is some vibration — this is normal until the stock is rounded. But if there is excessive vibration, turn off the lathe immediately. Try remounting the stock on different centers. If this doesn't work, discard the stock and try another piece.

Turning a Spindle

As you actually start to turn the stock, let's lay down just a few rules — *safety* rules:

● If you glue up turning stock, let the glue dry for *at least* 24 hours. If the glue has not properly cured, the wood may come apart on the lathe.

● Never turn stock with knots, checks, or other defects that might cause it to split out on the lathe.

● Round the wood at a slow speed, then steadily increase the speed as the turning takes shape. But never go above 2000 rpm — less for very large turnings.

● From time to time, stop the lathe and readjust the tool rest so that it remains close to the stock. Also check that the wood is still firmly mounted between the centers with no 'give'.

● When you turn off the lathe, let it stop by itself. Don't grab the wood and try to slow it down.

As you turn, you'll take your work through four steps — rounding, shaping, sanding, and parting. Here's a brief description of each step:

Rounding — Lay your gouge across the tool rest near one end or the other. Grasp it with *two* hands. Use one hand to keep the shank down on the rest and the other hand to control the handle. Hold the chisel firmly — but lightly. If you grasp is too tight, the chisel may jerk as you move it. Also, you'll tire quickly.

Angle the gouge so the cup faces up and slightly toward the other end of the tool rest. Carefully feed the cutting edge until it just kisses the spinning wood. Then draw it slowly across the rest. Angle the tool back the other way and repeat until the wood is completely rounded.

You can tell when the wood is round *without* constantly turning the lathe on and off. Just lay the shank of the chisel on top of the revolving stock. If the tool lays there, the stock is round. If it vibrates or jumps up and down, you

Figure 10. To tell if work is rounded without turning off the lathe, just lay the shank of the chisel across the top. If the chisel vibrates, you have some more work to do.

Figure 12. You can make chisels out of your molder knives to turn certain shapes. Just bolt them to a length of tool steel and fit a handle to the other end.

Figure 11. Beads and coves are made in a similar fashion, but with different tools. Feed the chisel into the work slowly and move the handle from side to side.

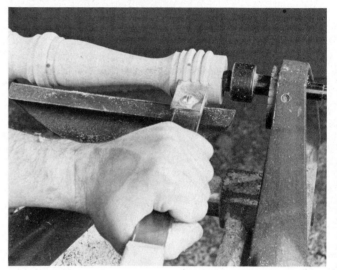

have a little more work to do. (See Figure 10.)

Shaping — After rounding, cut the beads, coves, and flats in your spindle, in that order.

Beads and coves are made in much the same way, even though you use different tools. Feed the chisel gently into the wood, gradually removing stock. As you do, move the handle from side to side to shape the curve the way you want it. (See Figure 11.)

Flats are made in a similar manner as rounding. Draw the chisel slowly and steadily across the tool rest. Be careful to keep the tip of the chisel at exactly the same distance from the center of the work, or you'll create unwanted curves.

If you have a molder for your table saw or radial arm saw, you can use the molding knives for shaping on the lathe. These will quickly cut the same coves, beads, and flats as they do when mounted in the molding head. Just drill a hole in the end of a piece of flat tool steel and bolt the knife to it. Make a handle for the other end, then use this home-made chisel with a scraping action. (See Figure 12.)

Sanding — Experienced woodworkers know that it's infinitely easier to sand a turning on the lathe than it is to remove it and hand sand it. But since you have to almost

touch the wood in order to do this, you must be extremely careful.

First, remove the tool rest from the lathe so that there's no 'pinch point'. Slightly increase the speed, and begin sanding with 100# paper. Don't use new sandpaper; this will score rings in your spindle. Use discarded paper from other projects — old, worn-out sanding belts make great sandpaper for lathe projects. Or rub two new sheets of sandpaper together to knock off some of the grit.

Move the paper back and forth on the spindle as you sand. Don't hold it still or you may burn the work. You may also want to 'double up' the sandpaper several times, or put a piece of felt or steel wool between the paper and your fingers as you sand. (See Figure 13.) This will help protect your hands from the heat that builds up during this operation.

As you progress up through finer and finer grits, tiny 'feathers' will develop on the surface of the wood because you're sanding *across* the grain. These feathers should be removed before you apply a finish.

To get rid of them, dismount the spindle from the lathe

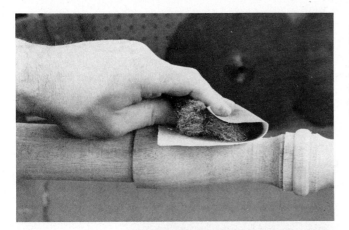

Figure 13. When you sand on a lathe, put a pad of steel wool or felt between you and the paper to protect your fingers from the heat.

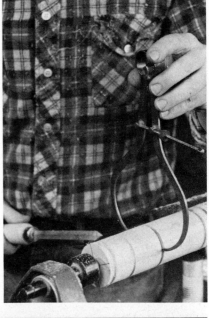

Figure 15. To turn a pattern or duplicate spindles, mark the diameters of the beads and coves with a parting tool. Measure these diameters with a pair of 'outside' calipers.

Figure 14. After the work is sanded, partially cut away the waste stock from the spindle with a parting tool. But *don't* cut the wood completely through on the lathe.

Figure 16. To measure the shape of a turning, first cut a 'negative' pattern in cardboard or hardboard. Compare this pattern to the spindle as you work.

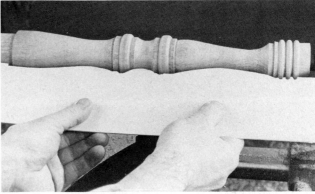

and flop it end for end. Remount it in the lathe with the drive center holding the end that used to be held by the cup center, and vice versa. Start the lathe and *briefly* sand the entire spindle with very fine paper. This reverses the rotation of the spindle so that you can knock off the feathers. But if you sand too long, you'll just create new ones.

If you're going to stain the work or finish it with a penetrating finish such as tung oil, don't 'burnish' the wood with extra-fine sandpaper. This closes up the pores and prevents the stain or oil from penetrating properly.

Parting — Once the turning is sanded, 'part' the finished spindle from the waste stock. With a parting tool, scrape or cut part way through the stock on either end of the work. (See Figure 14.)

But don't part the wood completely on the lathe! Stop parting when there's still 1/4"-1/2" of stock left and dismount the turning from the lathe. Saw through the last little bit of stock with a coping saw and remove the waste.

Pattern Turning

If you want to turn a particular pattern, or duplicate several spindles, carefully measure the diameter of all the coves, beads and flats you want to cut. Mark the position of these contours on the rounded stock with a pencil or crayon.

Using a parting tool, cut grooves at each mark stopping at the desired diameter. How do you know when you've reached this diameter? Set a pair of 'outside' calipers to the proper measurement and use it to test the diameter of the spindle from time to time as you cut. (See Figure 15.) When the calipers slip over the work at the bottom of the groove, you've reached the desired diameter.

When you've marked all the various diameters on your spindle, turn the contours. Be careful to stop cutting when you reach the bottom of the groove.

Sometimes you need more guidance than simply marking and cutting a diameter. You need to measure the actual *shape* of the spindle. If this is the case, make a 'negative' pattern cut of cardboard or thin hardboard. As you turn, hold this pattern up to the work from time to time and compare the contours. (See Figure 16.)

There's a lot more to be said about turning, of course. But once you get past the basics, it's mostly opinion. You'll find some of these opinions helpful, others less so. As we said before, lathe work is a form of *personal* expression. Find your own way, use good sense, and enjoy yourself. — *Nick Engler*

Mending Mistakes

Every woodworker makes mistakes. But what separates the craftsmen from the craftsboys is how well you mend them.

How many times has something like this happened to you? You're turning a spindle on the lathe — the seventh in a series of eight, so you're a little tired. You're in a hurry to get finished and you feed the chisel into the wood a little faster than you should. *Rip! Crack!* The chisel takes a big bite out of the stock, and suddenly you're working on the seventh spindle in a series of nine.

Well, we all make mistakes, sometimes pretty bad mistakes. There were times when I thought I'd completely ruined a project just when it was almost completed. But as I gained experience as a woodworker, I learned there are few mistakes so bad that they can't be mended if you have the time and the patience.

Raising Dents

Probably the most common mistake woodworkers make is denting the surface of the wood while they're working on it. This can happen any number of ways — clamping down too hard when you're gluing up, dropping a screwdriver or a hammer, laying the project on a screw or nail. Your first impulse will be to sand out the dent. But this just leaves a depression in the surface of the wood.

There's a much better (and much easier) way to get rid of dents. All a dent is is compressed wood. Swell the wood up and the dent will disappear. And what causes wood to swell? Water!

To raise a dent, first 'prick' the surface of the compressed wood with a pin in several places. Then put a few drops of water in the dent and let it soak in for a few minutes, as shown in Figure 1. (The pinholes help the water to penetrate the wood.) Place a piece of tinfoil over the wet dent (this seals in the water); put a piece of cotton cloth over the tinfoil (this protects the wood); then apply a hot iron for a few minutes. (See Figure 2.) When you remove the cloth and tinfoil, the dent will be gone! (See Figure 3.)

> **Tip ◆** For really stubborn dents, or dents in very hard woods, repeat this procedure several times.

Filling Cracks, Splits, and Gaps

Checked (or split) wood is another common problem. So are hairline gaps between boards where two surfaces don't quite butt up against one another. The solution to both these problems is to fill these voids with something that looks like wood.

Most woodworkers resort to wood putty or wood dough. But this substance rarely matches the wood, and it sometimes makes the gap *more* visible than if you had left it

Figure 1. To raise a dent, prick the dented surface with a pin, apply a few drops of water, and let the water soak in for a few minutes.

Figure 2. After the water has soaked in, put a piece of tinfoil over the dent, a cloth over the tinfoil, and apply a hot iron for a few more minutes.

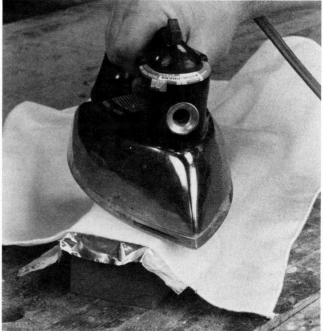

unfilled.

If the crack or gap is very small, I sometimes mix fine sawdust from the project with plastic cement (modeler's glue) or clear epoxy. This creates a putty-like substance that almost matches the color of the wood. It's usually just a shade darker, but not so dark that you'd notice it in a tiny crack.

For larger cracks, I use stick shellac. Stick shellac is a hard substance that can be easily melted into a void. It hardens just as soon as it cools and can be sanded immediately. It comes in a variety of wood tones, and you can mix two or more tones while the shellac is hot to match almost any wood surface.

Stick shellac is usually applied with a hot knife. There are 'shellac knives' available from several sources, but I find

Figure 3. When you remove the iron, the cloth, and the tinfoil, the dent will have raised up.

Figure 4. To fill a crack, first carve a piece of shellac off the stick with a hot knife.

Figure 5. Then smear the shellac around, forcing it into the crack. When the crack is filled, smooth over the surface of the shellac. If the knife cools, heat it up again with a torch.

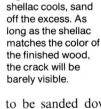

Figure 6. After the shellac cools, sand off the excess. As long as the shellac matches the color of the finished wood, the crack will be barely visible.

an old kitchen knife works just as well. Simply heat the knife up in a torch flame, then 'cut' a small piece of shellac off the knife as you would a pat of butter. (See Figure 4.) Smear the shellac into the void and smooth it over with the knife. (See Figure 5.) If the knife cools while you're cutting or smearing, simply heat it up again and continue. When you've filled the entire void and smoothed over the surface, sand off the excess shellac. (See Figure 6.)

Some woodworkers will tell you not to use stick shellac or other products to fill the cracks until *after* the project has been finished. That way, you can match the final color of the wood. However, I doubt this is such a hot idea for two reasons: First of all, a finish may keep the sawdust-and-glue mixture or stick shellac from adhering to the wood properly. And since both of these types of wood filler have

to be sanded down and the surfaces around them refinished, it just seems like I'd be creating more work for myself. So I usually go ahead and finish a piece of scrap from the project, then use this scrap to determine the right color when I'm choosing and mixing my fillers.

Replacing Gouged Wood

The worst and most dreaded mistake of all is gouged wood, where you've accidently cut a chunk out of the surface. You can't swell the wood up to hide the gouge, and a filler would just stand out like a sore thumb no matter how well you matched the color of the wood. The only thing to do in this case is to replace the missing wood.

If the gouge is fairly small, your best bet is to plug it. First, find a piece of scrap stock whose grain pattern and

Figure 9. After the glue dries, sand the plug flush with the surrounding surface. The grain of the plug and the grain of the surrounding area should run in the same direction.

Figure 7. To repair a small gouge, first cut a plug from scrap stock whose grain pattern and color match the gouged wood.

Figure 10. To repair a large gouge, rout out the gouged area to make an oblong groove.

Figure 8. Drill out the gouged area, then glue the plug in place. The plug should be just a little thicker than the depth of the hole.

Figure 11. Make an oblong plug on your bandsaw, then tap it into the groove. To get a good fit, cut the plug a little oversize and taper it on a sander.

Figure 12. When the glue is dry, sand the oblong plug flush with the surrounding surface.

color match the gouged area as close as possible. Cut a plug from the scrap with a 'plug cutter'. (See Figure 7.) Plug cutters commonly come in several different sizes, all the way up to 1″ — so that you can plug a gouge up to 1″ in diameter.

After you've cut the plug, drill out the gouge and fill the hole with the plug. The plug should be 1/16″-1/8″ thicker than the depth of the hole, so that a little bit of the plug sticks up above the surface. Also, be careful to glue the plug in place with the wood grain running in the same direction as the surrounding stock. (See Figure 8.) After the glue dries, sand the plug flush with the surrounding surface. (See Figure 9.)

If the gouge is too large to be replaced by a round plug, make an oblong plug on your bandsaw. Once again, find a piece of scrap whose grain and color match the gouge stock. Then carve out the gouged area with a router, making an oblong groove. (See Figure 10.) Carefully measure this groove and cut an oblong plug to fill it.

Tip ◆ To get a perfect fit, cut the plug slightly oversize, then taper the sides with a disc sander or belt sander. (See Figure 11.)

Apply glue to the inside of the groove and tap the plug in place with a mallet. Let the glue dry and sand the plug flush. (See Figure 12.)

Just knowing these few techniques will not only improve the appearance of your completed projects; it will help relieve your frustration when you make a mistake. I sure feel a lot better about my own limitations as a woodworker. I also get a feeling of smug satisfaction every time somebody inspects some of my home-made furniture and tells me, "It looks perfect!" If only they knew how much of that perfection is a lot of mistakes well covered. — *Nick Engler*

A Joinery Primer

Fine furniture is not built piece by piece, but joint by joint.

If you ever get to New York, be sure to take a tour of the new American Wing in the Metropolitan Museum of Art. They have a wonderful collection of classic furniture: Queen Anne, Chippendale, Windsor, Country, Shaker, Modern. Whatever you're interested in, it's there. But despite the differences in styles and design, this furniture all has something in common. Each piece is built with the same tried-and-true joints, carefully chosen, cut, and fitted. That's why the furniture lasted long enough to end up in a museum.

Obviously the craftsmen who built these pieces understood the subtleties of wood and woodworking. They knew that the strength, endurance and continued usefulness of furniture doesn't depend on the design or style so much as good, solid joinery. Use proper joinery techniques in your own workshop, and you can expect your own projects to be handed down for generations, too — maybe even end up in a museum.

Five Basic Joints

The fundamentals of joinery are simple, despite the fact that most cabinetmaking books show dozens of different joints, many of them quite difficult to make. But the truth is there really aren't dozens of joints — only *five*! (See Figure 1.) Here's a brief discussion of each joint:

Butt — A butt joint is the simplest of all woodworking joints to make. The end of the board is simply squared off, then butted up to another board. Butt joints have very little strength and often need reinforcement.

Miter — Wood is mitered when you cut it diagonally across the grain. Like butt joints, miter joints are weak and need reinforcing. They are used extensively to join two shaped pieces of wood (such as moldings or picture frames) so that the shaped design looks continuous.

Rabbet — A rabbet is a long notch in the edge of a board. It's often used to join wide boards to one another — one board sits on the 'shoulder' formed by the rabbet. In fact, rabbet joints are sometimes called shoulder joints.

Dado — When you cut a slot across the grain of the wood, it's called a dado. Use dadoes to join the middle members (such as shelves or rails) to a furniture frame or carcass.

Groove — Grooves are almost the same as dadoes, except that the slot runs *with* the grain. For this reason, grooves aren't used so much to join frame members as they are to join stock edge-to-edge or edge-to-side.

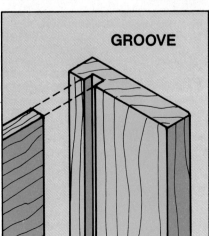

BUTT

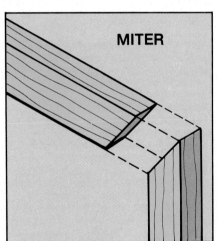

MITER

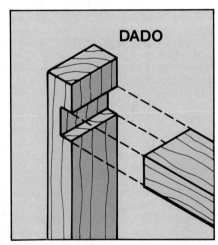

DADO

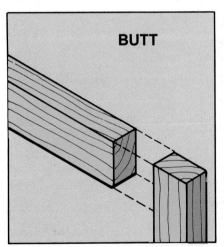

GROOVE

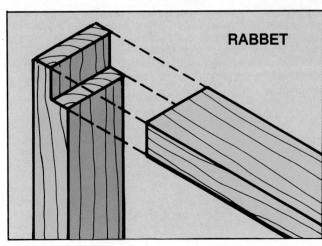

RABBET

Figure 1. There are just five basic woodworking joints: Butt, Miter, Dado, Groove, and Rabbet. All other joints are variations of combinations.

But what are those other joints that you read about — mortise-and-tenon joints, lap joints, dovetail joints? These are nothing more than a combination or variation on the five basic joints. Once you've learned how to make a butt, miter, rabbet, dado, and groove, you can make *anything*.

For instance: Cut four rabbets in the end of a board, and you've made a *tenon*. Rout a dado or a groove that's closed on both ends, and you've made a *mortise*. (See Figure 2.) To make a lap joint, cut two dadoes or rabbets in the sides of the boards you want to lap. Mitered dadoes, set side by side on the end of a board form what is commonly referred to as dovetails.

Five Necessary Tools

Just as there are five basic joints, there are also five tools that you need to make them:

Saw — The first and most important tool in joinery is, of course, the saw. You can't do without a good table saw or radial arm saw. You'll also want a good selection of blades. A garden-variety combination blade is okay for occasional woodworking, but it's not the greatest blade for accurate joinery. A *hollow-ground planer* blade makes smooth cuts across the wood grain, while a *rip* blade cuts with the grain. A *plywood* blade keeps the laminated layers of ply-

wood from tearing out or 'feathering' as you saw through it. And a *carbide-tipped* blade is a must if you work with hardwoods a great deal.

Jointer — Once you've sawn the wood, you'll need to true up the edges with a jointer. It's impossible to underestimate the importance of this tool to good joinery. You can get boards to fit together fairly well with a saw, but only a jointer will give you the professional fit you're after. Some jointers also have *rabbeting ledges,* making it easy to cut long rabbets. (See Figure 3.)

Dado Set — A dado set is not a tool so much as an important accessory for your table saw or radial arm saw. The set fits on your saw arbor and enables you to cut a much wider kerf than normal — from 1/8" to 3/4" or more. There are two types of dado sets available. The most common is the *wobble dado,* which is mounted at an angle to the arbor. To adjust the width of the dado, you simply change the angle. (See Figure 4.) However, wobble dadoes often

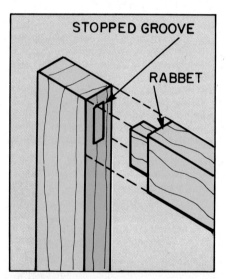

STOPPED GROOVE

RABBET

Figure 2. A tenon is formed by rabbeting all four sides on the end of a board. A mortise is a dado or groove closed at both ends.

Figure 3. Some jointers have 'rabbeting ledges' so that you can cut long rabbets easily. However, be very careful when using these ledges, since you may have to remove the knife guard.

Figure 4. To adjust the width of the kerf on a 'wobble dado' set, just turn the dial on the side of the accessory. This changes the angle of the blade to the arbor.

Figure 5. To change the width of the kerf on a 'dado knife' set, add or subtract chippers.

cut a kerf with a slightly rounded bottom, so most professional woodworkers prefer *dado knives*. A dado knife set comes with two small combination blades and several chipping blades. To change the width of the dado, you add or subtract 'chippers' from the setup. (See Figure 5.)

Router — You can't cut every dado with a dado set. Sometimes the board is just too big to handle on your table saw or radial arm saw. When that's the case, you need a router. Build a simple jig (or use a long, straight board) to serve as a guide, then rout the slot you want. (See Figure 6.) Routers are also indispensable for cutting dovetails. (See Figure 7.)

Drill Press — A drill press isn't always thought of as a joinery tool, but most experienced woodworkers know that it's invaluable for cutting small dadoes, grooves, and mortises. In the time it takes you just to set up a dado set or router to make a small mortise, you can drill a series of holes and square up the edges with a chisel. (See Figure 8.)

There are also *mortising attachments* available for most drill presses, enabling you to drill a mortise or square up the ends of a stopped dado *without* a chisel. (See Figure 9.)

. . . And Three Rules for Choosing Joints

If you have the proper tools and know how to make the five basic joints, how do you know which joint to use? How do you tell when to use a variation or combination of joints? There's no hard and fast answers for those questions, but there are three fundamental rules to help you choose the right joint for the job:

Whenever possible, glue the wood long grain to long grain. Every side of every board shows either the *long grain*

Figure 8. You can make a mortise on your drill press by drilling a series of holes, all at the same depth. Then square the edges and corners with a sharp chisel.

Figure 9. If you do a lot of mortising, you'll find a mortising attachment for your drill press comes in handy.

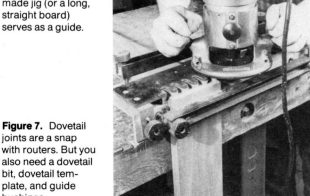

Figure 6. Use a router to cut dadoes and grooves in large boards. A homemade jig (or a long, straight board) serves as a guide.

Figure 7. Dovetail joints are a snap with routers. But you also need a dovetail bit, dovetail template, and guide bushings.

or the *end grain* of the wood. (See Figure 10.) A joint whose members are glued end grain to end grain is very weak; it won't hold up. Neither will a joint where the boards are glued end grain to long grain. To make a joint as strong and as long-lasting as possible, you have to glue the wood long grain to long grain.

Good joinery often increases the long grain to long grain gluing surface. For instance: A butt joint, when used to join two boards at right angles, butts end grain to long grain. But when you cut a series of dadoes in the end of each board to make a 'finger joint', long grain meets long grain between each finger.

Support the anticipated load. There's only one adjoining face in a butt joint. Consequently, it will stand up under continual stress coming from only one direction. There are many occasions in furniture design where this is perfectly acceptable — joining the top to a furniture carcass, for example. The only load on the joint will be whatever you decide to put on top of the piece when it's finished.

But the legs of that same piece require drastically different joinery. They will be bumped and pushed and pulled from many different directions. A mortise-and-tenon joint, with four or more adjoining faces between the legs and the carcass, will help to absorb this punishment.

Let the wood move. Wood is the product of a living being, and as such it still needs to 'breathe'. All wood expands and contracts with changes in humidity and temperature. These changes are imperceptible along the length of the grain in a board, but that same board will move up to 1/4″ for every 12″ of width *across* the grain. This movement may be unimportant where small boards (less than 3″ wide) are joined together; but larger pieces will swell and 'pop' the joint, or shrink and split out.

Where you can, align the wood grains of adjoining boards so that they expand and contract in the same directions. This lets the wood breathe and the joints remain stable. When you can't align the grains, leave room for the wood to move or make a series of smaller joints.

Some joints are especially designed to accommodate the movement of wood. The entire purpose of frame-and-panel joinery, for example, is to give the large panel room to breathe without distorting the frame. The panel sits loose in slots in the frame members, free to swell or shrink whenever it pleases. If you were to glue the panel in this slot, it might

split out, warp the frame, and ruin the entire project. (See Figure 11.)

Of course, there are some wood movements that you need to restrict. Lumber has a nasty tendency to warp and cup as it sits. Proper joinery will keep the boards in alignment while still letting the wood breathe.

None of this is as cut-and-dried as it sounds. There are always trade-offs. You can't design every joint in every project to fulfill all three of these rules. A dado joint provides no long grain to long grain gluing surfaces even though it shoulders a load from three directions and allows for the movement of the wood better than many other joints you could use. On the other hand, a snug mortise-and-tenon joint leaves no room for the wood to expand and contract, but it provides a healthy amount of long grain to long grain surface.

If you run into a dilemma where one of the basic joints won't meet a critical requirement, you may want to try a variation on a joint or a combination of two or more joints. But don't get hung up trying to decide among the myriad variations and permutations you'll see in some furniture design books — at least, not at first. There's one other rule you can call on if you need it: *Simple does just as well as fancy.*

Joinery Techniques

In many ways, what joinery you choose may be less critical than how you make these joints. *The wood has to fit.* A poor-fitting joint that fulfills all three of the fundamental requirements may weaken the project and cause it to deteriorate much faster than a well-made joint that only fulfills one or two.

The techniques involved in making a joint — layout, fitting, and assembly — are not difficult, but they require close attention to detail. They also require that you constantly keep in mind the three rules we just covered.

Laying out a joint — Measure with just *one* tool. Also, measure from just one reference point on any given tool. If you can possibly help it, don't butt a tape measure up against an inside edge to take one measurement, then hang it over the edge of a board to take another. (Most tape measures are made to give you fairly accurate results if you do this, but they won't be *precise* — and good joinery requires precision.) The slight variations you'll get from

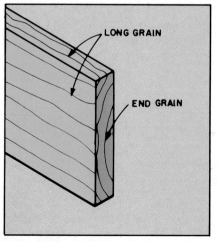

Figure 10. The face of a board shows either the *long grain* or the *end grain*.

LONG GRAIN

END GRAIN

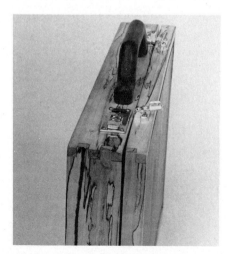

Figure 11. A panel must be free to expand and contract in a frame. The briefcase shown here was made with classic frame and panel joints. But the panel was glued in place. As a result, the top warped.

switching measuring tools and reference points can add up to big problems.

Keep a hard pencil to mark with — and sharpen it frequently. As the tip wears down, the line will broaden and make it harder to be precise. If you can get used to working with a *scratch awl,* so much the better. The metal point stays sharp; the line it scribes is always the same width; and it tears the grain when you outline a joint — this helps you eliminate unwanted feathers and splinters when you cut. (See Figure 12.)

As you lay out the various joints in a project, pay attention to which way the wood grain runs on various pieces. Not only do you want to mate long grain to long grain as often as possible; you want to avoid chopping up the long grains into *short grains.* (See Figure 13.) Short grains have little strength.

Fitting a joint — When it comes time to cut, remember that every piece of wood has its idiosyncrasies. Just the act of cutting will relieve tensions in the board, causing it to change shape. Usually these changes are minute, almost undetectable — until you try to fit the joints together.

Custom fit each board to the next. When it's practical, cut just a little wide of your mark then shave the joint down until you get the fit you're after. How do you know when you've got a good fit? When you can assemble a joint without a mallet and there's no slop — that's a good fit.

Some joints, of course, require a little slop. Dowel joints are customarily drilled a little deeper than the length of the dowels to leave room for the glue. Large panels in a frame need a lot of slop so they have room to expand and contract. Movable joints, such as a sliding dovetail, may need as much as 1/16"-1/8" of slop to slide freely. Remember which way the wood moves and fit your joints accordingly.

Assembling a joint — Always go through a dry run first. Clamp up the pieces without glue just to be sure of the fit. When you're satisfied, disassemble the joint and coat all the mating surfaces with glue. Apply a little extra glue to the end grains — end grains absorb much more glue than long grains. And even though these surfaces won't be as strong as the long grains when glued up, they will contribute to the overall strength of the joint.

Reassemble the joint and *clamp* it together while the glue dries. Glue is much stronger when it cures under pressure. But don't tighten the clamps too tight — too much pressure will squeeze the glue out from between the boards and cause a weak, 'starved' joint.

Often, it's a good idea to reinforce joints, particularly if you think they will be subjected to unusual stress. Glue blocks reinforce a joint where there is insufficient long grain to long grain contact. For example, if you back up a rabbet joint where two boards are joined at right angles, the long grain of each board will contact the long grain of the glue block — and the joint will be much stronger. (See Figure 14.)

Nails and screws act as tiny clamps that hold the boards together. But nails are rarely used in fine joinery. As the wood shrinks with age, the nails loosen up. Screws can be tightened from time to time.

A Parting Thought

There's much more that can be said about joinery, of course. But the fundamentals are nothing more than knowing how to make the basic joints and understanding the rules that govern when to use them. Once you understand that concept, you can design and build almost anything.

As you start out to make your own furniture, here's one last bit of advice: *Design your furniture around good, solid joinery; don't add the joints to fit the design.* Remember that when you next have a chance to inspect a piece of furniture that's lasted for generations — joinery is the heart and soul of fine woodworking. — *Nick Engler*

Parts of this chapter first appeared in HANDS ON! Magazine. Thanks to Shopsmith, Inc. for allowing us to borrow some good information.

Figure 12. Use a scratch awl to lay out a joint. The scribed line is always the same width and the awl tears the grain when you mark with it. This helps to eliminate 'feathers' when you cut.

Figure 13. Avoid chopping up the long grains into short grains. Short grains have little strength.

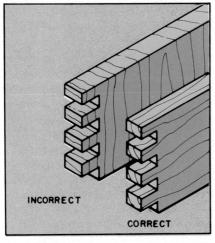

INCORRECT

CORRECT

Figure 14. Use glue blocks to reinforce joints where there is little or no long grain to long grain gluing surface. The long grain of the glue block contacts the long grain of the joined boards.

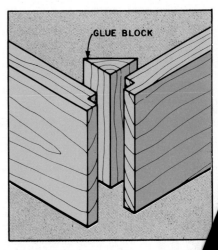

GLUE BLOCK

Index